Leadership in a Changing World - A Multidimensional Perspective

Edited by Muhammad Mohiuddin,
Bilal Khalid, Md. Samim Al Azad
and Slimane Ed-dafali

Published in London, United Kingdom

IntechOpen

Supporting open minds since 2005

Leadership in a Changing World – A Multidimensional Perspective
http://dx.doi.org/10.5772/intechopen.99304
Edited by Muhammad Mohiuddin, Bilal Khalid, Md. Samim Al Azad and Slimane Ed-dafali

Contributors

Hailan Salamun, Asyraf Ab Rahman, Luciana Mourão, Gardênia da Silva Abbad, Juliana Legentil, Anna Uster, Afatakpa Fortune, Okedare David Olubukunmi, Harold Andrew Patrick, Sunil Kumar Ramdas, Jacqueline Kareem, Ken Kalala Ndalamba, Euzália do Rosário Botelho Tomé, Elizabeth Addy, Audrey Addy, James Addy, Fatimah Saeed AlAhmari, Inusah Salifu, Eugene Owusu-Acheampong, Muhammad Mohiuddin, Bilal Khalid, Md Samim Al Azad, Slimane Ed-dafali, Muhammad Hoque, Job Jackson

© The Editor(s) and the Author(s) 2022

The rights of the editor(s) and the author(s) have been asserted in accordance with the Copyright, Designs and Patents Act 1988. All rights to the book as a whole are reserved by INTECHOPEN LIMITED. The book as a whole (compilation) cannot be reproduced, distributed or used for commercial or non-commercial purposes without INTECHOPEN LIMITED's written permission. Enquiries concerning the use of the book should be directed to INTECHOPEN LIMITED rights and permissions department (permissions@intechopen.com).
Violations are liable to prosecution under the governing Copyright Law.

[CC BY]

Individual chapters of this publication are distributed under the terms of the Creative Commons Attribution 3.0 Unported License which permits commercial use, distribution and reproduction of the individual chapters, provided the original author(s) and source publication are appropriately acknowledged. If so indicated, certain images may not be included under the Creative Commons license. In such cases users will need to obtain permission from the license holder to reproduce the material. More details and guidelines concerning content reuse and adaptation can be found at http://www.intechopen.com/copyright-policy.html.

Notice

Statements and opinions expressed in the chapters are these of the individual contributors and not necessarily those of the editors or publisher. No responsibility is accepted for the accuracy of information contained in the published chapters. The publisher assumes no responsibility for any damage or injury to persons or property arising out of the use of any materials, instructions, methods or ideas contained in the book.

First published in London, United Kingdom, 2022 by IntechOpen
IntechOpen is the global imprint of INTECHOPEN LIMITED, registered in England and Wales, registration number: 11086078, 5 Princes Gate Court, London, SW7 2QJ, United Kingdom
Printed in Croatia

British Library Cataloguing-in-Publication Data
A catalogue record for this book is available from the British Library

Additional hard and PDF copies can be obtained from orders@intechopen.com

Leadership in a Changing World – A Multidimensional Perspective
Edited by Muhammad Mohiuddin, Bilal Khalid, Md. Samim Al Azad and Slimane Ed-dafali
p. cm.

This title is part of the Business, Management and Economics Book Series, Volume 1
Topic: Business and Management
Series Editor: Taufiq Choudhry
Topic Editors: Vito Bobek and Tatjana Horvat

Print ISBN 978-1-80355-129-6
Online ISBN 978-1-80355-130-2
eBook (PDF) ISBN 978-1-80355-131-9
ISSN 2753-894X

We are IntechOpen,
the world's leading publisher of Open Access books
Built by scientists, for scientists

5,800+
Open access books available

142,000+
International authors and editors

180M+
Downloads

156
Countries delivered to

Our authors are among the
Top 1%
most cited scientists

12.2%
Contributors from top 500 universities

Selection of our books indexed in the Book Citation Index (BKCI)
in Web of Science Core Collection™

Interested in publishing with us?
Contact book.department@intechopen.com

Numbers displayed above are based on latest data collected.
For more information visit www.intechopen.com

IntechOpen Book Series
Business, Management and Economics
Volume 1

Aims and Scope of the Series

This series will provide a comprehensive overview of recent research trends in business and management, economics, and marketing. Topics will include asset liability management, financial consequences of the financial crisis and covid-19, financial accounting, mergers and acquisitions, management accounting, SMEs, financial markets, corporate finance and governance, managerial technology and innovation, resource management and sustainable development, social entrepreneurship, corporate responsibility, ethics and accountability, microeconomics, labour economics, macroeconomics, public economics, financial economics, econometrics, direct marketing, creative marketing, internet marketing, market planning and forecasting, brand management, market segmentation and targeting and other topics under business and management. This book series will focus on various aspects of business and management whose in-depth understanding is critical for business and company management to function effectively during this uncertain time of financial crisis, Covid-19 pandemic, and military activity in Europe.

Meet the Series Editor

Prof. Choudhry holds a BSc degree in Economics from the University of Iowa, as well as a Masters and Ph.D. in Applied Economics from Clemson University, USA. In January 2006, he became a Professor of Finance at the University of Southampton Business School. He was previously a Professor of Finance at the University of Bradford Management School. He has over 80 articles published in international finance and economics journals. His research interests and specialties include financial econometrics, financial economics, international economics and finance, housing markets, financial markets, among others.

Meet the Volume Editors

Dr. Muhammad Mohiuddin is an Associate Professor of International Business at Laval University, Canada. He has taught at Thompson Rivers University, Canada; University of Paris-Est, France; Osnabruck University of Applied Science, Germany; and Shanghai Institute of Technology and Tianjin University of Technology, China. He has published research in *Research Policy*, *Applied Economics*, *Review of Economic Philosophy*, *Strategic Change*, *International Journal of Logistics*, *Sustainability*, *Journal of Environmental Management*, *Journal of Global Information Management*, *Journal of Cleaner Production*, *M@N@GEMENT*, and more. He is a member of CEDIMES Institut (France), Academy of International Business (AIB), Strategic Management Society (SMS), Academy of Management (AOM), Administrative Science Association of Canada (ASAC), and Canadian council of small business and entrepreneurship (CCSBE). He is currently the director of the Research Group on Contemporary Asia (GERAC) at Laval University. He is also co-managing editor of *Transnational Corporations Review* and a guest editor for *Electronic Commerce Research* and *Journal of Internet Technology*.

Dr. Samim Al-Azad is a post-doctoral fellow and Stephen A. Jarislowsky Chair in International Business at Laval University, QC, Canada. He is also an Assistant Professor of Management Information Systems (MIS), at North South University, Bangladesh. His current research interests include artificial intelligence (AI), offshore IT outsourcing, IT adoption, and Industry 4.0. His research has been published in peer-reviewed journals including the *Journal of Global Information Management*, *International Journal of Logistics Research and Applications*, *Knowledge and Process Management*, and *Contemporary Management Research*. He has presented several papers at international conferences: Academy of International Business (AIB), *Pacific Asia Conference on Information Systems* (PACIS), and Administrative Science Association of Canada (ASAC). He was awarded best paper award twice for his papers at the t ASAC-2014 (IB) and ASAC-2015 (TIM) conferences. He also has experience working with BRAC (the world's largest development organization based in Bangladesh) on a number of projects funded by the World Health Organization (WHO) and the United Nations Development Programme (UNDP).

Dr. Bilal Khalid received a Ph.D. in Industrial Business Administration from KMITL Business School, Bangkok, in 2021, and a master's in International Business Management from Stamford International University, Bangkok, in 2017. Dr. Khalid's research interests include leadership and negotiations, digital transformations, gamification, eLearning, blockchain, Big Data, and management of information technology. Dr. Bilal Khalid also serves as an academic editor at *Education Research International* and a reviewer for international journals.

Dr. Slimane Ed-dafali is a Professor of Management (HDR) at the National School of Commerce and Management (ENCG), Chouaib Doukkali University, Morocco, where he conducts teaching and research activities. His current research is focused on entrepreneurial finance, innovation, knowledge management strategy, family business, and corporate governance. He has contributed to different research projects with various scholars and universities. Professor Ed-dafali has conducted applied research studies for institutional associations like the Moroccan Private Equity Association (AMIC). He is also a member of the International Academic Association of Governance (AAIG) and the Family Business Center. Dr. Ed-dafali also serves as a referee for several international journals.

Contents

Preface   **XV**

Chapter 1   **1**
Effective Management of Deportation of Undocumented Migrants
from South Africa
by Job Jackson and Muhammad Hoque

Chapter 2   **15**
Innovation Leadership in the 21st Century
by Fatimah AlAhmari

Chapter 3   **29**
Venture Leadership under Uncertainty: An Emerging Country
Perspective
*by Bilal Khalid, Md Samim Al Azad, Slimane Ed-dafali
and Muhammad Mohiuddin*

Chapter 4   **47**
Leadership in a Changing World: Relating Transformational Leadership
to Internal and External Environmental Issues in Technical Universities
by Elizabeth Addy, Audrey Addy and James Addy

Chapter 5   **63**
Leadership Values and Understandings from an Islamic Perspective
by Hailan Salamun and Asyraf Ab Rahman

Chapter 6   **79**
E-Leadership: Lessons Learned from Teleworking in the COVID-19
Pandemic
by Luciana Mourão, Gardênia da Silva Abbad and Juliana Legentil

Chapter 7   **101**
The New Institutional Approach as a Lens on Local Network Leadership
by Anna Uster

Chapter 8   **117**
Leadership Challenges among Undergraduate Students: Case Study
of Dominion University, Ibadan
by Afatakpa Fortune and Okedare David Olubunkunmi

Chapter 9   129
Positive Leadership Experiences of Software Professionals in Information
Technology Organisations
by Harold Andrew Patrick, Sunil Kumar Ramdas and Jacqueline Kareem

Chapter 10   145
Process Management: A Requirement for Organizational Excellence
in the Twenty-First Century Business Environment?
by Ken Kalala Ndalamba and Euzália do Rosário Botelho Tomé

Chapter 11   161
Improving Higher Education Instructional Delivery in the Developing
World: The Role of University Teachers as Digital Leaders
by Inusah Salifu and Eugene Owusu-Acheampong

Preface

Leadership plays an important role for organizations in the dynamic business ecosystem. Effective leadership is a valuable source of competitive advantage for organizations and a determining factor in workplace team resilience and efficiency. In the digital era, entrepreneurial teams, policymakers, and managers need to balance both digital and managerial leadership capabilities to overcome new challenges raised in the business environment of public, private, and hybrid organizations. For instance, leadership dimensions and orientations as strategic levers need to be considered in today's volatile and rapidly evolving marketplace, both for-profit and not-for-profit organizations.

Charismatic business leaders and managers in the Renaissance of the 21st Century must consider leadership as one of the key functions of management. On the top of classic management styles and approaches, it is important to consider diversity, environmental considerations, and different styles of leadership that ensure exemplary actions and influence other members of the organization. Leaders in the new era not only use rhetoric but also adhere to compliance with socially responsible practices. Leadership is more than just a simple management style and they need to develop a global mindset in the evolving business environment. Importantly, leadership is required for designing and implementing successful new business models for new ventures as well as established firms. Managerial and theoretical aspects of leadership should be focused on collective intelligence, strategic agility, and leadership styles that encourage both learning and knowledge sharing among collaborators to seize entrepreneurial opportunities and deal with geopolitical and socioeconomic challenges at different levels. The rapid advancement of technology, financial and economic crisis, serious disruptions to global value chains caused by the Covid-19 pandemic, and social and environmental transformation require today's leaders to embrace a new model of governance and leadership. Thus, the challenge for organizations is to develop effective leadership styles to generate expected economic, environmental, and societal benefits. This book explores the question of leadership in a changing world by adopting a multidimensional perspective. There are eleven chapters written by authors from across the globe.

In Chapter 1, Job Jackson and Muhammad Hoque investigate the effective management of deportation of undocumented migrants by discussing various aspects of immigration and deportation in the South African context as well as identifying challenges in managing the deportation of illegal immigrants.

In Chapter 2, Fatimah AlAhmari explores the various theories that have dictated innovation leaders over the years and investigates the connection between leadership, innovation, and creativity. The author puts into perspective a host of possible ways in which innovative leaders have brought revolutions in the field of entrepreneurship.

In Chapiter 3, Bilal Khalid, Md Samim Al Azad, Slimane Ed-dafali, and Muhammad Mohiuddin investigate the relevance of venture leadership by exploring the idea of venture leadership, leadership skills, and ethics in an emerging country context of Thailand. Specifically, they investigate how venture leadership thrives within the Thai business environment. They highlight that the quality of Thailand's leaders has a significant impact on the country's venture leadership success. Also, they conclude that the central skills of venture leadership should serve as a foundation for ongoing education.

In Chapter 4, Elizabeth Addy, Audrey Addy, and James Addy develop a conceptual model of the strengths, weaknesses, opportunities, and threats (SWOT) in technical universities about the features of transformational leadership. They reveal that transformational leadership is the key to the prompt development of tertiary technical education.

In Chapter 5, Hailan Salamun, and Asyraf Ab Rahman investigate the importance of understanding leadership values from an Islamic perspective. They advocate a significant relationship between the spiritual values of leadership with Rabbani's leadership practices. Specifically, they conclude that Rabbani's leadership model produces three components that influence the perspective of the leadership framework: the vision of leadership, the impact of leadership, and the core principles of effective leadership (Maqasid Shariah).

In Chapter 6, Luciana Mourão, Gardênia da Silva Abbad, and Juliana Legentil propose an E-Leadership Theoretical Model for Brazilian public service in the context of teleworking during the COVID-19 pandemic. The theoretical model proposed in this chapter can be used to plan and conduct research on relationships between antecedent variables (context, inputs), e-leadership processes, and their effects on essential criterion variables (outcomes for teleworkers and organizations).

In Chapter 7, Anna Uster provides an overview of current thinking on network leadership and related factors affecting local governance. The author concludes that leadership of inter-organizational networks requires organizational ability to achieve goals through collaboration with other organizations.

In Chapter 8, Afatakpa Fortune and Okedare David Olubunkunmi investigate leadership challenges among undergraduate students at Dominion University, Ibadan, Nigeria. The principal leadership challenges include lack of support for selected leaders, lack of respect, and incorrect perceptions. The chapter concludes that with the right kind of training, leadership skills acquisition can transform the plethora of challenges facing undergraduate leaders at Dominion University.

In Chapter 9, Harold Andrew Patrick, Sunil Kumar Ramdas, and Jacqueline Kareem investigate the software professional's emotions or perceptions about their positive leadership experiences in the workplace. This chapter provides an understanding of how virtuous behavior is vital in the workplace and how virtuous behaviors are the basic qualities that enhance the well-being and happiness of employees.

In Chapter 10, Ken Kalala Ndalamba and Euzália do Rosário Botelho Tomé examine the importance of process management as a requirement for organizational excellence. The authors develop six testable propositions that address the nature of process management and organizational excellence.

In Chapter 11, Inusah Salifu and Eugene Owusu-Acheampong use the context of Ghana to examine the kinds of digital technology tools university teachers in the developing world often use in their teaching as digital leaders, and whether the tools were effective in promoting academic work. Results reveal high average usage of laptops, mobile devices, and apps by digital leaders.

We believe our respected readers will find this book helpful for understanding the role and types of leadership needed to guide organizations in the rapidly changing economic, social, and environmental business ecosystem.

Muhammad Mohiuddin
Department of Management,
Laval University,
Quebec, Canada

Md Samim Al Azad
Post-doctoral Fellow,
Stephen A. Jarislowsky Chain on International Business,
Laval University,
Quebec, Canada

Assistant Professor,
School of Business,
North-South University,
Bangladesh

Bilal Khalid
KMITL Business School,
Bangkok, Thailand

Slimane Ed-dafali
Department of Management,
ENCG,
Chouaib Doukkali University,
El Jadida, Morocco

Chapter 1

Effective Management of Deportation of Undocumented Migrants from South Africa

Job Jackson and Muhammad Hoque

Abstract

The problem of migration into the Republic of South Africa took shape at the dawn of democracy and it has since then become overly complex to manage. South Africa has witnessed an unprecedented, undocumented population over the past three decades. The illegal migrants are economic migrants who enter the republic illegally for greener pastures. There are possible repeat deportees commonly known as the "revolving door" syndrome. The number of repeat deportees and the reasons for their continuous return is not known. The deportation process is currently faced with numerous challenges of re-entry after deportation and serious budget cuts to fulfil the mandate. This has significant impacts on the management of deportation in the country. This chapter provides various aspects of immigration and deportation from a South African context and also identifies challenges faced to manage the deportation of illegal immigrants.

Keywords: asylum seekers, corruption, fraudulent entry, social networks

1. Introduction

There is only a small percentage of the world's population that live outside their countries of birth or origin, but migration is still an important phenomenon on the political agenda of some countries. The movement of people across borders is a potential problem for almost all countries as it is nearly impossible to completely control immigration flows. The management of deportation is a mandatory function of the Department of Home Affairs (DHA) in the Republic of South Africa in terms of Section 34 of the Immigration Act 13 of 2002 as amended [1]. The DHA has two core businesses which are civic services and Immigration Services (IMS). Deportation management falls under the branch of IMS. IMS has further three business units namely, Port Control, Permitting (Visas), Asylum Seekers Management and Inspectorate. Inspectorate is established in terms of Section 33 of the Immigration Act 13 of 2002 as amended. The management of deportation is one of the functions of the Inspectorate, which is the law enforcement arm of the department [2]. The responsibility of the inspectorate is to comply with the Immigration Act. It is the responsibility of the deportation directorate to deport Illegal Foreigners (IFs) who are detected and arrested for contravening the Immigration Act.

2. Migration

2.1 Global migration

An immigrant is someone who voluntarily chooses to leave his or her own country and make a new life in another country. Movement is the established pattern of migration and is both a strategy of survival and livelihood and inseparable from identity. The daily mobility rate has declined with increasing age and duration of residence. Forced migration is defined as the coerced movement of a person or people away from their home or home region to another country [3].

The literature has shown that elderly people who live with adult children leave the country due to poverty or their disabilities [4]. Moreover, some scholars have suggested that many of the extended households mainly benefit the child in migration [5]. In addition, migration internally shows movement within the country and this is called internal displacement.

The recent policies such as liberalisation, macro-economic reforms, decentralisation, and regionalisation, and food security, for example, are likely to influence population movements. The government must plan for migrations because there is a correlation between development and population movement. Policy documents do not provide sufficient reference to migration and the controlling and limiting of migration remains a state objective [6].

In current development planning, the development-migration relationship plays out in two main ways. First, development strategies are proposed to reduce population movements that are harmful to development. Second, population movements are consequences, often unintended, of development interventions. For example, structural adjustment measures indirectly induce displacement. It has also been noted that sometimes forced population displacement is justified to further development and provide an opportunity for national poverty reduction measures. It was found that infrastructural development projects directly bring about population displacement and resettlement or for the alleviation of overcrowding and land-tenure reform in South Africa [7].

The most notable characteristic of deportation statistics in South Africa is their consistency in rankings and growth patterns. Mozambicans continue to pose the greatest challenge as they comprised 87% of all deportations in South Africa in 1996. However, Zimbabweans remain the second major problem as they have steadily increased as a percentage of the total from 8% in 1996 to 43% by 2004 [8].

The exponential increase in deportations from 1994 to 1996, reflects the restrictions represented in the 1995 amendments to the Aliens Control Act, 96 of 1991 [9]. The end of the Apartheid regime with the beginning of democracy in South Africa and the promise of higher employment rates, had an impact on illegal migration as it clearly increased the number. The amendments show the government's harsh perceptions of illegal migrants in South Africa [10]. Moreover, statistics on the immigrants who were detained at the Lindela Repatriation Centre indicate that the average age of detainees is 25.8 years. Moreover, the proportions of males to females are equal [11].

2.2 Impact of global migration

Various governments consider numerous methods to decrease access by foreigners. Sometimes this is an inevitable result that immigrants continue to cross barriers and live within the country without proper documentation. This constitutes illegal immigration [12]. There was mass migration in the onset of nineteenth- and

Effective Management of Deportation of Undocumented Migrants from South Africa
DOI: http://dx.doi.org/10.5772/intechopen.101768

twentieth-century patterns of mass migration that were much lower compared to the present. This was caused by the increasing income inequality and the widening gap between rich and poor countries that only intensifies the pressure on those who can find employment in other countries. An important theme that comes strongly across in global migration and the world economy is the potential gain in terms of global income if migration controls and restrictions were to be released [13].

The data from the international migration network show that overall, there has been a reduction in migration. However, whilst migration flows are high in absolute terms, in relative terms they are not. The long view of migration compares mass migrations before the First World War and the Second World War. At both stages, globalisation promoted the movement of people but also increased the development gap between sending and receiving countries. The main difference between the two periods of world history lies in the fact that it was more favourable in the first period compared to the restrictions on immigration characteristic of the recent period. Presently, there is a massive return of migrants to their countries of origin. In previous depressions there was always somewhere else to go, but not this time [14].

It has been estimated that between 2.5 million and 5 million or up to 7 million irregular migrants are present in South Africa as reported by the Department of Home Affairs [15]. There are many types of migration occurring in the country. The different types of migration can be characterised as highly skilled migration, qualified and educated professionals, and unskilled and illegal migration. Unskilled and illegal migrants enter the country after the political transitions from the Apartheid regime to democratic South Africa in 1994 [16]. These foreign migrants experience harassment by police officials. Police officers abuse their power by requesting bribes or by abusing the migrants when checking migrants for their identity document (ID) which is against their human rights [17].

Moreover, migrants are at the risk of being unnecessarily arrested and detained for longer periods which violates the law [18]. Usually, illegal migration is less beneficial for immigrants as they do not have access to a full range of employment. They must accept lower wages for the same job and pay for higher immigration costs.

The movement of migrants fluctuates because of factors that include geographic proximity, the precedent, sociocultural issues, communications and technology, and demographic, environmental, economic, and political considerations.

South Africa has seen increased pressure on resources such as housing, strains of overpopulation and resultant transmissions of disease leading to increased expenditure and social and political tensions. Migrants, therefore, are marginalised and have a low-status in society with low-paid employment [19].

Many people enter South Africa illegally. One way of controlling this movement is by deportation. Deportation is the expulsion of a person or group of people from a place or country. Therefore, South African and international literature will be used to identify factors that lead to ineffective management and factors that influence illegal immigrants to enter a country. Thus, saving South Africa millions of rands in revenue [20].

2.3 International immigration theory

The literature suggests that there are three theories of migration, in which the purposes of migration are not the same and do not supersede another. The first one is macro theories which emphasise the structural, objective conditions that act as "push" and "pull" factors for migration. The push factors are the things about a country that make it not desirable and make people want to leave for reasons such as political and economic factors which leads to unemployment conditions, poor wages, or poor per capita income and political persecution compared to the host country. The pull factors are the characteristics of the host country that make it desirable and people want to be in that country for those benefits. These pull factors may include labour and migration legislation situations, better amenities, living conditions, education, health care, and many others [21].

In addition, forced migration may be caused by factors such as state repression or fear of persecution or civil war. All these theorists agree that macro conditions such as those are vital because they cause forced migration and pioneer voluntary migration. Pioneer migrants are the first individuals or groups of migrants from a given country or area moving to another country or area. These migrations are not voluntary but rather forced upon the individuals [3].

Although migrants are persistent in their quests to enter South Africa they are ill-equipped in dealing with the economic conditions and legislation in receiving countries. Rates of flow differ from mass emigration to almost no mobility [3]. These rates are influenced by political instability and the pursuit of economic opportunities.

The systems and networks are particularly important for meso-theory analysis regarding the population size. Groups of countries can be linked economically, politically, and culturally which further influences migration flows. These networks refer to the individual and collective factors with symbiotic ties that link them together [22].

Besides, once formed, social networks can substantially influence the direction and volume of migration flows, providing resources that help people to move, such as information, contacts, economic, and social support.

The micro-theories are factors that attract or give reasons for individuals to migrate, weighing the cost-benefits of migrating. This may include the financial resources invested in migrating and integration in the country of destination, while benefits could include a higher wage. The micro-perspective provides a critical analysis in terms of pointing out how people internally process and assess the options for migration. There are forms of check or control for macro- and meso-theories, in relating to how individuals make decisions on the fact of objectivity [23].

3. Methodology

This was a policy document and literature review study. South African Immigration Act, legal framework documents were reviewed. The literature review was conducted between October and November 2020 using Google Scholar and Ebscohost search engine. The following keywords were used to search the literature: Immigration, Migration, Deportation, and illegal foreigners. Initially, a total of 250 abstracts were retrieved for relevance. After careful consideration, 53 articles were found suitable for the study. Based on the policy and legal documents, together with literature, we summarised the management of illegal deportation of undocumented migrants as well as, the challenges faced by the DHA of South Africa.

4. South African context

4.1 Republic of South Africa immigration act of 2002

The Immigration Act manages how foreigners enter, depart from, and reside in South Africa. People who do not follow the Immigration Act can be arrested, detained at the Lindela Holding Facility, and then deported. The detention and deportation procedure are conditional to many legal protections that shield the constitutional rights of foreigners who are in detention or who are going to be deported [24].

The Immigration Act defines an 'illegal foreigner' as a person who enters South Africa in breach of the Immigration Act, or someone who does not have the correct documentation such as an asylum seeker permit, legal recognition of refugee status, or a valid permit or visa in their passport. The term 'illegal foreigner' is an issue as it creates the perception that the person is a criminal. A person cannot be 'illegal' just because they do not have the correct documents in terms of a country's immigration laws [25].

An illegal foreigner may involuntarily have to leave South Africa via a deportation process administered by the Department of Home Affairs under detention legislation outlined in the Immigration Act. Generally, this person would be returned to their country of origin. The Lindela Holding Facility would detain the migrant until this occurs, as set out by Sections 32 and 34 of the Immigration Act.

The Department of Home Affairs works with officials from the foreigner's country of origin to guarantee they will be received once they return as part of the process of deportation. Deportation is the function of the state and should be done by following the law [26].

4.2 The legal framework for migration in South Africa

During the Apartheid regime, South Africa had a set of legislation to control the movement of the non-White population that was linked to employment opportunities that only allowed low to semi-skilled work known as the pass laws. The Act only permitted the White population into urban areas while all non-White adult men had to always carry passes to justify their presence in those areas. Anyone found without the correct documentation were to be arrested and sent to rural areas. This law was created to restrict the control of movements of the non-White population within the country. This included constant coercion and the presence of a submissive workforce only when and where it was needed [27].

Moreover, from 1960, this system of controlling the movements of the non-White population was extended to the foreign migrants known as the 'two gates' policy. The Aliens Control Act almost did not allow any non-White migrant workers to enter the country. There were also a set of mutual agreements with countries across the border of South Africa. These agreements allowed foreign migrants into the country as they were needed by economic sectors such as mining or commercial farming [28].

The Aliens Control Act has evolved since 1937 with updates occurring in the 1960s and 1970s. The original focus involved restricting Jewish immigration to South Africa by enforcing police controls at various entry points and arresting those migrants who did not have the relevant documentation [29]. During this period, this Act was only available to White inhabitants employing migrants. Since South Africa's democratic government came into power in 1994, a new Immigration Act was adopted in 2002 that replaced the Refugees Act of 1998 [30]. However, scholars have reported that public officials, such as migration and police officers, may retain historical attitudes on South African migration policies [31].

After the demise of the Apartheid era, new regulations replaced the previous legal framework concerning migration. At present, these regulations are outlined in the 2002 Immigration Act, the 1998 Refugees Act and the Constitution of 1996. The former, which was amended in 2004, defines the enforcement and monitoring principles as well as the general objectives of the migration policies regarding temporary and permanent residence.

It is reported that during Apartheid the Alien Control Act opened a path for foreigners to become South African residents. The Act did not solely focus on opposing illegal migration and it particularly outlined the protection of migrants' rights [32].

There were numerous ways to receive temporary residence in South Africa. For example, employment, education, visiting or meeting family, applying for asylum, and cross-border travels as outlined in the Immigration Act of 2002 [33]. The Act also establishes special work permits, which are easier to obtain for people with exceptional skills or qualifications as it benefits South Africa to increase their professional and skilled workers. Moreover, the Immigration Act also maintains the category of 'corporate work permit'.

Corporate companies may employ migrants by applying directly to the Department of Home Affairs while placing financial guarantees. However, due respect regarding the migration regulations needs to be granted by the provision of numbers employed and their job descriptions [34]. In some cases, such as in the mining and agricultural sectors, the Act enables the government to waiver, reduce, or even end certain requirements with foreign countries regarding permits for work migrants.

The Immigration Act provides a robust mechanism to maintain a balance between the needs of the South African economy and the high level of unemployment in the country [35].

4.3 Illegal migrant/illegal foreigner

According to the Immigration Act (2002), an illegal or legal immigrant will temporarily or permanently settle in the Republic of South Africa. Regularisation of an illegal immigrant in South Africa occurs as soon as he/she receives the proper documentation, which is in accordance with the Immigration Act. Following the successful completion of this process, the applicant's immigration status changes to permanent residence.

Any foreign national or immigrant who is not properly documented according to the Immigration Act is liable to an offence of contravening the Immigration Act and will be either forcefully or voluntarily deported. This is to ensure the efficiency of planning and budgeting by the state. To create a history of sustainability for humans, good national governance is an important component [36].

An issue of immigration is to ascertain the extent of illegal immigration and its main features, which is fundamental for efficient management of the phenomenon. However, the official figures are inadequate, leading many experts to estimate the data through direct measures [37].

Illegal immigrants face numerous hindrances by being compelled to work in the informal economy as comparatively having a legal status opens up a wide variety of employment opportunities with resulting higher wages and lower immigration costs. Illegal immigrants feel that they need to pay for false documents to avoid employment in poor working conditions.

Moreover, on average, their wages are lower than those paid to legal immigrants.

Even though illegal immigrants have different status results and characteristics from legal immigrants, their motivations to migrate are the same; they look for ways to improve their economic and social situations.

Other studies have debated issues such as national security and civil rights but in this chapter, the emphasis is on the economic consequences of illegal immigrants and their effect on goods and services, social benefits and welfare, and income distribution [38].

Employers benefit from illegal labour that is abundant, inexpensive and flexible, with illegal immigration responding faster to economic incentives compared to

Effective Management of Deportation of Undocumented Migrants from South Africa
DOI: http://dx.doi.org/10.5772/intechopen.101768

legal immigration. Ebbs and flows in the markets of the expanding and contracting economic periods in both the host and the sending economies are more visible in illegal immigration [39].

4.4 Reasons for illegal migration into South Africa

The process for acquiring documentation poses logistical and financial issues, and what is required for people is not necessarily clear. For some people, the fee of R430 for a visa application may be high and may discourage migrants from applying for this at all which makes illegal entry into the country more appealing [40].

Furthermore, there may be cross-border ethnic similarities and the absence of solid barriers, which may lead to an extension of internal migration that is still considered to be irregular immigration. People who live along borders may cross these borders often without the proper documentation to carry out their daily business of trading, visiting family, attending school, or doing shopping. A potential solution is to create a cross-border system that facilitates movement within a prescribed area across a border. The Immigration Act makes an exception regarding a cross-border permit for South Africa's immediate neighbours. However, the regulations neither provide a clear indication on how to make an application, nor do they contain an example of the permit itself [41].

In addition, it may be difficult or impossible for some migrants to meet the requirements to attain a permit. For example, many of the migrants who want to enter South Africa in search of employment may not qualify for a work permit. This may lead to documents being forged or tampered with. Fraudulent entry has been accomplished either by going undetected or with the complicity of corrupt officials in South Africa.

The record of arrests of department officials on charges of corruption generally indicates where the corrupting influence comes from and has significantly implicated Chinese, Pakistani, and Nigerian migrants. The intention of securing services or rights to which they are not entitled within South Africa encourages fraud. A specific issue is that where the department must handle is fraudulent citizenship obtained through the delayed registration of births [42].

Moreover, the issue is the registering of fraudulent marriages between foreigners and South Africans. In both these situations, corruption within the department makes it possible for irregular migrants to establish their presence through fraudulent means. Moreover, a lack of resources and inefficiency of the department, causing delayed, incorrect or invalid delivery of citizenship or residential services result in migrants not having the proper documentation which may lead to their irregular or illegal migrant status [43].

4.5 Deportation

Deportation is the action or procedure aimed at illegal foreigners to leave the country in terms of the Immigration Act (Immigration Act, 2002). Some authors define deportation as the removal of an alien out of the country. This is simply because his or her presence is deemed inappropriate with the public welfare. Also, this happens without any punishment being imposed or contemplated under the laws of the country. In the USA, most of the people who are deported are normally those who have also committed crimes within the country [44].

4.6 Re-migration after deportation

The data from the Department of Home Affairs have shown that there is a pattern of illegal migrants who re-enter South Africa after being deported once within six months [45]. Most of these returnees are from the SADC countries who simply jump the borders such as Zimbabweans. This phenomenon has been termed the 'revolving door syndrome'. The porous borders greatly contribute to this phenomenon. In November 2003 media briefing, the Director-General began to draw attention to this concept as it was an increasing challenge for the country. The revolving door syndrome is a difficult concept to measure. The recent introduction of the fingerprinting system should be an attempt to address this problem [46].

Furthermore, this phenomenon implies that the deportation process does not have much preventative effect. If irregular migrants are not stopped by their experience of deportation, the process becomes redundant. It has also been noted that some illegal immigrants present themselves to immigration officers for arrest and deportation around the Christmas season as a way of receiving a free ride home. This has led the department to pause deportations over this period [47].

The effectiveness of the deportation process is questioned by the human rights community, as while touring the Lindela Holding Facility, the South African Human Rights Commissioner opined that the system of detention and resulting deportation was unsuccessful and this was concurred by the Lawyers for Human Rights. The detention and repatriation process was believed to promote illegal migration into South Africa according to the Deputy Chairperson of the Commission. This process has been termed as the 'revolving door syndrome' [48].

Pull and push factors influence the success of the migrants to return to their countries of origin. For instance, having a family in the receiving country would motivate them to return to South Africa. Also, should there be a lack of support, financial and otherwise, from family members, migrants would be motivated to return to the receiving country again, in this case, South Africa. Similarly, if the repatriated family member had committed a major criminal offence, the relatives would be loath to support them [49].

4.7 The management of the deportation process in South Africa

The Linda Holding Facility is the largest detention centre for undocumented migrants in South Africa. Literature shows that the current management of deportation is unfair and ineffective [50]. There are various issues experienced by detainees during their arrests such as the arrest and detention of foreigners with valid documents, failure to take various steps to verify immigration status, failure to inform suspected illegal foreigners of the reason for their arrest, physical harm during the arrest process, lack of access to cell phones and refusal to allow detained suspects to call relatives or friends, systemic problems with the DHA's record-keeping and lack of communication between the DHA and the police, and lastly detention of suspected illegal foreigners for more than two days which is a violation of their human rights law as well as the immigration law. These issues illustrate that problems in the detention and deportation process are not limited to the actions of the DHA alone [26].

The best alternative to resolving some of the issues mentioned above is through coordination and cooperation with other departments, particularly, the South African Police Services. Moreover, one of the main issues identified was the lack of effective verification of an individual's immigration status before being sent to Lindela Holding Facility. This is due to various reasons, including corruption and abuse of power, insufficient resources, and the failure to follow legal procedures by providing individuals with an opportunity to confirm their status with supporting documents when it is reasonable and practicable. Due to these issues, individuals with illegal immigration status frequently find themselves at the Lindela Holding Facility. This increases the burden on the DHA, in terms of verification, transport, and administration [51].

The inefficiency and abuse that is evident in the Lindela Holding Facility reflect poorly on the vision of a democratic South Africa as it jeopardises the rule of law and is directly in conflict with the country's respect for human rights, regardless of an immigrant's legal status. This aspect is a vital contribution to a functioning democracy [52].

The Lawyers for Human Rights (LHR) frequently visit this facility and have represented many of the individuals illegally detained there. It is in the interest of the government to remedy the causes of these legal violations as most of them have resulted in costs and punitive damages against the DHA. The overall cost of detaining migrants has raised the costs of detention [53].

Detainees at the Lindela Centre have expressed feelings of frustration and legal uncertainty [54]. Despite the numerous South African laws that protect illegal immigrants, abuses of power are still evident. Detainees have prolonged, indefinite periods of detention with a lack of information on their legal status. Some individuals were aware of the appeal process through reviews which would enable them to challenge their circumstances. However, others reported being unable to access these rights due to the barriers in the facility. Immigration officials within the DHA holding facility were unavailable to detainees who reported only having contact with Bosasa staff who were responsible for the daily operations there. Corruption was a common theme that prevented them from exercising their rights of review and appeal [53].

Asylum seekers in Lindela who are at risk of prosecution could be sent back to their countries of origin by the DHA which is a direct violation of the international prohibition against non-refoulement [55]. Those asylum seekers who were released from the facility and told to report to the refugee reception office were rearrested which indicates a lack of communication between officials in Lindela and the reception offices [56].

There are implications from the literature on the migration patterns in South Africa. First and foremost, the Department of Home Affairs must address its ineffective administrative processes and fulfil its mandate cost-effectively and legally that upholds the rights of all individuals. A total of 29% of the respondents were not advised on the reasons for their arrest, and 10% reported being injured during the arrest. Those arrested by the SAPS were more than twice as likely to have suffered an injury during the arrest which indicates that these police personnel frequently abuse their power by causing physical harm to the migrants which is a violation of their human rights. Individuals arrested by immigration officials could make calls more often (57%) than those arrested by the SAPS (41%) [57].

Furthermore, it has been reported that there were problems with the verification process when the individuals were arrested on suspicion of being illegal foreigners. The statistics reported that 53% of the respondents had asylum permits and only 21% of the respondents were undocumented [58].

In some cases, the individuals detained as illegal foreigners did hold valid refugee IDs, asylum seeker permits, or even South African IDs [59]. This highlights the deficiencies in the verification process as it is evident that these individuals have not had their legal status verified. This study illustrates that the management of deportations within Lindela is shown to be ineffective.

4.8 Corruption

Requests for funds were reported by 21% of the detainees to avoid being physically harmed, further detained, or arrested. These requests arose from interactions with DHA officials (35%), Bosasa employees (8%), and police officers (50%). At the facility itself, requests for money was mentioned to secure their release and avoid deportation waiting periods [60].

5. Conclusion

The DHA officials should understand immigration laws while performing official work. The tracing of people in the Republic of South Africa is important but illegal immigrants are not easy to detect because they do not have a permanent place of residence for illegal immigrants in South Africa. The arrest of illegal immigrants must be done according to the law and the constitution. Several pull factors lead to re-entry into South Africa after deportation and these include property in the republic, and family and social networks, among others. These pull factors must be addressed during the deportation process so that they are not tempted to get back to the republic. The DHA official must understand these pull factors whilst executing the deportation processes.

There are several challenges to illegal immigration in South Africa, but the most important ones include poor border control systems. South Africa has more than 100 gazetted entry points and the controls are poor. Moreover, IT systems are not integrated and resources are limited.

This study has provided insights into the management of deportation of an undocumented illegal immigrant in South Africa which was lacking in the literature. In addition, policymakers may use the findings of this study to design robust policies to secure the border and protect citizens from the negative consequence of illegal migration such as drugs, fraud and others which is on the rise in the Republic of South Africa.

Author details

Job Jackson and Muhammad Hoque*
MANCOSA Graduate School of Business, Durban, South Africa

*Address all correspondence to: muhammad.hoque@mancosa.co.za

IntechOpen

© 2022 The Author(s). Licensee IntechOpen. This chapter is distributed under the terms of the Creative Commons Attribution License (http://creativecommons.org/licenses/by/3.0), which permits unrestricted use, distribution, and reproduction in any medium, provided the original work is properly cited. (cc) BY

References

[1] Republic of South Africa. Department of Home Affairs. Temporary Residency Visa. Available from: http://www.dha.gov.za/index. php/notices/10-immigration-services?start=30 [Accessed: 20 March 2021]

[2] Ngozi O. The face of violence: Rethinking the concept of xenophobia, immigration laws and the rights of non-citizens in South Africa. BRICS Law Journal. 2017;**4**(2):40-70

[3] Piguet E. Theories of voluntary and forced migration. In: Routledge Handbook of Environmental Migration and Displacement. London, New York: Routledge, Taylor & Francis Group; 2018. pp. 17-28

[4] Escarce JJ, Rocco L. Immigration and the Health of Older Natives in Western Europe (No. 228). GLO Discussion Paper. Maastricht; Global Labor Organization (GLO); 2018

[5] Thapa DK, Visentin DC, Kornhaber R, Cleary M. Migration of adult children and quality of life of older parents left behind in Nepal. Geriatrics & Gerontology International. 2020;**20**(11):1061-1066

[6] Oishi N. Skilled or unskilled?: The reconfiguration of migration policies in Japan. Journal of Ethnic and Migration Studies. 2020;**47**(10):2252-2269

[7] Suit JM. 2017. U.S. Patent No. 9,678,803. Washington, DC: U.S. Patent and Trademark Office

[8] Farley A. South African Migration Policy: A Gendered Analysis. South African Institute of International Affairs. 2019. Available from: https:// www.africaportal.org/publications/ south-african-migration-policygendered-analysis/ [Accessed: 12 February 2021]

[9] Moyo I, Nshimbi CC. Of borders and fortresses: Attitudes towards immigrants from the SADC region in South Africa as a critical factor in the integration of southern Africa. Journal of Borderlands Studies. 2020;**35**(1): 131-146

[10] Alfaro-Velcamp T. "Don't send your sick here to be treated, our own people need it more": Immigrants' access to healthcare in South Africa. International Journal of Migration, Health and Social Care. 2017;**13**(1):56-68. DOI: 10.1108/ IJMHSC-04- 2015-0012

[11] Hunter-Adams J, Modisenyane M, Vearey J. Towards a migration-aware health system in South Africa: A strategic opportunity to address health inequity. South African Health Review. 2017;**2017**(1):89-98

[12] Griffin L. When borders fail: 'Illegal', invisible labour migration and Basotho domestic workers in South Africa. In: Constructing and Imagining Labour Migration. London, New York: Routledge, Taylor & Francis Group; 2016. pp. 33-56

[13] Ramji-Nogales J, Spiro PJ. Introduction to symposium on framing global migration law. AJIL Unbound. 2017;**111**:1-2

[14] Risam R. Beyond the migrant "problem": Visualizing global migration. Television & New Media. 2019;**20**(6): 566-580

[15] Mobius M. South Africa: Key Issues and Challenges. Franklin Templeton. Advisor Perspectives. 2017. Available from: https:// emergingmarkets.blog. franklintempleton.com/2017/03/16/ south-africa-key-issues-andchallenges/ [Accessed: 14 June 2021]

[16] Schutte C, Shaw M, Solomon H. Public attitudes regarding

undocumented migration and policing/crime. Africa Security Review. 1994;**6**(4):4-15. DOI: 10.1080/10246029.1997.9627731

[17] Geldenhuys K. Undocumented foreign nationals–looking for a better life. Servamus Community-Based Safety and Security Magazine. 2018;**111**(3):16-21

[18] International Federation for Human Rights. 2008. Available from: https://www.fidh.org/en/about-us/What-is-FIDH/ [Accessed: 12 May 2021]

[19] Kanayo O, Anjofui P, Stiegler N. Push and pull factors of international migration: Evidence from migrants in South Africa. Journal of African Union Studies. 2019;**8**(2):219

[20] Cobbinah C, Chinyamurindi WT. Motivational factors for engaging in dirty work entrepreneurship among a sample of African immigrant entrepreneurs in South Africa. SA Journal of Human Resource Management. 2018;**16**:9

[21] Burstein A, Hanson G, Tian L, Vogel J. Tradability and the Labor-Market Impact of Immigration: Theory and Evidence from the US (No. w23330). Massachusetts Avenue, Cambridge: National Bureau of Economic Research; 2017

[22] Munshi K. Social networks and migration. Annual Review of Economics. 2020;**12**(1):503-524

[23] Windzio M. The network of global migration 1990-2013: Using ERGMs to test theories of migration between countries. Social Networks. 2018;**53**:20-29

[24] Pokroy J. Are changes to South Africa's Migration Policy imminent? HR Future. 2017;**2017**(7):44-45

[25] Crush J, Peberdy S. Criminal Tendencies: Immigrants and Illegality in South Africa. AfricaPortal. Southern African Migration Project. 2018. Available from: https://www.africaportal.org/publications/criminal-tendencies-immigrants-and-illegality-south-africa/ [Accessed: 30 August 2021]

[26] Hiropoulos A. Migration and detention in South Africa. In: A Review of the Applicability and Impact of the Legislative Framework on Foreign Nationals. APCOF Policy Paper No. 18. Available from: http://apcof.org/wp-content/uploads/018-migration-and-detention-in-south-africa-alexandra-hiropoulos.pdf. 2017 [Accessed: 20 March 2021]

[27] Kaziboni A. The Lindela Repatriation Centre, 1996-2014. Applying theory to the practice of human rights violations. SA Crime Quarterly. 2018;**66**:41-52

[28] Chiumbu SH, Moyo D. "South Africa belongs to all who live in it": Deconstructing media discourses of migrants during times of xenophobic attacks, from 2008 to 2017. Communicare. 2018;**37**(1):136-152

[29] Bright RK. A 'Great Deal of Discrimination is Necessary in Administering the Law': Frontier Guards and Migration Control in Early Twentieth-Century South Africa. Journal of Migration History. 2018;**4**(1):27-53

[30] Biavaschi C, Facchini G, Mayda AM, Mendola M. South–South migration and the labor market: Evidence from South Africa. Journal of Economic Geography. 2018;**18**(4):823-853

[31] De Haas H, Czaika M, Flahaux ML, Mahendra E, Natter K, Vezzoli S, et al. International migration: Trends, determinants, and policy effects. Population and Development Review. 2019;**45**(4):885-922

[32] Mbiyozo AN. Gender and migration in South Africa: Talking to women

migrants. ISS Southern Africa Report. 2018;**2018**(16):1-36

[33] Anderson K, Apland K, Yarrow E. Unaccompanied and unprotected: Systemic vulnerability of unaccompanied migrant children in South Africa. In: The United Nations Convention on the Rights of the Child. Brill Nijhoff; 2017. pp. 361-389

[34] Kaplan D, Höppli T. The South African brain drain: An empirical assessment. Development Southern Africa. 2017;**34**(5):497-514

[35] Bradlow E. Empire settlement and South African immigration policy, 1910-1948. In: Emigrants and Empire. Manchester, UK: Manchester University Press; 2017

[36] Vigneswaran D. The complex sources of immigration control. International Migration Review. 2020;**54**(1):262-288

[37] Crush J, Williams V. Making Up the Numbers: Measuring "Illegal Immigration" to South Africa. Southern African Migration Project. 2018. Available from: https://www.africaportal.org/publications/making-numbers-measuring-illegal-immigration-south-africa/ [Accessed: 10 July 2021]

[38] Kollamparambil U. Happiness, happiness inequality and income dynamics in South Africa. Journal of Happiness Studies. 2020;**21**(1): 201-222

[39] Vanyoro K. Activism for migrant domestic workers in South Africa: Tensions in the framing of labour rights. Journal of Southern African Studies. 2020;**47**(4):663-681

[40] Alfaro-Velcamp T, McLaughlin RH, Brogneri G, Skade M, Shaw M. 'Getting angry with honest people': The illicit market for immigrant 'papers' in Cape

Town, South Africa. Migration Studies. 2017;**5**(2):216-236

[41] Crush J, Tawodzera G, Chikanda A, Ramachandran S, Tevera D. South Africa Case Study: The Double Crisis – Mass Migration From Zimbabwe And Xenophobic Violence in South Africa. Vienna: International Centre for Migration Policy Development and Waterloo, ON: Southern African Migration Programme; 2017. pp. 1-93, Rep. Available from: https://scholars.wlu.ca/samp/4/ [Accessed: 30 June 2021]

[42] Van der Straaten J. South Africa ID Case Study. Washington, D.C.: World Bank Group; 2019

[43] Mawodza O. The implications of Nandutu and Others v Minister of Home Affairs and Others. ESR Review: Economic and Social Rights in South Africa. 2019;**20**(4):14-17

[44] Landgrave M, Nowrasteh A. Criminal immigrants: Their numbers, demographics, and countries of origin. Immigration Research and Policy Brief. 2017;(1):1-7

[45] Thebe V. "Two steps forward, one step back": Zimbabwean Migration and South Africa's Regularising Programme (the ZDP). Journal of International Migration and Integration. 2017; **18**(2):613-622

[46] Malatji TL. Poor coordination among government departments and border control agencies: Its impact on South African porous borders. In: International Conference on Public Administration and Development Alternatives (IPADA). The 5th Annual International Conference on Public Administration and Development Alternatives, 07 - 09 October 2020, Virtual Conference 2020, University of Limpopo, South Africa; 2020

[47] Crush J, Skinner C. Rendering South Africa Undesirable: A Critique of

Refugee and Informal Sector Policy (No. 79). Ontario, Canada: Southern African Migration Programme; 2017

[48] Dlamini NP. An assessment of the effects of xenophobia on social integration in Isipingo, KwaZulu-Natal province [Doctoral dissertation]. University of Zululand; 2018

[49] Martinez O, Wu E, Sandfort T, Dodge B, Carballo-Dieguez A, Pinto R, et al. Evaluating the impact of immigration policies on health status among undocumented immigrants: A systematic review. Journal of Immigrant and Minority Health. 2015;**17**(3): 947-970

[50] Adugna F, Deshingkar P, Ayalew T. Brokers, Migrants, and the State: Berri Kefach "Door Openers" in Ethiopian Clandestine Migration to South Africa. Migrating Out of Poverty Research Programme Consortium. United Kingdom: University of Sussex; 2019

[51] Feltes T, Musker S, Scholz P. Regional governance of migration in the Southern African Development Community: Migration regimes and their implications for the experience of refugees and migrants in South Africa. In: Refugees and Migrants in Law and Policy. Cham: Springer; 2018. pp. 555-575

[52] Kalla T. The Criminalisation of Asylum Seekers: Arbitrary Detention in South Africa. Faculty of Law, Department of Public Law. 2019. Available from: http://hdl.handle. net/11427/31414 [Accessed: 14 February 2020]

[53] Ibrahim A. Bridging the international gap: The role of national human rights institutions in the implementation of human rights treaties in Africa. Obiter. 2018;**39**(3):701-726

[54] Ekambaram SS. Foreign nationals are the 'non-whites' of the democratic

dispensation. In: Racism After Apartheid: Challenges for Marxism and Anti-Racism. South Africa: The Wits University Press; 2019. pp. 217-236

[55] Eghosa EJ. The securitization of asylum in South Africa: A catalyst for human/physical insecurity. In: Borders, Sociocultural Encounters and Contestations: Southern African Experiences in Global View. London: Routledge; 2020. pp. 112-138

[56] Marek E, D'Cruz G, Katz Z, Szilard I, Berenyi K, Feiszt Z. Improving asylum seekers' health awareness in a Hungarian refugee reception centre. Health Promotion International. 2019;**34**(5):36-e46

[57] Masebo W. Accessing ART in Malawi while living in South Africa–A thematic analysis of qualitative data from undocumented Malawian migrants. Global Public Health. 2019;**14**(5):621-635

[58] Pineteh EA. Illegal aliens and demons that must be exorcised from South Africa: Framing African migrants and xenophobia in post-apartheid narratives. Cogent Social Sciences. 2017;**3**(1):1391158

[59] Amit R. Paying for Protection: Corruption in South Africa's Asylum System. Migration Policy Institute. 2015. Available from: https://www. migrationpolicy.org/article/paying-protection-corruption-south-africa%E2%80%99s-asylum-system [Accessed: 15 November 2020]

[60] Plaatjie SR, Mogashoa M. South Africa and xenophobia: Coalescence of "myths" and coloniality. In: Impact of Immigration and Xenophobia on Development in Africa. Pennsylvania, United States: IGI Global; 2021. pp. 38-55

Chapter 2

Innovation Leadership in the 21st Century

Fatimah AlAhmari

Abstract

It is a well-known fact that innovation is hard to execute without convincing people of new ideas. It is not something that can come about without collaborations. How then do we create an atmosphere where creativity and ideas lead to innovations within the organizations? The answer lies in innovation leadership. Innovation leadership is a conception and manner that consolidates different leadership styles to motivate people to generate creative ideas, outcomes, and services. This chapter will assist you in understanding who an innovation leader is. It will help you explore different theories of innovation leadership like the Path-Goal theory and Leader-Member Exchange theory, followed by different strategies that innovation leaders have adopted over the years. This will shed light on some of the leadership styles that have emerged commonly in entrepreneurs and how it has helped them build their empire, for instance, directive, supportive, and participative leadership. The chapter will end on the best practice recommendations that research has proven are the most effective for being an effective leader and bringing about innovation in your organization.

Keywords: leadership, innovation, model, creativity, strategy, 21st century

1. Introduction and need for innovation leaders

Since time immemorial, people have steered clear of change because of its complexity and the need to adapt to completely different mindsets. Any kind of change is difficult to accept because it demands that people leave behind the ideas and concepts, they trust and substitute them for something that is new but uncomfortable to them. The question then is not about turning up with something novel, but about persuading people to accept that change. This requires building trust and collaboration, as no change or innovation would be successful without joint action or collusion. The present century is one of adventure, excitement, and many challenges. Financial insecurities, social embarrassments, and a need to jump out of comfort zones are major factors driving a need for change and have decreased the adoption time for people. This has major implications on society because now more than ever, consumers are willing to put a premium on innovation. And innovation is the starting point for a revolution. Thus, it is essential to understand what exactly is meant by innovation?

Before moving on further, let us explore what innovative thinking is. One way it can be defined is as a "potentially powerful influence on organizational performance". More importantly, to introduce innovation within an organization, there is a need to look for people who believe in something, who are willing to cooperate, and who are passionate. Innovation leadership is thus the ability to inspire productive action in yourself and others during times of creation, invention, uncertainty, ambiguity, and risk [1]. It is a necessary competency for organizations that hope to develop truly innovative products and services [2]. Often, innovation is confused with invention and the generation of new ideas. Like invention is the conception of a new product, innovation is about making the existing product function better. Like they teach you in design strategy classes in MBA, the invention is the first boat ever pushed out to sea: it may be profound or fill a significant void in history. However, is it consequential? Can it be easily accessed by people in day-to-day life? Even though a prodigious new discovery in a lab might be a wonderful invention, yet if it does not create value in the market, if people do not trust it, it is not an innovation. Coming up with advanced tech products every year to gain profit is of no use if its usefulness to society is nil. Innovation is thinking out of the box. And how do you know if something you created is of use to someone? How do you stay relevant as an organization? That is where innovation leadership comes into play. Because as they say, "From the idea to the invention, concept to creation...... Execution is the key".

Ever wanted to augment your creative potential to tackle the escalating technological as well as social challenges that we are facing today? Ever wanted to equip your team or employees to take "leaps of faith " that would enable them to overcome these complex obstacles and create a better product for society? That is what innovative leaders' practice. Even though innumerable definitions of innovation leadership exist, still one that explains it all is the fact that innovation leaders help people translate their ideas into reality. Innovation is not just doing something new for the sake of it, but to add value or solve a problem within an existing system or organization. George Cuoros defines innovation as a way of thinking to create new and better things. Innovation can result from either "invention" (all new) or "repetition" (change of what already exists), but if it does not correspond to the idea of "new and better", it is not innovative [3].

The words that come to your mind when you hear about the word "leadership" include mentor, vision, support, manager, ethics, influence, etc. "A leader is someone who builds their team, mentors them, and then advocates for them," [4]. What then is meant by innovation in leadership? Innovation leadership involves synthesizing different leadership styles in organizations to influence employees to produce creative ideas, products, services, and solutions. These innovators who use their creative capacity enough to advance, help us to make big strides and lead us to a new age of betterment. One of the things that every great innovator has is that not one of them accepts the status quo. Innovative leaders cultivate an environment where ideas can be developed, and better yet where they can blossom. They are visionaries who lead by example and more importantly foster collaboration, creating a culture of trust and venturousness where those under them are not afraid of trying out new ideas, as they know the leader has their back. In his memoir, "The Long Walk to Freedom," Nelson Mandela compared the roles of leader and shepherd as follows: "I piloted from behind." [5]. Innovation leaders basically commit to making organizations work for the greater good and innovation leadership takes its inspiration from a vast array of sources. This chapter will explore the various theories that have dictated innovation leaders over the years, how creativity begets conception of new ideas, look at case studies to understand strategies that have helped in the evolution of certain companies, and sum it all up with the best practices that should be promoted to create innovative leaders.

Innovation Leadership in the 21st Century
DOI: http://dx.doi.org/10.5772/intechopen.101932

1.1 Innovation leadership theory

We believe innovation leadership provides particularly powerful lessons to those wanting to address the big challenges of developmental reforms within their organizations. We can define leadership as the ability to influence a group towards the achievement of its goals. In management terms, if you achieve the aim of an organization, through its members by the use of your authority, then that is called leadership. There are various theories prevalent today that dictate how leadership should look like. It is essential to really understand these theories to meet our organizational goals and groom leaders within organizations.

1.1.1 Path-goal theory

This theory has been around since 1970 when Martin Evans developed it while Robert House improved it in 1971. The Path-Goal model emphasizes the importance of the leader's ability to interpret followers' needs accurately and to respond flexibly to the requirements of a situation [6].

The basic argument that this theory offers is that it is the chief responsibility of the leader to motivate the followers to conclude their tasks, and the leader does that by removing any obstacles in their path. To reiterate it, if the followers are motivated enough to attain a sense of fulfillment after they accomplish a task, and if all the negating factors in their way get cleared, they could take these tasks to completion. In the most simplistic terms, Path-Goal theory is about "how leaders motivate their followers to accomplish goals" [7].

Why is it called the Path-Goal Theory? Because it emphasizes the fact that leaders should change their leadership styles to their subordinates or adopt a path based on the situations, they face to achieve a goal. It is molded on the Expectancy Theory of Motivation. Breaking it down for the layman, when will your employees or your team be motivated enough to work towards a task? First, when they believe that the goals, they have received are attainable (Expectancy). Second, when there is a promise of a reward (Instrumentality). And third, if that reward holds any value for them (Valence).

Therefore, in the Path-Goal theory, leaders go about looking for ways to motivate their teams to achieve their objectives, eliminate any roadblocks or ambiguities in their way and make sure that the fruit these efforts bear is desirable. It is similar to the way a parent removes obstacles from a child's path so that he can attain excellence in the best environment possible.

Now, depending on the situation a leader faces and the kind of employee or teammate he has under him, there are four kinds of behaviors that he may need to adapt to increase productivity and thus the possibility of innovation within his organization. It would also improve job satisfaction and performance. According to (House and Mitchell 1974, p. 83), this approach has focused on "directive, supportive, participative, and achievement-oriented leadership behaviors" [8].

- Directive- Like old-fashioned management, this includes planning, organizing, specifying standard protocols, or making policies based on the task.

- Supportive- When there is a warm and friendly surrounding, it enables open communication between team members and the leader.

- Participative- Like one-on-one peer sessions in classrooms, this behavior style asks for inputs from subordinates, enables an open discussion between them,

17

and juggles ideas in a way that each member has an active involvement in the decision-making process.

- Achievement-oriented- A style where the main focus is on the attainment of the goal.

Thus Path-Goal theory is instrumental in dictating the responsibility that a leader has towards the organization and the users [9]. But how do leaders then decide which style to follow?

For example, if your followers have known how to approach a situation and are skilled, but they are not confident about their approach, then in this state you adopt a participative style, engage in an open discussion with them, get them to talk, discuss ideas and guide them on a clear path.

On the other hand, if your followers are unskilled, not in control of the situation, completely naive, then it's time to adapt the directive leadership style. Apple's culture of fairness to the employee was nurtured by Steve Jobs. As the leader, he adopted the participative style and understood that he needed to work with highly motivated employees. He did not only act as a leader but he offered guidance to the employees giving them a sense of direction [10].

1.1.2 Leader-member exchange theory (LMX)

The Leader–Member Exchange (LMX) literature is hardly at its infancy, but the field is still under progressive development [11]. This theory suggests that leaders automatically develop a relationship with each of their subordinates, and the strength of these relationships strongly influences the productivity within the organization. It encompasses two-way communication between the leader and the team member. The more trust, loyalty, and support present in this bond, the better the performance of the team members will be.

A study done in 2017 found that this theory fully mediates the relationship between abusive supervision and intrinsic motivation; intrinsic motivation partially mediates the relationship between LMX and creativity, and LMX and intrinsic motivation sequentially mediate the relationship between abusive supervision and individual creativity [12]. There are three stages through which this leader-subordinate relation passes-

- When a team member joins the group and the leader gauges how skilled he is, the manager is still forming an initial assessment of the team member, just like in real life when we meet someone new for the first time. This stage is called Role Taking.

- Based on his assessment of the team, he will divide them into two groups, one that forms his inner circle i.e., people close to him who proved their loyalty or trust. And another group is the outer circle, which has not formed as strong bonds as the inner group. This stage is called Role Making

They based this theory on the assumption that each individual is different and thus has different communication needs. Or in other words, that every member of the team is unique and must be treated differently. The findings of a study published in the International Journal of Organizational Leadership demonstrated that there exists a significant and positive relationship between LMX and organizational change management [13].

Innovation Leadership in the 21st Century
DOI: http://dx.doi.org/10.5772/intechopen.101932

A proper understanding of these theories thus helps foster the right environment for innovation by providing a general direction on necessary leadership functions.

And innovation climate (top management support, resource supply) mediates the relationship between transformational leadership and organizational innovation because effective leadership should build a supportive climate for innovation [14]. Organizational innovation is the implementation of a method that has not been used before in the organization, it results from the strategic decision that management has taken [15].

1.1.3 Creativity, leadership, and innovation- what is the connection?

Now that we clearly understand innovation, leadership, and the roots behind these concepts, let us ponder on the significance of "creativity" for promoting innovation.

Although almost identical on face value, creativity and innovation hold different connotations in real life. While every innovation involves creativity, not all forms of creativity lead to innovation. And understanding the clear distinction between these ideas helps leaders flourish in their organizations. One of my favorite analogies to make this easier to understand is the invention of pasta. Creativity involves coming up with an entirely new dish or recipe of the Italian pasta. Whereas innovation is modifying what is already known about pasta to make it more appealing to the market. Like changing the shape of the pasta, or making it more colorful to attract children.

It is safe to assume that there is truly a connection between creativity, leadership, and innovation? The use of Apple products has been rampant in the past few decades, and iPhone has emerged as one of the greatest inventions in recent years, especially among youth. He was a man who did not accept conventional wisdom about cell phones that existed and challenged it. He did not respect it and struggled to work around ways of turning that invention into innovation through his creative ideas. When thinking about tablets, smartphones, and laptops, it's almost inevitable that Apple and its companion Steve Jobs will appear. But instead of seeing Jobs as the inventor, it's better to see him differently because Walter Isaacson's biography calls him a "tweeker." [16, 17]. His creative flair led him to go out of his comfort zone, challenge the existing deficiencies and lead to the creation of a new innovative product.

Rajendra Prasad, who is a common name in the field of fashion and architecture, believes that the gap between being a fashion symbol and taking the entire fashion industry by storm lies in the realm of creativity. It lies in the ability of ordinary people to do extraordinary things and lies in the minds of the out-of-the-box thinkers who take the first courageous leap into the unknown and bring back something spectacular. These people are nothing short of leaders, who, through their creative mindsets, give birth to amazing innovations. In the process of creative entrepreneurship, apart from using creativity to build a business, these entrepreneurs also need to strike a balance between creative ideas, creativity, and entrepreneurship, which is achieved through the management and leadership behavior of creative entrepreneurs [18]. A creative leader hears something in one place, hears something else in another place, and somehow assembles it to come up with an innovation. That is how creativity, leadership, and innovation gel so well together.

To sum it up, creativity leads to innovation, and innovation gives birth to leadership. There is a basic formula to becoming a leader or starting entrepreneurship. It is a function of two major things- an initial idea and a willingness and creativity to engage in and sell that idea. Also, heroic creativity and leadership feature strongly in the careers of creative workers, optimizing well-being, satisfaction, and career coping strategies.

2. Strategic model for innovation leadership

Having come to this point in the discussion, let us rewind to what we started this discussion with. The notion that it is the people and their cooperation that leads to the best kinds of innovations. Combine that with a creative mindset and the right direction, and you get innovative leaders to lead the team forward. Ever then wondered why some companies or organizations succeed at doing this while others fail. From research over countless years and by many researchers, it all boils down to having the right strategy. And not only that but also being able to implement that strategy.

Many models of promoting innovation leadership in organizations have come into play in recent times. There are varied opinions regarding the same. Some belief in implementing an innovation culture by motivating your teammates to seek advancement. But this wastes resources and is based on a dependence on skillful people who can leave the team anytime. Another model that some companies use is of hiring what they call an "inventor" or innovation consultant, who propose ideas that are then taken to realization. This again means relying on external sources for the successful leadership of your organization. To give a better frame of reference, some corporations use mixed tactics that include open and closed innovation approaches.

The most important question to ask for the leaders while devising an appropriate strategy is related to their expectations from their organization and themselves in the future. How do they want to reinvent their team? Is the plan of action they have aligned with their goals for the company? If yes, a strategic model for innovation leadership is then nothing more than a roadmap for a team's coveted future. Strategic innovation takes the road less traveled – it challenges an organization to look beyond its established business boundaries and mental models and to participate in an open-minded, creative exploration of the realm of possibilities [19, 20].

Here, I will give you a basic structure on how organizations should choose the best strategy. First of all, start with making sure you are selecting the leadership styles or practices that you are more equipped to execute than your counterparts. One relatively solid framework for making those strategic choices and choosing those behaviors is the strategy choice cascade [21]. It is described in the strategy book titled Playing to Win by. Former P & G CEO Lafley and Roger L. Martin, Dean of the Rotman School of Management at the University of Toronto.

One of AG Lafley's specific suggestions is that organizations build and develop an entire list of strategic decision-makers who know what it takes to attract and connect with participation and a more conscious structure. Innovation is one of the most difficult to align with strategy. It's chaotic in nature, and its team-oriented approach sometimes pushes the boundaries, challenging a variety of established positions and becoming seemingly contradictory. Achieving alignment requires some better options that repeatedly trace back to innovation activities and strategic needs [22].

This requires a selection cascade model. In this model, understanding flows through coordinated cascade decisions. Its purpose is first to give the "decision-maker" the opportunity to make individual decisions so that they can move it upstream again by stimulating and facilitating different levels of common sense or best judgment. Roger Martin and Hillary Clinton proposed "the art of integrated

Innovation Leadership in the 21st Century
DOI: http://dx.doi.org/10.5772/intechopen.101932

thinking [23]. To sum it all up, just as in battles, businesses or governments, similarly a good strategy put to work is what separates a successful innovation leadership from a poor one. This makes strategic leadership one of the most important components of innovation in the 21st century.

3. Innovation leadership in a digital environment

The days of brainstorming on whiteboards and sticky notes are long gone. Innovation in leadership looks slightly different in this century, especially when we talk about digitalization. But what exactly is digital transformation? "It is the integration of digital technology into all areas of a business, fundamentally changing how you operate and deliver value to the customer ". This transformation has also come about as a cultural change that requires companies to constantly challenge the present state of affairs, and observe and gracefully accept failure. Since users are now at the center of every digital experience, it has now become all the more important to develop leaders that cultivate a work culture that rewards innovation which in turn drives efficiency and thus better delivery of services to the users. Rapid growth in mobile connectivity and remarkable strides in the cloud has reduced the costs incurred in establishing global platforms since it has become simpler to dismantle technological barriers. In fact, as research by the MIT Sloan School of Management shows, 14 out of the top 30 brands by market capitalization in 2013 were platform-oriented companies. These organizations thrive on digitalization in innovation leadership [24].

Also, businesses are now being measured by the outcomes of the services they deliver which has increased the importance of selling results that appeal to the customer. A rising enterprising culture means that hundreds of start-ups have emerged that have overshadowed the traditional markets that could not keep up with digitalization [25]. Include a list of Uber, Twitch, Tesla, Hired, Clinkle, Beyond Verbal, Vayable, GitHub, WhatsApp, Airbnb, Matternet, Snapchat, Homejoy, Waze, and more. These startups can scale much faster than traditional analog companies. It took 20 years for Fortune 500 company to reach an average market capitalization of $ 1 billion, but Google achieved that in 8 years, and companies such as Uber, Snapchat, and Xiaomi achieved it within 3 years [26]. What is the reason behind this tremendous growth? Maybe because these enterprises have the foundational stability and the 360-degree vision to enter and dominate as-yet unidentified niche markets which will forever remain shut to the slower moving, more traditional stalwarts of the industry.

To put this concept into perspective, as Zeike et al. (2019) mention, we measure the holistic vision of digital leadership as an overlap between digital literacy (i.e., computer literacy, ICT literacy, digital competence, etc.) and digital leadership itself. In simpler terms, leadership capabilities are the ways in which managers are driving change [27].

I will end this on a case study of the leading aerospace company in the world and how it was transformed for the digital age. Boeing is sitting in the gold mine of the data. A single trip on one of the company's 787 Dreamliners can generate up to 1 terabyte of data. It takes hundreds of planes and tens of thousands of trips a year … well, you understand what's important. However, to use all this data to improve features such as product development and value-added services for customers, a 102-year-old company needed to redefine its an approach to software [28]. Bill Boeing created the company in 1916 with the clear philosophy "build something better ". Niki Allen, a 14-year veteran of the aerospace company lead the effort to transform Boeing's approach towards digitalization. To execute this, Allen developed a "master plan"

Leadership in a Changing World - A Multidimensional Perspective

that was based on the Three Es: Engagement, Excellence, and Enablement. Her approach is illuminating to other organizational executives embarking on digital transformation journeys at their enterprises and sheds light on how innovation leadership in a digital world looks like [29].

4. Innovation leadership- best practice recommendations

The radical transformation of 21st century organizations is nothing less than a modern-day industrial revolution wherein innovation now plays a critical role in determining organizational success (Cascio & Aguinis, 2008, 2019). Disney's animation studio Pixar uses cutting-edge technology and creative collaboration to create a competitive advantage. Pixar movies (Finding Nemo, Finding Dory, Toy Story 3, etc.) are one of the top 50 movies to date, with Toy Story 3 recording $ 1.06 billion in 2010 sales (Mendelson, 2017), as it became the third-highest animated film in history. The secret to Pixar's success is the founder's innovation leadership. Edwin Catmull and Alvy Ray Smith inculcated an environment where creative ideas could be turned into innovations by following certain best practices [30].

So how do you become an innovator if you are not already that? Do these innovation leaders follow certain practices or show certain behaviors that make them different from their counterparts? Well yes, they do. To begin with, these leaders create a safe space for innovation by developing an environment that allows for the respectful sharing of ideas. If the subordinates are not afraid of being reprimanded for presenting their thoughts, they would be more open to sharing them. For instance, Toyota encourages innovation by removing some of the pressure for short-term returns. Toyota's decade-long investment in its Prius sub-brand ultimately succeeded in strengthening the company's reputation as a respected product innovator while allowing Toyota to capture a first-mover advantage in the fast-growing hybrid category [31]. Secondly, these leaders observe the world like an anthropologist and learn from their setbacks. They are not afraid of pushing their boundaries. An example of an employee's performance assessment is "productive failure" if an employee tries something and fails, but learns valuable lessons or can adapt from what did not work to what worked [McKinsey Global Institute, 2014]. At Dow Chemical's risk-taking is not only accepted, it is encouraged, which helps the company to stay agile and innovative. Dow sources said: "Empowerment really helps to stay agile. We encourage you to take the courage to lead and keep asking "what if " and "why?". We recognize opportunities for our employees and challenge them to push the boundaries."

Thirdly, innovation leaders are known to be persuasive. They present their ideas with such eloquence that the team is forced to follow them at the drop of a hat. On top of that, they display their vision for the future with excellence and alacrity. Finally, innovation leaders are courageous and trust themselves enough to trust others in the team. They have full faith in their ideology and the expectations they have from their organizations. Along with being courageous, they exhibit intellectual humility which is the ability to listen to others and admit your own mistakes. In a recent op-ed piece, [for example, Thomas Friedman 2014] recounts the five attributes internet giant Google looks for in new employees. They include intellectual humility – an ability to recognize and admit mistakes to others. Gardner recognizes the environment and potential for change in the future and believes that there are five minds that must be cultivated for the success of the 21st century. These five spirits are a disciplined mind, a synthetic mind, a creative mind, a respectful mind, and an ethical mind. Gardner acknowledges that he could have broadened the use of the word mind and perhaps used more accurate perspectives and skills, but the

Innovation Leadership in the 21st Century
DOI: http://dx.doi.org/10.5772/intechopen.101932

word mind is an individual action, thought, emotion, or action. It reminds me that it is created in my mind. Gardner pays no special attention to any one of these minds, emphasizing that their development is equally important.

5. Putting it all together

According to the Center for Creative Leadership creativity experts David Horth and Dan Buchner, creating an innovative organization "is about growing a culture of innovation, not just hiring a few creative outliers." This chapter puts into perspective a host of possible ways in which innovative leaders have brought revolutions in the field of entrepreneurship. This chapter draws on the way some companies have achieved spectacular successes through behaviors to promote innovation and creativity. It distinguishes innovation and invention and sheds light on the various theories that have been put forward in recent years. It emphasizes the importance of providing enough autonomy to allow leaders with the development ideas to test innovative solutions in their teams. Innovative leaders have certain behaviors that set them apart from their counterparts and enable them to bring a change in their organizations. Entrepreneurs should be able to balance vision with managerial skill, passion with pragmatism, and proactiveness with patience. They should be able to build a high trust environment that promotes and fosters innovation. The implications of not establishing a high-trust environment among team members are huge because trust is the gateway to candor – the honest and frank exchange of ideas vital for "getting to the best idea". Professors and Ph.D. students in ecology and evolutionary biology, Iain Couzin and Albert Kao, respectively, have discovered that "popular wisdom" does not always lead to better decisions. Instead, the results of studies of individuals within the group, whether human or other animal species, suggest that small groups maximize decision-making accuracy in many situations. (Kao and Couzin, 2014, cited in Zimmer, 2014).

This chapter also brings to attention the connection between leadership, innovation, and creativity and how it all adds up to bring exponential growth in conglomerates. Innovative leaders like Steve Jobs and A.G Lafley lead by example and show the world how the correct choices in leadership and the perfect alignment of goals could yield massive results. They called it the Cascade of Choices. To put cherry on top, digitalization has made life easier. Although there are still certain ambiguities involved, yet with the crossing of technological barriers, traditional organizations have been left behind and new start-ups are starting to emerge and evolve. Advancement in digital technology has also enabled better access to remote areas and communities which has made it easier to cater to their user demands. As a result, small companies have flourished and gained momentum, which they would not have been able to do earlier. Going forward with the motto of creating something better, innovation leaders have started to evaluate the expectations they have from their teams and organizations and help these direct the course of action they want to take. Boeing is an example of such a conglomerate. In a review of great entrepreneurs like Steve Jobs of Apple, Bill Gates of Microsoft, Jeff Bezos of Amazon, Martha Stewart, Jack Bogle of Vanguard, and Howard Shultz of Starbucks, CNBC's chief editor Eric Schurenberg (2014) notes "the thread that stands out, partly because it's unexpected, is a failure. Or more precisely: the ability to absorb failure and – by determination, grit, pugnacity, whatever – turn it into success." (for example, Myers et al., 2014).

The chapter ends meaningfully on the best practice recommendations that every leader should follow to bring about innovation in his sphere, whether it be through creating a safe culture for his subordinates that promotes discussion or be it through pushing boundaries and challenging the status quo. His team members must be encouraged to show their vulnerabilities, to reveal what they know or think, and to accept their mistakes and willing to correct them. There should be elimination of a hierarchy system that leads to an atmosphere of fear within the organization. Inculcating these practices can bring about positive changes towards innovation.

Conflict of interest

The authors declare no conflict of interest.

Author details

Fatimah AlAhmari
King Faisal Specialist Hospital and Research Center, Riyadh, Saudi Arabia

*Address all correspondence to: fatimahsa@hotmail.com3

IntechOpen

© 2022 The Author(s). Licensee IntechOpen. This chapter is distributed under the terms of the Creative Commons Attribution License (http://creativecommons.org/licenses/by/3.0), which permits unrestricted use, distribution, and reproduction in any medium, provided the original work is properly cited. (cc) BY

References

[1] Gliddon D, Rothwell W. Innovation Leadership. 1st ed. Routledge; 2020. DOI: 10.4324/9781315178219

[2] Cone T. What is Innovation Leadership? How the Most Effective Innovation Leaders Show Up, Do Great Work, and Superpower Their Teams. Lightshed. 2019. Available from: https://medium.com/lightshed/what-is-innovation-leadership-8094f79620ca

[3] Cuoros G. The Innovator's Mindset: Empower Learning, Unleash Talent, and Lead a Culture of Creativity. 1st ed. Dave Burgess Consulting, Inc.; 2015. https://www.perlego.com/book/867937/the-innovators-mindset-pdf

[4] Hoey JK. Build Your Dream Network: Forging Powerful Connections in a Hyper-connected World. Tarcher Perigee; 2018. https://www.phoenixbooks.biz/book/9780143111498

[5] Ioannis. The Leadership Style of The Future. The People Development Magazine. 2019. Available from: https://peopledevelopmentmagazine.com/2019/10/16/leadership-style-of-the-future/

[6] Developing Leadership Skills. Available from: http://oer2go.org/mods/en-boundless/www.boundless.com/management/textbooks/boundless-management-textbook/leadership-9/developing-leadership-skills-74/developing-leadership-skills-365-3463/index.htmlContent and user contributions on this site are licensed under CC BY-SA 4.0 with attribution required

[7] Anderson P. What is Path-Goal Theory? PSYCH 485 blog. 2016. Available from: https://sites.psu.edu/leadership/2016/06/29/what-is-path-goal-theory/

[8] Northouse PG. Leadership: Theory and Practice. 7th ed. Thousand Oaks,

CA: Sage; 2016. p. 494. Available from: https://journalhosting.ucalgary.ca/index.php/cjeap/article/view/42995

[9] Hom Jr HL, Abigail L, Nuland V. Evaluating scientific research: Belief, hindsight bias, ethics, and research evaluation. Applied Cognitive Psychology. 2019;**33**(4):675-681. DOI: 10.1002/acp.3519

[10] Martin R, Epitropaki O, Erdogan B, Thomas G. Relationship based leadership: Current trends and future prospects. Journal of Occupational and Organizational Psychology. 2019;**92**:465-474. DOI: 10.1111/joop.12286

[11] Meng Y, Tan J, Li J. Abusive supervision by academic supervisors and postgraduate research students' creativity: The mediating role of leader–member exchange and intrinsic motivation. International Journal of Leadership in Education. 2017;**20**(5):605-617. DOI: 10.1080/13603124.2017.1304576

[12] Arif M, Zahid S, Kashif U, Sindhu MI. Role of leader-member exchange relationship in organizational change management: Mediating role of organizational culture. International Journal of Organizational Leadership. 2017;**6**(1):32-41. DOI: 10.33844/ijol.2017.60339

[13] Uddin MA, Fan L, Das AK. A study of the impact of transformational leadership, organizational learning, and knowledge management on organizational innovation. Management Dynamics. 2017;**16**(2):43-45

[14] Meroño-Cerdán AL, López-Nicolás C, Molina-Castillo. Risk aversion, innovation and performance in family firms. Economics of Innovation and New Technology. 2018;**27**(2):189-203. DOI: 10.1080/10438599.2017.1325569

[15] Chu M. The Steve Jobs Method of Innovation: Why You Should Stop Making Things From Scratch. Jumpstart your Dream Life; 2019. Available from: https://medium.com/jumpstart-your-dream-life/the-steve-jobs-method-of-innovation-why-you-should-stop-making-things-from-scratch-26c6f583a031

[16] Dios AD, Kong L. Handbook on the Geographies of Creativity. 1st ed. ElgarOnline; 2020. DOI: 10.4337/9781785361647

[17] OECD. Innovating Education and Educating for Innovation: The Power of Digital Technologies and Skills. Paris: OECD Publishing; 2016. DOI: 10.1787/9789264265097-en

[18] Dani R. When ideas trump interests: Preferences, worldviews, and policy innovations. Journal of Economic Perspectives. 2014;**28**(1):189-208

[19] Mueller J, Melwani S, Goncalo JA. The bias against creativity: Why people desire but reject creative ideas. Psychological Science. 2011;**23**(1):13-17. DOI: 10.1177/0956797611421018

[20] Dearlove D. The Chief Strategy Officer Playbook. Thinkers50 Limited; 2018. DOI: 10.1787/9789264265097-en

[21] Taylor A. Strategy Implementation: How To Cascade Your Strategic Plan. Strategy Management Consulting; 2019. Available from: https://www.smestrategy.net/blog/how-to-cascade-your-strategic-plan

[22] Scene. Scenes from An Interview-AG Lafley. Sarasota Scene Magazine; 2021. Available from: http://www.scenesarasota.com/magazine/clean-scenes-interview-ag-lafley/

[23] Martin R. The Opposable Mind: How Successful Leaders Win Through Integrative Thinking. Harvard Business School Press; 2017. http://www-2.rotman.utoronto.ca/rogermartin/Becominganintegrativethinker.pdf

[24] Brown S. How to Master Two Different Digital Transformations. Ideas Made to Matter; 2020. Available from: https://mitsloan.mit.edu/ideas-made-to-matter/how-to-master-two-different-digital-transformations

[25] Companies with Better Digital Business Models HaveHigher Fnancial Performance, Center for Information System Research, MIT Sloan Management. Research Briefing. July 2013;13(7)

[26] Nauwijn B. New Way of Digital Business Models. TJIP; 2017. Available from: https://www.tjip.com/en/publications/new-way-of-digital-business-models

[27] Zeike S, Bradbury K, Lindert L, Pfaff H. Digital leadership skills and associations with psychological well-being. International Journal of Environmental Research and Public Health. 2019;**16**(14):2628. DOI: 10.3390/ijerph16142628

[28] Shivdas S, Shepardson D. U.S. FAA Confirms Boeing Halt to 787 Dreamliner Deliveries. Reuters; 2021. Available from: https://tanzu.vmware.com/content/blog/boeing-and-the-three-e-s-of-digital-transformation

[29] Kelly J. Boeing and the Three Es of Digital Transformation. Vmware Tanzu; 2018. Available from: https://tanzu.vmware.com/content/blog/boeing-and-the-three-e-s-of-digital-transformation

[30] Watkinson J. Who Inspired the Founders of Pixar? Innovation at Work; 2014. Available from: https://innovationatwork.wordpress.com/2014/10/01/who-inspired-the-founders-pixar/

Innovation Leadership in the 21st Century
DOI: http://dx.doi.org/10.5772/intechopen.101932

[31] Toyota. Prius Was Only the Beginning as Toyota Bets Big on Hybrids. Toyota Newsroom; 2020. Wordpress. Available from: https://pressroom.toyota.com/prius-was-only-the-beginning-as-toyota-bets-big-on-hybrids/

Chapter 3

Venture Leadership under Uncertainty: An Emerging Country Perspective

Bilal Khalid, Md Samim Al Azad, Slimane Ed-dafali and Muhammad Mohiuddin

Abstract

Strategic planning and entrepreneurial leadership are needed for effective navigation into the volatile business environment in an era of the knowledge intensive and fast-changing business eco-system. The growing volatile and competitive business climate demands a new sort of "leadership" different from the conventional form of leadership. As a result, having either management or entrepreneurial traits in venture leaders is insufficient for business success. Leaders must be capable of both entrepreneurship and management skills to excel. This study emphasizes the notion of venture leadership that refers to entrepreneurial leadership combining leadership characteristics with an entrepreneurial mindset. In addition, venture leadership involves developing new business processes, new products and prospects for growth in established businesses, collaborating with other social institutions to combat neglected social issues, engaging in political and social movements, and contributing to the modification of prevailing policies and schemes executed by the government and civil organizations. Venture leadership is an emerging concept in business management that challenges the status quo. As a result, the relevance of venture leadership is addressed in this paper by investigating the idea of venture leadership, leadership skills, and ethics in the emerging country context of Thailand.

Keywords: venture leadership, leadership skills, leadership ethics

1. Introduction

Business eco-system is fast changing due to increased competition, rapidly changing advanced technology, global diversity and a multipolar economic order contributing to rapidly changing market circumstances. To maintain a competitive edge, businesses must be more versatile to respond rapidly to the effects of these developments. As a result, the venture leadership role and responsibilities are becoming less structured and require leaders with multi-skills, flexible, receptive, sensitive, and open to managing rapid changes [1]. Also, venture leaders play a critical role in the creation of new enterprises that propel growth in the global community. In many aspects of life, venture leaders employ a combination of technological inventions to create a new and productive way of doing things. A major challenge of leaders when the enterprise experience massive growth, is the ability to transition seamlessly from a sole entrepreneur to a leader of an expanding business. Many venture leaders are usually not equipped or prepared to take on this new responsibility.

Several start-ups' leaders lack traditional management or leadership experience, while others are most productive when working alone on difficult technical challenges. However, they are capable of learning and mastering effective leadership skills. Also becoming a successful leader of a business venture does not necessitate an advanced formal education but the instinct of identifying opportunities, taking risk and transforming uncertainty into opportunities [2]. Although, many emerging entrepreneurs rely on learning on the job, this may be dangerous. Expanding ventures typically have limited tolerance for error and must function efficiently from the start to prosper [3]. If the leader is a novice and just acquiring management and leadership skills for the while on the job, the business will suffer and it may also make the stakeholders and investors feel frustrated with the process. Although, venture leaders must have basic experience in the craft and skill of leading and managing, a few insights from literature and experts may also be beneficial. Currently, the demand for venture leaders in organizations is rising daily, and studies should explore the topic of venture leadership [4]. This study elucidates more about the importance of venture leadership and the characteristics of venture leaders. While there have been papers exploring the venture leadership question, this study expands the scope by offering perspectives from an ASEAN emerging country such as Thailand.

It attempts to answer the question of how venture leadership thrives within the Thai business environment. Within this context, the concept of leadership is briefly discussed as well as the skills required to be an effective and successful leader. It covers some basic concepts for leading and managing a venture. The fundamental principles and leadership approaches presented here are meant to give a foundation for comprehending the wide range of challenges that always occur in new enterprises [5]. These concepts should not only be applied to leadership also the outcomes must be tracked and evaluated. Every one of the abilities, roles, and strategies presented here should be altered and adjusted as specific cases emerge. The discussion begins with the concept of leadership then it reviewed numerous sought-after skills that venture leaders require to control and organize the business work environment. Leadership guidelines, as a subcategory of organizational principles, can play a vital role in influencing employee perceptions, morals, and attitudes, and the relationship between leadership and followership. They can be used to help establish a common leadership culture.

2. Venture leadership and influence

Leading in a fast-changing, usually hostile corporate environment is what venture leadership entails. This leadership method is extremely important when you are, launching a global high-growth business, or leading a significant shift or an innovation venture. Therefore, leadership is becoming increasingly crucial. Businesses must focus on leadership to actualize their goals and maintain their sustainability. Leadership is commonly described as the practice of influencing businesses' personnel to attain organizational objectives [6]. It refers to the capacity to influence people so that certain objectives and goals can be achieved. Leadership is also the capacity to inspire others to support and believe in the firm's aims. Leadership involves the act of influencing and directing team members on the right path. To attain business goals, the leader influences group members by displaying leadership skills. Persuading others to do something needs a variety of persuasive abilities. Leadership requires having the power to influences others. Several studies have established that the professional skills and competence that made venture leaders effective in the beginning stage of the business can inhibit them as the business expands needing more leading and managing [7, 8]. Scholars have also identified that several leaders are successful in starting and creating a business alone. Although, when the business expands and demands more workers, they more not have the essential skills to inspire and motivate their team members [9].

Ventures leaders with business acumen and entrepreneurial abilities are like captains in a soccer game who plays along with the team member to achieve a goal. Leaders do not make decisions, provide orders, and monitor their employees, they must also choose to be leaders who direct the team and point to the way. Leaders who take risks and grasp chances are critical for the future success of the firm [10]. They identified six attributes that characterized effective venture leadership. The first characteristic is the support of entrepreneurial skills. Successful venture leaders recognize the source of entrepreneurial skills to be the human element and give their full support to the acquisition of this skill. They recognize the human factor as the basis of entrepreneurial activity and work to foster its growth. The second characteristics are how they interpret and perceive business opportunities. Venture leaders can detect opportunities from afar and inculcate their value as part of the goals of the business. They defend the breakthroughs that pose a challenge to the present business model. Disruptive technology is considered an organizational and personal danger by individuals [11]. However, an effective venture leadership can successfully communicate to others about the prospective advantages of disruptive innovations. To find a new valuable opportunity and ensure that the company is positioned successfully, venture leadership is continually questioning the assumptions underpinning the prevalent logic. Venture leaders also continuously evaluate the questions regarding identifying opportunities and employing the resources required to maintain the existence of the organization, business, developing a strong relationship with partners, and defining the business achievements and goals. In addition, effective leaders think that to produce more value, a business should strategically employ entrepreneurship skills.

Additionally Young Entrepreneur Council [12] also identified 12 significant traits that are required for an effective venture leader. The first feature is that a leader should be flexible and willing to adjust plans as work progresses. The second important feature is humility. An effective venture leader must have a modest demeanor. They should examine their role if the business fails and not point accusing fingers at others. Also, if the company succeeds, this should not be viewed only as their accomplishment. Rather it should be considered a collective effort. Another important trait of venture leaders is their ability to focus on important issues. They concentrate their energy and time on the success of the business. They are also keen on making decisions that will add maximum benefit to the business. Another trait is their die-hard attitude. Leaders are not in haste rather they are determined and resolute in their willingness to succeed. Apart from this, they are vision carriers, they are like the eagle that can see what is afar [13]. They also make sure that their team members understand this vision and are ready to run with it. Successful leaders can strike a good balance between anxiety and trust. They never abandon both their pragmatic and imaginative beliefs. Venture leaders own their achievements. They exert control over external forces. This is one of the requirements they must embrace. Venture leaders see daily occurrences favorably. And they encourage their staff to remain upbeat. Venture leaders can successfully communicate and promote their business. They can persuade customers to buy items from their businesses. Lastly, venture leaders understand their strengths and weaknesses [14].

Moreover, Jaiswal and Dhar [15] in their study identified personality traits of a successful venture leader and suggested nine aspects of venture leadership. These are decisiveness, teamwork, risk-taking, persistency, ability to identify consumers' needs, visionary, innovation, problem-solving ability, and adaptability to changes. Generally, leadership as a concept applies to a wide range of social situations, including politics, sports, organizations, and business enterprises. It is undoubtedly agreeable that the characteristics and actions that influence the individual to be a successful political leader differ greatly from the ones that influence another individual to be an excellent sports team captain. This is also true for business executives. The qualities and actions required of leaders of huge corporations differ from what is required of leaders of business ventures [16].

The use of influence is at the heart of effective leadership. Influence is the key instrument used by leaders in advancing the venture toward achieving its objectives. To drive a venture ahead, the leader also uses methods such as remuneration, employee assessment and feedback, and organizational structure. For venture leadership positions, seven influence techniques have been identified as essential. The first technique is logical reasoning. This is the use of data and evidence to construct a logically sound argument. The second is friendliness which is the use of encouragement, praise, and fostering of goodwill. The third is a coalition which involves the mobilization of other team members [17]. The fourth technique is bargaining, this involves making deals using favors or rewards. The fifth is assertiveness which is taking a forthright and aggressive stand. The sixth is obtaining the backing of higher authority in the business hierarchy to lend weight to their proposal. The last technique is sanctioning which involves both the use of incentives and punishment.

Venture leaders must master a range of influence techniques. As the company expands, they will be unable to rely exclusively on the confidence that comes with being the founder. According to research, allowing employees to influence how the business operates increases their motivation. Todorovic and Schlosser [18] identified that the biggest challenge for leaders is not if they make wise judgments and take bold action, but it is whether they educate and motivate people to become leaders and develop an enterprise that can maintain success even in their absence. Venture leaders should wield influence without creating hubris or a sense of superiority. This might be challenging for new leaders who are unaccustomed to influence and responsibility. To summarize, tyrants seldom inspire substantial effort among followers [19]. People are more influenced by frontiers that genuinely care about their progress. A business leader is not expected to be preoccupied with personal progress in non-business domains like an individual personal financial ability or romantic life. Generally, individuals are more responsive to leaders that can give them a steady supply of difficult assignments that match their existing capabilities, temperament, and skills [20].

3. Leadership skills

Achievement in a new or expanding venture is not by happenstance. It is made possible by dedicated and skilled leaders who play strategic roles in the venture. As a leader of a developing venture, you impact performance by establishing objectives, detecting and reducing impediments to established objectives' accomplishment, and successfully organizing, planning, and regulating resources to achieve elevated levels of success. The focus of this section is the leadership skills needed in the daily situations that arise in a start-up venture. For many leaders, leading successfully as the business expands may be a challenging issue. The majority of first-time leaders do not have traditional management training. Their sole reference point might be

Venture Leadership under Uncertainty: An Emerging Country Perspective
DOI: http://dx.doi.org/10.5772/intechopen.102870

those who have led and supervised them at one time or the other along with their careers. They might have not been also exposed to professional leadership training. Although, professional leadership training is not required to be a good leader, however, the principles and skills offered by formal training can result in more successful performance. Leaders that do not adjust to a leadership position as they ought to, usually have to relinquish management of their business to more experienced individuals. This is something that can be done, and several venture leaders have done it. However, acquiring personal leadership capabilities and skills will be critical for leaders that desire to be at the front seat of the decision-making for their company for the long term [18].

The value of leadership in ventures is generally acknowledged by seasoned entrepreneurs and most investors [21]. In determining the success of a venture, only real performance counts. Wishes, good intentions, and promises are meaningless to the investors if good implementation and performance are absent. Moreover, the majority of the critical skills and talents required for execution are teachable, and any leader that is open to learning these skills has the highest chance of success [22]. Most leaders learn to lead others through learning and analyzing, as well as on-the-job experience. Irrespective of the type of venture, leaders must have and continue to cultivate several fundamental skills. A skill is an ability or expertise to do a certain activity. Leadership skills should be acquired and honed. Generally, leaders must strive to cultivate skills in these key areas as leaders: Team building, conceptual, self-awareness, communication, analytical, resilience, and decision making.

3.1 Team building skill

It is rare to see a leader who can operate like a hermit and yet be successful. Most ventures are too complex for an individual to run without assistance. Successful leaders are those who have mastered the skill of team building. They have the ability to intimate others with their idea, therefore, enabling them to grow into a cohesive team that is entirely centered on one goal. Team building focuses on recognizing the skill and talent gaps needed for the business venture to thrive, and then selecting individuals who possess these qualities. Successful leaders possess the ability to recruit workers, investors, and advisors who fill gaps in the venture's skill pool and help it meet its objectives. Building an effective team needs all of the skills listed above, as well as a healthy dose of humility. Successful leaders emphasize the necessity of employing and encouraging people who are more skilled than them. Indeed, the most successful leaders are not intimidated by the idea of recruiting workers that are better skilled than them. This remark may appear self-evident, yet it is not unusual for leaders to feel intimidated by individuals that more skilled than them. Before now, leaders have been used to competing with others all through their formal professional training. That competition does not simply vanish, a leader will need to realign their thought to subdue the competitive instinct. Replace sentiments of rivalry among their contemporaries with sentiments of team building which requires sacrificing personal pride and employing competent individuals to assist the venture to achieve its set goals and succeed against competitors. The basis of an effective team is straightforward: clear objectives and responsibilities. Exceptionally brilliant individuals are typically self-motivated. They desire to perform excellently and love working on well-defined, quantifiable goals. Leaders in ventures have discovered that they can anticipate a high level of dedication from bright individuals devoid of administrative interference. That is, brilliant individuals typically perform optimally when leaders set goals for them without interference. Self-organization is common among teams formed around specific tasks and goals [23].

3.2 Conceptual skills

The capacity to envision the fuller picture, the intricacies of the entire business system, and different parts are linked together are all examples of conceptual skills. Leaders utilize conceptual skills to build long-term visions for businesses. Conceptual skills also help the leader to forecast how future activities will impact the business years to come. Leadership, particularly visionary leadership, is one of the most essential cornerstones of success in ventures today. Every venture must create a vision and purpose to drive the various decisions that must be taken now and in the future. Visionary businesses have principles that are founded on an unchanging fundamental concept that spans immediate consumer needs and market realities. People are guided and inspired by the unifying concept of innovative firms. A uniting concept, when combined with a strong "cult-like" ethos, fosters great camaraderie and corporation. Tolerance for uncertainty and ambiguity is another important skill that the venture leader must cultivate. In reality, a leader should cultivate the capacity to absorb uncertainty, allowing the other team members to concentrate on the core aim. The ambiguity that all ventures face can be alleviated over time by market investigation and discovery. To facilitate positive growth, the venture leader must select which trials the business will undertake and the interpretation of the findings. The most successful technology ventures have frequently been founded by visionaries. Steve Jobs, the founder of Apple, is arguably the most well-known among the visionaries. Steve's underlying vision was to develop an "incredibly wonderful product." For over 20 years, this basic vision aroused great dedication and commitment from staff and has presented the world with a steady stream of new and ground-breaking products.

3.3 Self-awareness skill

Self-improvement in any capacity necessitates taking charge of establishing your self-identity through personal analysis. To do this, the individual needs to consider circumstances that they were successful and identify elements that contributed to their success. Was it hard work, sound planning, problem-solving ability, patience? Critical examination of past experiences necessitates self-talk, contemplation, and analysis. Sadly, recollections of memories frequently leave out important facts, information, and occurrences. Keeping a daily notebook is a wonderful way of tracking important aspects of one's achievement. Maintaining a diary for 5–10 days on daily interactions with others requires discipline [24]. The diary may be easily organized by including a date and summarizing remarks on what you did daily, whom you interacted with, the kind of thoughts you had, and the method you employed in solving problems faced. Concise and simple diary entries will aid in the evaluation and analysis process. At the very least, a daily entry of 10 days gives a picture of your thinking and behavior pattern. Another way to obtain self-awareness data is by completing self-assessment questionnaires. This can be a piece of private information that is only accessible to you. Invariably, feedback is required to develop any skill. Online tests of attitude, personality, talents, and skills can also be a source of eye-opening information, colleagues and friends can also provide feedback. However, some co-workers and acquaintances may be hesitant to offer genuine, revealing thorough and accurate comments. As a result, you can develop a short memo explaining why their feedback is essential to your growth. Following this method can convince them to be willing to help. Comparing other people's comments with the personal analysis you have conducted on self-awareness is instructive and useful. You will discover directly how people see you, allowing you to compare this knowledge to the way you see yourself. There might

Venture Leadership under Uncertainty: An Emerging Country Perspective
DOI: http://dx.doi.org/10.5772/intechopen.102870

be disagreements that must be properly assessed. After completing and analyzing the review, it is time to evaluate the skills that need to be developed. The evaluation system will undoubtedly reveal areas that require improvement. Overall, the self-evaluation should concentrate on three key areas to improve leadership skills: attitudes, values, and personality.

3.3.1 Personality

Individual uniqueness is created by a set of psychological and physical variables known as personality. An essential personality factor is a self-concept which is the way you see yourself as a spiritual, social, and physical being. Self-sufficiency and self-esteem are two related parts of self-concept. The belief in one's worth is referred to as self-esteem. Self-esteemed people believe they are vital, valuable, and important. Self-sufficiency is an individual believes that they can complete an activity, a job, or task, successfully [25].

3.3.2 Values

A person's values are their preferences for correct options. Values depict a person's perception of what is right, correct, or fair. Generally, a person's values are influenced by teachers, friends, parents, role models parents and, mentors. Because everyone's learning and experiences are different, so are individual values. There are two broad value categories. A person's preferences for "ends" to be achieved are reflected in terminal values. Instrumental values express a person's preferences for the methods that will be used to achieve their desired outcomes [26].

3.3.3 Attitudes

Attitudes can be described in a variety of ways. First, attitudes remain the same in individuals unless effort is made to change them. Second, attitudes can be positive or negative. Third, attitudes are usually aimed at a specific object and reflect the beliefs and feelings of the individual. As a result, attitudes are a continuous tendency to feel and act in a certain way toward a specific object. Information, behavior, and emotion are the three components that make up an individual's attitude.

3.4 Communication skills

Considering venture leaders need others to accomplish their goals, their ability to communicate with, collaborate, and appreciate others is critical [27]. Effective oral and written communication is critical for venture success. The ability is essential for success in any enterprise, but it is more important for leaders who must accomplish results via the contributions of others. Communication abilities include the capacity to communicate in an understandable way, as well as the willingness to pursue and use feedback gotten from others to guarantee that you are being understood [28]. Also, a leader's communication skills will be put to test when interacting with shareholders, investors, and stakeholders. Fundraising is one of the most important continuous responsibilities of a venture leader. To raise funds, the leader must be able to convey a concise story on the venture's products and market, its business strategy, and value proposition. This brief description of the company is frequently called the elevator pitch. Aside from the elevator pitch, a leader must also have the ability to explain the venture's goal and direction through a documented business plan. Nicole [29] hints that when engaging with potential lenders, investors, or other important stakeholders, a business plan is essential. You can also reduce the business plan into significant writing skills. Although, there are companies that offer these services, research has shown that the leader should produce these documents themselves [30]. Lastly, a leader must be adept at pitching the plan or executive summary to potential investors and other stakeholders [31]. The linguistic capacity to explain the business's objective and goals, as outlined in the strategy, necessitates understanding and adapting the style of communication to one's audience. Several technological venture leaders, for example, need to present their company ideas to individuals that are diverse and not technically savvy like them. In such circumstances, utilizing technical language or sophisticated visuals to explain a business idea is unlikely to generate the intended outcomes. The venture leader must modify communications to meet the other people's capabilities to participate in the conversation.

3.5 Analytical skill

Analytical skills are the ability to address organizational issues utilizing repeatable methodologies or procedures. Analytical skills centers on the capacity to recognize important elements influencing venture success, comprehend how they interface, and manage them to meet venture goals. It also includes the capacity to detect and analyze difficulties that arise on a day-to-day basis for the venture. Analytical skills are essential to comprehending challenges and devising a solution with action plans. Analytical abilities include the capacity to identify and comprehend how numerous complicated factors interact, as well as the ability to devise methods that would make these factors interface in a preferred manner [32]. These skills also enable you to assess your potential and the expertise of those involved in the venture. A leader that can assess and embrace their weakness and strength is in the best position to meet performance objectives. Also, leaders who have properly assessed their skills will recruit individuals who fit their strengths and mitigate their deficiencies. Most leaders may already have excellent analytical abilities; however, they are primarily concerned with technological issues instead of business concerns [33]. Managing a venture necessitates changing the focus from studying the main technology to assessing the business. In terms of technology, a venture may offer the best product or services. But from a business standpoint, the leader must analyze and evaluate the market potential, the associated costs of introducing the product or services to the market, the financial capacity that is needed to build and expand the venture, the scalability of the venture over time, and a variety of other factors [34].

3.6 Resilience skill

Another essential trait of a venture leader is resilience. The physical, financial, and emotional turmoil that most ventures face is frequently difficult to handle. Leaders must be able to maintain the venture's stability in the face of turmoil. Every human is equipped with the ability to maintain strength amid stress, ambiguity, and uncertainty. A leader must be fully aware of their limitations and try to improve them by engaging in personal development, reflection, and experience. Most leaders will eventually cultivate greater resilience as they fail, struggle, and recover [35]. However, there are things that a venture leader can and should do to improve personal resilience. For instance, peradventure the venture experiences difficulties with their finances, the leader needs to put their feelings concerning the difficulty under control so that it does not affect the venture team's performance. Walking around as a leader with a sad face or loud complaints concerning the state of finance will likely affect the team morale and subsequently, their performance

Venture Leadership under Uncertainty: An Emerging Country Perspective
DOI: http://dx.doi.org/10.5772/intechopen.102870

will suffer too. Whereas at such times, team performance is important more than ever, however, the leader's lack of self-control has the potential to undermine that performance [36].

3.7 Decision making skill

Every leader will have to decide at one point or the other and the quality of the decision, it will determine their effectiveness. The ability of a leader to focus and navigate the venture despite conflicting information and conditions has a significant impact on their decision-making ability. The ambiguity of emerging ventures is one of their defining characteristics [37]. They are frequently ambiguous about their value proposition, competition, market, and endurance capacity. When issues and challenges arise, venture leaders must learn to reject the pressures for a temporary fix. They need to learn how to cope with ambiguous situations, as well as to identify the most subtle differences between successful and unsuccessful actions [38]. In almost all cases, decision-making in ventures is made while confronting unresolvable ambiguity. Every leader must come to terms with this. The ambiguity of several of the challenges that a leader faces, however, should not result in paralysis or inaction. A leader must possess a proclivity for action as well as the ability to make decisions based on incomplete data. Finally, a leader needs the ability to act once a decision was taken [39].

4. Venture leadership and ethics

In a business textbook, ethics is usually a tricky topic to discuss. A large portion of individuals who succeed in business is unfamiliar with these concepts. Also, because there are several different points of view on the subject matter, many business executives regard it as "muddled" and hard to grasp [40]. Ethics can be easy or difficult. It is easy when people decide to live by a few principles guiding them irrespective of the situation. On the other hand, ethics is difficult for people who believe ethics can be bent and that situations should be assessed separately to determine the best plan of action [41]. Essentially, integrity is defined as acting based on your word and saying only what you intend to mean or intend to do. Integrity is a great starting place when developing ethical standards. It would be tough to claim that integrity is unimportant or that integrity is not critical to success in the venture. The majority of successful leaders will affirm the importance of integrity. The majority of business is conducted within a structure of trust. Leaders believe that those they work with will implement the commitments they have both agreed on. Honesty is another principle that should be closely linked to integrity. The virtue of honesty can also be referred to as "transparency" in business [21]. When a leader practices this ethic, this means that the business will be functioning properly. Humility is a final ethical principle to be discussed and appears to be critical for business success. Humility is frequently described as a personality trait, but it can also be defined as an ethical principle. A person who demonstrates humility recognizes that many of the good and bad things that happen in life and business are often the result of random events. The majority of success is due to a complex combination of personal ability, luck, and happenstance. Leaders who understand this will be successful in maintaining a genuine humility during the success period while also being more stable individually during a time of difficulty. Many authors coined the term "ergonomics" to describe the importance of controlling one's pride and cultivating humility [42]. Four red flags that show when a person's ego has taken charge are listed by these authors: Being defensive, being comparative, seeking acceptance, and showcasing brilliance. It is critical to understand the way humility fits into the range of possible character identities, ranging from a vacant ego to self-indulgence. Humility reflects a balanced and perceptive understanding of one's own distinct skill and talent while avoiding the destructive power of arrogance and egoism.

5. Leadership in the Thai context

Thailand is a vital business hub in the Southeast Asia region. It is a collectivist nation where people value and commit to their relationships. It is more important and valued to be accepted than it is to grab attention among the crowd, therefore an assertive and competitive attitude is not supported or considered desirable. The individualism vs. collectivism scale is a cultural dimension developed by Hofstede et al. [43], individualist cultures mostly refer to themselves as "I," whereas collectivist societies view themselves in the context of "we." People are more likely to subordinate their personal goals to those of their group in collectivistic societies. The style of communication is implicit and is dependent on the context of what is said. The self-perception of belonging to an in-group implies that people consider their job and the organization for which they work to be a part of their self-identity [44]. The subordinate-superior relationship is based on an exchange of loyalty for protection [43].

Thai society is known for being resistant to change and for being risk-averse, which is why there is control over everything, which is manifested by strict laws, policies, rules, and regulations [45, 46]. Thailand, with its collectivist culture, is an ideal setting for transformational leadership to thrive. Transformational leadership has more chance of success in collectivist cultures than in Western individualistic cultures, Schmidt [47] reiterated that Followers in collectivist societies expect their leaders to look after them while identifying with their leaders' vision and showing their loyalty. This aligns with several studies that show a positive significant effect of transformational leadership on collectivists' employee creativity than individualists' [48]. This leadership style is the secret to venture leadership in Thailand [49]. Good leaders motivate their workers to challenge the system and try new and innovative approaches to their work. They put a lot of effort into intellectually stimulating their workers [50, 51].

For instance, these leaders challenge employees' imagination and inspirations, while recognizing their innovative values, mindset, and beliefs, as well as developing the capabilities of individual and work teams. They also provide support and resources as well as energize followers to put more effort to meet higher goals. Vora and Kainzbauer [49] while identifying themes in Thai humanistic leadership in culture-specific ways infer those leaders must engage in humanistic leadership practices that are appropriate for the Thai context to be successful. Human resource departments may want to focus on these behaviors when recruiting, selecting, and developing new employees. The success of the Thai economy which recorded a growth rate of almost 7% in the late 80s and early 90s, with an even better GDP performance of double digits making Thailand the fastest growing economy in the world over the same period was tied to the strategic leadership management of business entities [52]. In Thailand, family-run businesses frequently retain senior management for decades, and the predictable result is that they seek consistency rather than greatness. Leaders must shift their focus away from functional issues and toward developing independent thinkers and future successors.

They can stop telling people what to do and start listening to insightful feedback and ideas if they foster creativity [53]. According to studies, employees' perceptions of empowerment and support are major sources of innovation [48].

All of this contributes to the followers' development of a creative identity. As a result, the quality of Thailand's leaders has a significant impact on the country's venture leadership success. In organizational learning, the transformational leader will act as a facilitator, trainer catalyst, and coach. The Thai leadership nexus has keyed into this paradigm, where the leaders are open to technological reforms in business industries such as agriculture, automobile, bioengineering, biotechnology, electronics, healthcare, and nanotechnology, and increasing the development of new technologies such as aviation, digital innovations, logistics, and robotics. These are indications that the leadership model operated in Thailand emphasizes innovation and creativity [14, 54]. Studies have revealed that creative leaders are more effective at promoting positive change and inspiring their followers than leaders who are not creative [32, 55]. Hofsteede [56] stated that in Thailand, the people are used to an imbalance of power in organizations because they accept easily that power is distributed unevenly based on some of the characteristics outlined below:

- Being reliant on a hierarchy.

- Unequal rights for power holders and non-power holders.

- Inaccessible superiors.

- Leaders are commanding.

- Management exercises control and delegates authority.

- Power is centralized, and managers rely on their team members' obedience.

- Employees expect to be told what to do and when to do it.

- Managers are respected for their position.

- Communication is indirect, and negative feedback is hidden.

- Co-workers would expect the boss or manager to be clearly directed.

What is discernible from the above narrative is that privileges are assigned a rank and are respected accordingly. Employees demonstrate loyalty, respect, and obeisance for protection and security. Each rank is accorded its own set of benefits, and employees are expected to demonstrate loyalty, respect, and deference to the leadership, giving rise to a paternalistic management relationship between leaders and followers [56]. As a result, the attitude toward managers has become more formal. The flow of information is hierarchical and managed with the leaders at the top of the totem pole because of the privileges and functions ascribed to them in society. Somech [17] further affirms that leaders are the main drivers that either support or hinder organizational innovation management. According to Bel [25], various leadership styles tend to have different effects on employee loyalty and participation, influencing the climate for innovation management. Exploring from the work of Deschamps [40], he highlights that the failure of innovation projects is most likely due to ineffective leadership skills.

There are assertions in the growing literature on change leadership that the root cause of many change problems is leadership behavior [48]. Trust and lack of trust, in particular, are regarded as major factors in failed change projects. In general, trust in leadership has been identified as an important role in innovation and change research [13, 32]. Leadership is important in increasing organizational creativity, launching, driving, and implementing innovation projects, and overcoming resistance [24, 41]. These have been all evident in growing the Thai economy as discussed from the studies reviewed. Employee perceptions of how much creativity is encouraged at work and how much organizational resources are devoted to supporting creativity influence their creative performance. The perception of an innovative climate among employees encourages risk-taking and the challenge of using creative approaches at work. For the sustenance of the innovations in the economic and end technology sectors, Thailand must continuously produce the right leaders with a mind-set of enhancing creativity and innovation and setting the right examples for followers.

6. Conclusion

The concept of venture leadership has been discussed thus far. Discussions have revealed that leadership is built over a lifetime of training, adjustment, and reflection, as discussed throughout this section. There are no absolute facts in leadership; no one can be a leader in all situations. Each leader must identify the practices that fit them given the circumstances. Although, there are no absolutes, there are leadership principles that are highly applicable to the success of a venture and have been passed down across generations. For instance, in line with the basic rules of smart business practice, the ethical codes of humility, integrity, and honesty, apply to every type of venture. Furthermore, the central skills of venture leadership should serve as a foundation for ongoing education. As previously stated, many venture leaders have never received formal management or leadership training. As a result, many people master the skills and craft of management and leadership while on the job. Although, this is admirable and tolerable, however the venture environment in most cases is far too challenging to allow for such an inefficient and slow learning process. Although, formal leadership training is not required for ventures, having a conceptual model to analyze the situations or events that occur during the operation of a business is beneficial. Conceptual frameworks give order to the chaos of leadership. The fundamental skills discussed in this section are only intended to serve as a springboard for further reading and investigation into the principles and concepts that define effective management and leadership.

Venture Leadership under Uncertainty: An Emerging Country Perspective
DOI: http://dx.doi.org/10.5772/intechopen.102870

Author details

Bilal Khalid[1*], Md Samim Al Azad[2], Slimane Ed-dafali[3]
and Muhammad Mohiuddin[4]

1 KMITL Business, Bangkok, Thailand

2 North South University, Dhaka, Bangladesh

3 Chouaib Doukkali University, El Jadida, Morocco

4 Laval University, Quebec, Canada

*Address all correspondence to: khalidb9998@gmail.com

IntechOpen

© 2022 The Author(s). Licensee IntechOpen. This chapter is distributed under the terms
of the Creative Commons Attribution License (http://creativecommons.org/licenses/
by/3.0), which permits unrestricted use, distribution, and reproduction in any medium,
provided the original work is properly cited. (cc) BY

References

[1] Duening TN, Hisrich RD, Lechter MA. Technology Entrepreneurship: Taking Innovation to the Marketplace. 2nd ed. Cambridge, Massachusetts, United States: Elsevier; 2015

[2] Thanh TL, Mohiuddin M, Quang HN. Impact of uncertainty and start-up opportunities on technopreneurial start-up success in emerging countries. Transnational Corporations Review. 2021:1-11

[3] Browning R. Capitalism and the technology entrepreneur. 2016. Retrieved from: https://web.stanford. edu/group/techventures/1e/book/ dor53530_ch01.pdf

[4] Birdthistle N, Hynes B. Managing the new venture. In: Cooney TM, Hill S, editors. New Venture Creation in Ireland. Dublin: Oaktree Press; 2002. pp. 111-130

[5] Johansson F. The Medici Effect, with a New Preface and Discussion Guide: What Elephants and Epidemics Can Teach us about Innovation. Boston, MA: Harvard Business Review Press; 2017

[6] Esmer Y, Dayi F. A new paradigm in management: Ethical leadership, academic perspective. International Peer-reviewed Journal of Social Sciences. 2016;57:38-54

[7] De Queiroz Brunelli M. Social venture leadership: Understanding attributes and processes for innovation in social organizations. 2021. Retrieved from: https://doi.org/10.17771/PUCRio. acad.54808

[8] Gharibvand S, Mazumder MNH, Mohiuddin M, Su Z. Leadership style and employee job satisfaction: Evidence from Malaysian semiconductor industry. Transnational Corporations Review. 2013;5(2):93-103

[9] Hughes DJ, Lee A, Tian AW, Newman A, Legood A. Leadership, creativity, and innovation: A critical review and practical recommendations. The Leadership Quarterly. 2018; 29(5):549-569

[10] Phaneuf JE, Boudrias JS, Rousseau V, Brunelle E. Personality and transformational leadership: The moderating effect of organizational context. Personality and Individual Differences. 2016;102:30-35

[11] Sternberg RJ. A systems model of leadership: WICS. American Psychologist. 2017;62(1):34-42. DOI: 10.1037/0003-066X.62.1.34

[12] Young Entrepreneur Council. 12 Essential traits of successful start-up leaders. 2016. Retrieved from: http:// www.inc.com/young-entrepreneur- council/12-traits-of-successful-start-up- leaders.html [Accessed: 13 October 2021]

[13] Banks GC, Dionne SD, Sayama H, Mast MS. Leadership in the digital era: Social media, big data, virtual reality, computational methods, and deep learning. The Leadership Quarterly. 2019;30(5):1-2. DOI: 10.1016/S1048- 9843(19)30520-X

[14] Baxter W. Thailand 4.0 and the future of work in the kingdom. Vol. 29. 2017. Retrieved from: https://bit. ly/2GV4t37

[15] Jaiswal NK, Dhar RL. The influence of servant leadership, trust in leader and thriving on employee creativity. Leadership and Organization Development Journal. 2017;38(1):2-21

[16] Kumar R, Shukla S. Creativity, proactive personality and entrepreneurial intentions: Examining the mediating role of entrepreneurial self-efficacy. Global Business Review.

2022;**23**(1):101-118. DOI: 10.1177/0972150919844395

[17] Somech A. The effects of leadership style and team process on performance and innovation in functionally heterogeneous teams. Journal of Management. 2006;**32**(1):132-157. DOI: 10.1177/0149206305277799

[18] Todorovic WK, Schlosser FK. An entrepreneur and a leader! A framework conceptualizing the influence of a firm's leadership style on a firm's entrepreneurial orientation— Performance relationship. Journal of Small Business & Entrepreneurship. 2017;**20**(3):289-307

[19] Sutton RI. The No Asshole Rule: Building a Civilized Workplace and Surviving One that Isn't. New York: Business Plus; 2017

[20] Csikszentmihalyi M. Flow: The Psychology of Optimal Experience. New York: Harper Publishing; 2018

[21] Lapointe É, Vandenberghe C. Examination of the relationships between servant leadership, organizational commitment, and voice and antisocial behaviors. Journal of Business Ethics. 2018;**148**(1):99-115

[22] Singh S. Practical intelligence of high potential entrepreneurs: Antecedents and links to new venture growth. Academy of Management Proceedings. 2018:1-6

[23] Westphal JD, Fredrickson JW. Who directs strategic change? Director experience, the selection of new CEOs, and change in corporate strategy. Strategic Management Journal. 2018;**22**(12):1113-1137. DOI: 10.1002/smj.205

[24] Pimonratanakan S, Intawee T, Krajangsaeng K, Pooripakdee S. Transformational leadership climate through learning organization toward the organizational development. Journal of Administrative and Business Studies. 2017;**3**(6):284-291. DOI: 10.20474/jabs-3.6.3

[25] Bel R. Leadership and innovation: Learning from the best. Global Business and Organizational Excellence. 2019;**29**(2):47-60. DOI: 10.1002/joe.20308

[26] Rokeach M. The Nature of Human Values. New York: Free Press; 2018

[27] John RD, Steven AB. Enhancing entrepreneurial leadership: A focus on key communication priorities. Journal of Small Business & Entrepreneurship. 2017;**20**(2):151-167

[28] Boatman J, Wellins RS, Liu L, Phang N. Global Leadership Forecast 2011. Pittsburgh, PA: Development Dimensions International, Inc.; 2019

[29] Nicole LT. Sounds like a plan. Entrepreneur. 2016;**33**(3):102-104

[30] Lange JE, Mollov A, Peralmutter M, Singh S, Bygrave WD. Pre-start-up formal business plans and post-start-up performance: A study of 116 new ventures. Venture Capital. 2007;**9**(4):237-256

[31] Bossink BA. Leadership for sustainable innovation. International Journal of Technology Management & Sustainable Development. 2017;**6**(2):135-149. DOI: 10.1386/ijtm.6.2.135_1

[32] Newstead T, Dawkins S, Macklin R, Martin A. We don't need more leaders-we need more good leaders. Advancing a virtues-based approach to leader (ship) development. The Leadership Quarterly. 2019;**32**(2021):1-11. DOI: 10.1016/j.leaqua.2019.101312

[33] Conger JA. Charismatic and transformational leadership in organizations: An insider's perspective on these developing streams of research.

The Leadership Quarterly. 2016;**10**(2):145-179. DOI: 10.1016/S1048-9843(99)00012-0

[34] Bruton C. What kind of leaders do Thai workers prefer? Adecco survey results. 2018. Retrieved from: https://bit.ly/2OhF7QG

[35] Cummings A, Oldham GR. Enhancing creativity: Managing work contexts for the high potential employee. California Management Review. 2017;**40**(1):22-38. DOI: 10.2307/41165920

[36] Dellner A. Cultural Dimensions: The Five-Dimensions-Model According to Geert Hofstede. Munich, Germany: GRIN Verlag; 2017

[37] Yosem EC, McMullen JS. Strategic entrepreneurs at work: The nature, discovery, and exploitation of entrepreneurial opportunities. Small Business Economics. 2007;**28**(4):301-332

[38] Ucbasaran D. The fine 'science' of entrepreneurial decision making. Journal of Management Studies. 2008;**45**(1):221-237.2

[39] Tidd T, Bessant J. Managing Innovation: Integrating Technological, Market, and Organizational Change. Chichester, UK: John Wiley & Sons; 2019

[40] Deschamps J-P. Different leadership skills for different innovation strategies. Strategy & Leadership. 2018;**33**(5):31-38. DOI: 10.1108/10878570510616861

[41] Stoker J, Looise JC, Fisscher O, Jong R, d. Leadership and innovation: Relations between leadership, individual characteristics and the functioning of R&D teams. International Journal of Human Resource Management. 2018;**12**(7):1141-1151. DOI: 10.1080/09585190110068359

[42] Marcum D, Smith S. Ergonomics: What Makes Ego Our Greatest Asset (or Most Expensive Liability). West Yorkshire: Fireside Publishing; 2017

[43] Hofstede G, Hofstede GJ, Minkov M. Cultures and Organizations: Software of the Mind. 3rd ed. New York: McGraw-Hill; 2010

[44] Matsumoto DR. Culture and Psychology. Pacific Grove: Brooks/Cole Pub. Co; 1996

[45] Esmer Y, Dayi F. Entrepreneurial leadership: A theoretical framework. In: 25th International Academic Conference in Paris; 6-9 September 2016. 2017

[46] Persons LS. The Way Thais Lead. Chiang Mai, Thailand: Silkwormbooks; 2016

[47] Schmidt K. Are leaders in Thailand prepared for Thailand 4.0? International Journal of Business and Administrative Studies. 2019;**5**(6):341-351. DOI: 10.20469/ijbas.5.10004-6

[48] Mercer. Leadership development trends 2019. 2019. Retrieved from: https://bit.ly/2vGfVx4

[49] Vora D, Kainzbauer A. Humanistic leadership in Thailand: A mix of indigenous and global aspects using a cross-cultural perspective. Cross Cultural & Strategic Management. 2020;**27**(4):665-687. DOI: 10.1108/CCSM-01-2020-0008

[50] Khalid B, Kot M. The impact of accounting information systems on performance management in the banking sector. IBIMA Business Review. 2021:1-15. DOI: 10.5171/2021.578902

[51] Meekaewkunchorn N, Szczepańska-Woszczyna K, Muangmee C, Kassakorn N, Khalid B. Entrepreneurial orientation and SME performance: The mediating role of learning orientation. Economics &

Venture Leadership under Uncertainty: An Emerging Country Perspective
DOI: http://dx.doi.org/10.5772/intechopen.102870

Sociology. 2021;**14**(2):294-312.
DOI: 10.14254/2071-789X.2021/14-2/16

[52] Sheehan B. Entering into a business relationship or joint venture in Thailand—A cultural perspective. Management Research News. 1996;**19**(8):49-60. DOI: 10.1108/ eb028487

[53] Egremont J. Successful leadership in Thailand's unique cultural environment. Connexus Global; 2021. Retrieved from: https://www.connexus-global.com/ blog/2021/10/successful-leadership-in-thailands-unique-cultural-environment

[54] Maierbrugger A. Thailand drafts roadmap for "Digital Economy". 2016. Retrieved from: http://investvine.com/ highlights/news/

[55] Hairudinor, Hidayati N, Muspiron, Tampubolon E, Humaidi. The influence of transformational leadership and compensation on psychological well-being (study at private hospital nurses in South Kalimantan Province). International Journal of Business and Economic Affairs. 2017;**2**(5):317-326. DOI: 10.24088/ijbea-2017-25006

[56] Hofsteede G. Culture's Consequences: Comparing Values, Behaviors, Institutions, and Organizations across Nations. New York, NY: Sage; 2001

Chapter 4

Leadership in a Changing World: Relating Transformational Leadership to Internal and External Environmental Issues in Technical Universities

Elizabeth Addy, Audrey Addy and James Addy

Abstract

This paper seeks to relate the characteristics of transformational leadership (TL) to the strengths, weaknesses, opportunities and threats (SWOT) analysis of technical universities (TUs) in Ghana. The low performance of TUs in Ghana, has necessitated the need for effective TL. Using the qualitative approach, a documentary review and content analysis of 10 TUs were employed for the study. The study found that, the strength of the TUs were the qualified and experienced staff, the university structure, ICT services and flexible academic programmes. The main weaknesses were the inadequate staffing and low research output with opportunities identified as collaborations with industry and other institutions, whilst threats included the low and negative perceptions by the public about the TUs. Comparatively, it was revealed that the TUs in the southern part had more strengths than those in the northern part of Ghana. The TL was therefore key in providing transformation to the TUs by strengthening their SOs and minimizing their WTs. This study contributes to the technical tertiary education in the area of internal and external environmental conditions that could enhance performance of TUs. The content and SWOT analyses added another dimension to the qualitative documentary case study for the TUs.

Keywords: transformational, leadership, technical universities, strengths, weaknesses

1. Introduction

In a rapid transforming world, universities require a blend of unique features of transformational leadership styles to be innovative, and ensure sustainable performance to succeed. Transformational leadership (TL) have been known to be directive, participative and democratic [1]. Every organization has its strengths, weaknesses, opportunities and threats (SWOT) for which the same applies to technical universities (TUs). Leadership in technical university education has become critical because of intense competitions among tertiary institutions for sustainable performance and innovations. Each staff and student in a tertiary education is a potential leader and must work towards the vision and goals of the institution. Universities are required to transform people through the generation and application of knowledge, develop technological innovations for the performance and productivity of the institution [2, 3]. Scholars have argued that, there has been a paradigm shift in leadership styles to a more integrated approach for innovations [4, 5]. Other authors argue that, the growing demand for transformational leadership practices in organizations are to ensure high performance and productivity [6–8]. Studies on the qualities of TL emphasizes on its strengths and benefits for innovations, with limited studies on the weaknesses and threats that could hinder performance [7, 9–11].

In Ghana, TUs have undergone many transformational changes and is still underway, which requires TL to address such deficiencies [12]. The transformational changes in TUs, who were formerly polytechnics, began with their establishment in the 1960s as technical institutes to train people in craftsmanship [13]. They were re-designated into polytechnics to run non-tertiary programmes in 1963, and in 1992, the PNDC law 321, upgraded the polytechnics into a tertiary status. In 2007, the Polytechnic Act (Act 745) was passed to replace the PNDC Law 321, for a clear mandate to the polytechnics [12, 14]. The Technical University Act, 2016 (Act 922), converted the polytechnics into TUs to provide high skill training of students for industry [15]. Currently, Ghana has ten (10) public TUs located in ten (10) regions of Ghana.

These status transitions and low performance of the TUs require transformational leadership approaches to stimulate and accelerate the development of TUs in Ghana. This paper therefore aims to develop a conceptual model of the SWOT in TUs in relation to the features of the TL. It contributes to the internal and external environmental conditions which could enhance or hinder performance of TUs in Ghana. With the introduction in the Section 1, the Section 2 discusses the theoretical frameworks, whilst Section 3 presents the methods. Section 4 analyses the results with discussions in Section 5. The limitations to the study is in the Section 6 and the conclusion in the final chapter.

2. Theoretical framework

2.1 Transformational leadership theory

Many scholars have argued that transformational leadership theory is one of the prominent leadership theories that results in change and innovative work behaviour in organizations [16–20]. It also has been associated with managerial effectiveness during organizational change [1, 21]. The theory has evolved from the great man theory [22, 23], the trait theory [24, 25], the behavioural theory [26], situational theory [27, 28], and the transactional theory [29, 30].

Other scholars have classified TL into four areas: idealized influence, individualized consideration, intellectual stimulation and inspirational motivation [31, 32]. Podsakoff et al. [33] also identified six themes which corroborates with the four categories identified, with additional two on fostering acceptance of group goals and expectation of high performance. This means that, TL is comprehensive, dynamic and continue to expand with seven characteristics identified, which supports the views of earlier scholars. Extended and integrated literature on the seven TL are envisioning a new future (visionary), persistent communication, model desired behaviour, empower employees, meaningful changes and strategy, integrity and creating a sustainable organization (**Figure 1**) [17, 34–37].

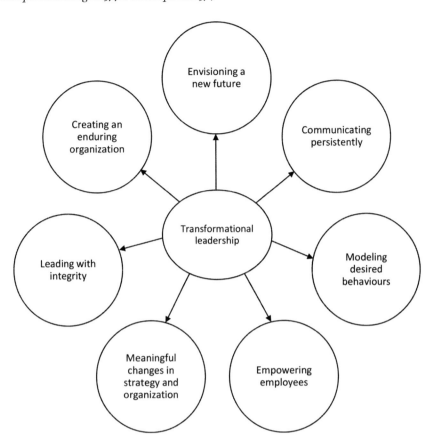

Figure 1.
Characteristics of transformational leadership. Adapted from: Hill and McShane [34].

Visionary: transformational leaders have a different and purposeful future for the organization they lead. This new vision transitions into the strategy and architecture of the organization.

Persistent communication: the new vision is communicated to employees consistently. They ensure that, there is information dissemination of their new vision to employees and they adopt and implement the vision. Top-down approach as well as bottom-up approach is accepted in such organization.

Model desired behaviour: the transformational leaders lead by example. They practice what they communicate to their employees. Their self-leadership style are exhibited by their followers.

Empower employee: the transformational leaders implement the grand strategic vision and by that they motivate employees to be innovate and apply various approaches to enhance organizational performance.

Meaningful changes: the changes effected by transformational leaders include the structure, processes, controls and incentives to promote work behaviours that is required to implement their strategic vision.

Lead with integrity: transformational leaders believe that they would have followers if people believe and trust their leadership vision. They build reputation for the organization, ensure fairness and firmness and behave in an ethical manner.

Sustainable organization: requires that organizations continue to operate efficiently and effectively to ensure continuous operations of the organization.

2.2 SWOT analysis theory

Theoretically, the SWOT analysis methodology identifies the internal and external environment in which the organization exists [34, 38]. Arguably, the application of SWOT analysis for the TUs is relevant due to the many actors or stakeholders involved.in determining the TL qualities that would promote innovation performance of the TUs. As such the cooperate strengths and opportunities could improve the performance of the TUs whilst the cooperate weaknesses and threats could inhibit performance. The strengths and weaknesses are internal factors and the opportunities and threats the external factors. The main goal of the SWOT analysis is to develop a systematic assessment of the phenomenon which would support decision-making related to strategic dimensions of the goals. In this study the SWOT analysis amount to assessing theoretically, the methodology and application of TLs in TUs. In general, a SWOT helps to develop the assessed phenomenon for further sequences of improved goal achievements and has an exploratory aspect which have not been noticed by other means of analysis. This exploratory force originates from the requirement to identify and distinguish overtly the four different categorization dimensions of the SWOT in the TLs [3].

Nevertheless, the SWOT analysis approach was the appropriate for this research due to the dynamic and comprehensive nature of the TL and the diverse stakeholders associated with the TUs to derive a holistic results on the phenomenon. The SWOT will help identify the total general strengths and opportunities of the TUs as well as the overall weaknesses and threats that could facilitate or inhibit the performance of the TUs.

3. Method

The study adopted the qualitative documentary approach and content analysis. According to Yang and Hwang [39] document review forms part of the qualitative case study. Data was collected from the strategic plans, reports from the vice-chancellors, policy documents on the operations of the TUs and sub-committees of ten (10) technical universities in Ghana. The strategic plans and other document of the 10 TUs were employed for the study which covered a 5-year period. It contains the vision, mission, core values, strengths, weaknesses, opportunities, threats and the strategic thrust which exist in the TUs. The TUs implement the strategic plans based on the approval by the TU council. The vice-chancellors, management and staff take full responsibilities of the implementation of the plan. Information was also obtained from the websites of the TUs.

The 10 TUs comprise of Accra, Takoradi, Cape Coast, Koforidua, Ho, Kumasi, Sunyani, Tamale, Wa and Bolgatanga. The northern part consist of three TUs, which are Tamale, Wa and Bolgatanga, whilst the southern part includes Accra, Takoradi, Cape Coast, Koforidua, Ho, Kumasi, and Sunyani.

The focus of the study is a comparative analysis on the strengths and weaknesses of the TUs that affect their environment positively or adversely for performance. A comparison was made on the strengths and weaknesses of the TUs in the southern part as against the northern side. Though interviews and survey may have revealed the individual's perceptions of what strengths and weaknesses exists in the TUs and the style of the TL practiced, the scope of the study is limited to the TU documents for the content analysis.

Leadership in a Changing World: Relating Transformational Leadership to Internal...
DOI: http://dx.doi.org/10.5772/intechopen.102574

4. Results and analysis

4.1 Strengths of transformational leadership and technical universities

The strength of transformational leadership is based on the premise that, leaders exhibit positive work behaviours of commitment, readiness, transparency and support that generate innovations and improvement of the organization [5]. First, the theory is comprehensive and all-inclusive because it covers broad descriptions of leadership qualities from different perspectives at the management levels [40]. Some of the leadership qualities are the ability to influence followers, integrity, provide motivation and morality at the organization [26, 41]. In the TUs, the characteristics of the TL are embedded in the analysis of the strategic plan, with key theme being the experienced and qualified staff, who are of integrity, innovativeness, commitment and excellence. The quality of staff reflects in the increasing number of students in the TUs. Another strength is the communication flow between the leaders and their subordinates with the aim of adopting moral standards that guide favourable interactions [4]. Effective communication flow is the one of the hall marks of a TL. Each of the TUs have an organogram or organizational structure which indicates the reporting lines of authority and channels of communication. Each faculty or administrative department has a head of department, supervisors, and subordinates. As such there is continuous flow of information from leaders to subordinates. Third, the TL motivates their followers to go beyond their limits and attain higher heights [42–44]. Hu et al. [44] argue that inspirational motivation encourage employees to exert more efforts to tackle challenges, work towards achieving their goals, and create more opportunities. The TUs have motivated staff whose aim is to achieve the goals of the university. Fourth, TL are encouraged to be innovative, creative and solve problems [8, 45]. Hu et al. [44] assert that, creativity and innovation occur in organizations whose leaders practice transformational styles. In the TUs, creativity and innovation have become essential because of the need to sustain relevance and competitive advantage in today's higher educational institutions for growth of new knowledge, ideas and research in a globalized world [8, 46]. Fifth, TLs are strong in their support they provide to members and help them develop their career, overcome personal fear and take on difficult and situational challenges [47]. The TUs have staff development policy for which they encourage staff to pursue further studies by offering scholarships, seminars, workshops and conferences for staff. Six, transformational leaders serve as role models to their followers and adopt proactive means to realize the vision [48, 49]. In TUs, the teaching and non-teaching staff follow the vision enshrined in their strategic plan inspire their followers to espouse the ownership of the TU goals in harmony with their personal goals for a follower transformation [28, 50]. All the 10 TUs have a vision, which are similar and reflect on their TL styles (**Figure 2**; **Table 1**) [51, 52]. For instance the visions of five of the TUs were stated as:

> *"A world-class technical university recognized for excellence, innovation and societal relevance (TU 1)".*

> *"A world-class technical university devoted to science, technology and entrepreneurship education (TU 2)".*

> *"Recognized as the top technical university in Ghana, with strong regional influence (TU 3)".*

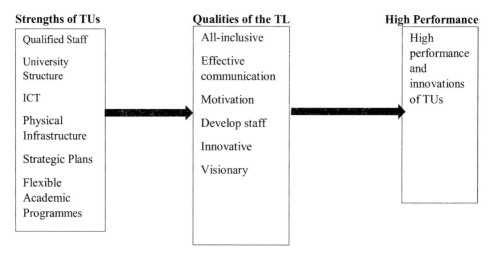

Figure 2.
Strengths of TUs in relations to TL. Source: Author's Construct (2021).

Strengths of transformational leadership	Author, year	Strength of technical universities
Comprehensive and all-inclusive	Burns, 1978; Bass, 1985; Siangchokyoo et al., 2022; Yukl et al., 2013; Korejan and Shahbazi, 2016	Leadership, staff, students, resources
Communication flow	Siangchokyoo et al., 2020; Khattak et al., 2019	1. Hierarchical structure/organogram 2. University's websites open to staff, students and the general public 3. ICT-internet services
Motivation	Klaic et al., 2020	Motivated staff
Innovation, creativity and problem solving	Avolio et al., 2014; Benmira and Agboola, 2021	Provide entrepreneurship/employable skills Has entrepreneurship centres
Career/staff development	Bass, 1985; Owusu-Agyeman, 2021	Qualified and experienced staff Staff development policy
Visionary	Bass, 1999; Hill and McShane, 2008	All the TUs had a vision and strategic plan with strategic thrusts

Source: Author's Compilation (2021).

Table 1.
Strengths of transformational leadership in technical university education.

> "The vision of the university is to become an internationally reputable institution of excellence in the provision of technical education (TU 4)."

> "University is to become a leading global tertiary institution that offers high quality career oriented programmes in… (TU 5)".

4.2 Weaknesses of TUs and relations with TL

Weaknesses or challenges of transformational leadership (TL), though exist, is limited in literature. Leaders have challenges of integrating the situational conditions with the group goals which allow individuals to work outside of the group goals [4]. In TUs, the administration system is associated with the committee work

Weaknesses of transformational leadership	Author, year	Challenges/weaknesses of technical universities
Lack integrative situational conditions	Owusu-Agyeman, 2021	Rigidly follow their statutes, strategic plan and policies
More theoretical than practical	Yukl et al., 2013	Inadequate resources to practice TL (human, physical, funding, teaching and learning materials)
Lack of consistent behaviour of leadership	Bass and Avolio, 1990; Hill and McShane, 2008	Changes in academic and administrative leadership
Differentiation of TL with other the leadership behaviour	Karadag, 2019	Many different leadership styles practiced by the leadership—no well-defined structure and model for leadership

Source: Author's Compilation (2021).

Table 2.
Weaknesses of transformational leadership in technical university education.

and teamwork. As such, urgent emerging situational conditions which require immediate attention, delay due to the bureaucracies.

Second, the qualities of the TL, is conceptual and closely related to each other, and this may be quite difficult to observe and its impact on the followers [20]. The concept of the TL has not been fully embraced in the TUs as other leadership styles may be employed by leaders in the TUs.

Third, it may be difficult to consistently adopt to the TL behaviours to achieve the goals of the TUs as leadership changes periodically [53]. After every 4 years, academic and administrative leadership changes occur in the TUs and may result in the lack of continuity of activities of the TUs.

Fourth, the employees may have difficulty in differentiating between various TL behaviours as they may perceive them to be in the same leadership sphere [54]. Leadership in TUs could exhibit charismatic, transactional, servant leadership or a blend of them which will be difficult to associate them with TL style. **Table 2** shows the weaknesses of TL in TUs. There has not been any cutting edge type of leadership adopted by the TUs (**Figure 3**).

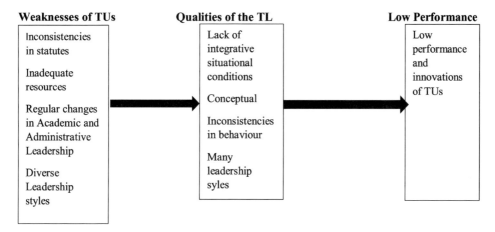

Figure 3.
Weaknesses of TUs in relations to TL. Source: Author's Construct (2021).

4.3 Opportunities of TUs in relation with TL

Opportunities exist for leaders of TUs who practice transformational leadership styles. **Table 3** shows the opportunities that exist for TL in TUs. TL are able to establish collaborations in the organization and externally [55]. They support the idea of working together to achieve a common goal. Leadership of the TUs form collaborations and partnerships with institutions both nationally and internationally for industrial attachment, scholarships, research and development of projects. All the TUs have collaborations with industries and international institutional linkages.

In creating a new future, TL sets new goals and select different behaviours for diverse followers for continuous improvement of their institutions [11]. The TUs, began as technical institutes involved in trades and craftsmanship programmes, and in technical and vocational education training (TVET), and later introduced the entrepreneurship education concept in their curriculum [2]. All the 10 TUs have entrepreneurship centres established to offer entrepreneurship training to the students for skills development.

Opportunities of transformational leadership	Author, year	Opportunities of technical universities
Establish collaborations	Korejan and Shahbazi, 2016; Asabri et al., 2020	Collaborations Partnerships Industrial attachments
Create a new future	Yang, 2014; Korejan and Shahbaz, 2016	Entrepreneurship education
Persistent communication with diverse stakeholders	Gupta et al., 2012	Language centre Consultancy services
Creating an enduring organization	Ramalingam et al., 2021	Strategically positioned-good location Global, national, regional, and local impact based on their programmes offering and have created a niche

Source: Author's Compilation (2021).

Table 3.
Opportunities of transformational leadership in technical university education.

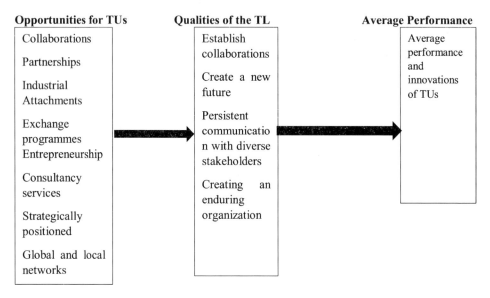

Figure 4.
Opportunities of TUs in relations to TL. Source: Author's Construct (2021).

Leadership in a Changing World: Relating Transformational Leadership to Internal...
DOI: http://dx.doi.org/10.5772/intechopen.102574

For the TL, links with the external environment is critical for innovation. The actors in the external environment include the governmental, non-governmental organizations, the private sector, and the general public. The TUs therefore have established language centres and offer consultancy services for stakeholders. The TU's websites and portals have been made accessible to the general public for the needed information.

Creating an enduring organization is meant to ensure sustainability of the performance for the institution [56]. The TUs are strategically positioned for easy accessibility and attraction to many clients. Each of the TUs have a niche in their programme offerings, and makes them unique and desirable to potential students, industry, institutions at the local, national and international level and have a global impact (**Figure 4**).

4.4 Threats of technical universities in relation to TL

TL are faced with threats that hinder them from exhibiting all the behavioural qualities for continuous improvement and innovations in the organization. **Table 4** shows the key threats which affects the TL in TUs. Issues of leadership bias, low transformational behaviours, no meaningful changes in strategy of the organization [11, 57]. In the TUs, there are threats of lopsided perceptions about the concept of the TUs by government giving more attention to traditional public universities than the TUs. There is discriminating against the TUs in terms of remuneration, resources, programme offerings and job placement [2]. Due to this, there is instability in the TUs due to the many strikes. The TUs have been inhibited by accreditation challenges for some of their programme offerings from the Regulators. Furthermore, the low transformational behaviours of the TU leaders make it difficult to compete with other tertiary institutions both nationally and internationally for students and projects. The poor public perception about TVET and the TUs has been one of the major threats of the TUs, which accounts for the low enrolment of students as compared to the traditional public universities (**Figure 5**).

4.5 SWOT analysis of TUs

Figure 6 presents the SWOT analysis of TUs on two main themes on the strengths, weaknesses, opportunities and threats of the TUs. On the strengths of the TUs, the two key features identified in the strategic plans were experienced and qualified staff and flexible academic programmes.

The weaknesses in the TUs were inadequate teaching and industrial experienced staff resulting low research output and innovation. These weaknesses affect the number of staff required in attaining the goals of the university. Many of the TU staff after training leave to the traditional public universities. Inconsistencies in the TU statues and policies affected the stability of staff.

Threats of transformational leadership	Author, year	Threats of technical universities
Leadership bias	Meindl et al., 1985	Skewed perceptions of the TU concept by government
Low transformational behaviours	Lieven et al., 1997	Competition from other tertiary institutions Nationally and internationally
No meaningful changes in strategy of the organization—low ability and achievement	Yang, 2014	Low public perception about TVET

Source: Author's Compilation (2021).

Table 4.
Threats of transformational leadership in technical university education.

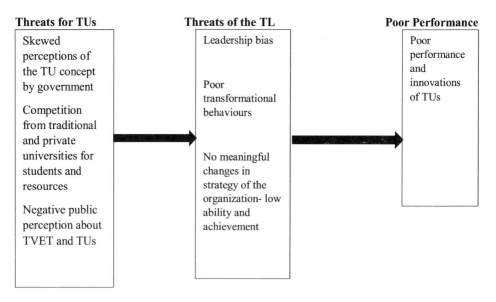

Figure 5.
Threats of TUs in relations to TL. Source: Author's Construct (2021).

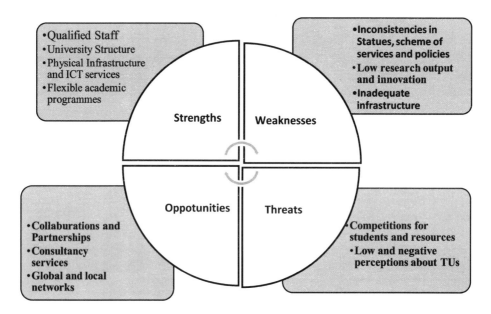

Figure 6.
SWOT analysis of the TUs. Source: Author's Construct (2021).

Opportunities which exists in the TUs are the collaborations and partnerships with institutions and industry and offering of consultancy services to the public. The opportunities include sponsorships and skills development for staff and students.

On threats, the TUs, are faced with competitions with other public tertiary institutions for students. The negative public perceptions of the TUs was revealed as one of the main threats for the TUs (**Figure 6**).

5. Conclusion

TU transformational leadership is key to the prompt development of tertiary technical education. By linking the TL to the TU leadership, a model of the technical

Leadership in a Changing World: Relating Transformational Leadership to Internal...
DOI: http://dx.doi.org/10.5772/intechopen.102574

university transformational leadership (TUTL) concept was developed for the weaknesses and threats of the TUs as well as the strengths and opportunities that exist were identified for the internal and external conditions that would enhance performance for innovation. The TUTL concept must be adopted by the TUs. The TU leaders should critically consider and apply the strengths and opportunities that exist and link them up with the TL qualities available. The SWOT analysis of the TUTL provides a clear direction for all leaders at the TUs which would enhance performance for innovations.

Major findings on the strengths for the TUs include qualified staff, university structure, physical infrastructure and information and communication and technology (ICT) services and flexible academic programmes. The performance of the TUs would greatly increase when TLs utilize these strengths of the TUs. This would encourage new ideas, creativity and innovations and initiative [7, 58]. These strengths are deepened and facilitated by the opportunities that exist for the TUs. Major findings of the opportunities include the collaborations and partnerships, consultancy services, global and local networks, exchange programmes and entrepreneurship education. Hill and McShane [34] and Ramalingam et al. [56] argue that the features of TL are capable of churning the strengths and opportunities for an improved environmental conditions and performance of the TUs. Though all the 10 TUs had similar strength, the document reviews revealed more strengths and opportunities in the southern than the northern part, in areas of many qualified and experienced staff and high student numbers.

Comparatively, weaknesses and threats do exist in the TUs for which TL should be able to mobilize followers or employees to address the problems and minimize the negative conditions. This finding confirms a study on evaluation on the weaknesses of transformational and charismatic leadership theories [59, 60]. Major findings for the TU weaknesses include inadequate infrastructure; frequent changes in leadership and staff; inconsistencies in statues, scheme of services and policies and high turnover. These weaknesses are aggravated by the threats which exist among the TUs, which are low and negative public perception of TUs; national and international competition for students and resources. The weaknesses and threats were more pronounced in the northern area of the TUs than the southern area in the areas of high turnover and inadequate facilities, national and international competition for students and resources.

This study highlights on the documentary review of the TUs in relation to the characteristics of the TL based on their strategic plan, reports from management and websites. This study contributes to the technical tertiary education in the area of environmental factors that could enhance performance. The content and SWOT analysis added another strategy to the qualitative document case study for the TUs.

6. Limitations

The study employed one leadership theory for the study. Other leadership theories such as situational, transactional and charismatic leadership styles were not adopted as part of the study. In addition, the study was limited to the qualitative conceptual model and documentary analysis concept. The SWOT analysis provided an examination into the environmental conditions of the TUs. Subsequent research could include interviews and direct observations from participants. Further limitations are that, the SWOT analysis may not prioritize issues, may generate many ideas for which not all may be important to solve the problem [61, 62]. However, the content analysis and the SWOT of the TUs in relation to the TL provided robust results in determining the environmental conditions which could influence or inhibit performance in the TUs.

7. Implication for policy and future research

Management and staff of the TUs could focus on the SWOT analysis model to develop policies that will enhance the environmental conditions of the TUs for performance and innovations. The conceptual model can be used in future researches, by testing and explaining the relationships between the SWOT analysis of the TUs. The relationships could be empirically tested in private and traditional universities. In addition, academicians and administrators in the TUs can use the additional knowledge in the theory of TL and SWOT to enhance creativity and innovations in the TUs.

Author details

Elizabeth Addy[1*], Audrey Addy[2] and James Addy[3]

1 Faculty of Built and Natural Environment, Koforidua Technical University, Koforidua, Ghana

2 Department of Management and Organizational Development, Kwame Nkrumah University of Science and Technology, Kumasi, Ghana

3 Eye Care Unit, Ghana Health Service, Accra, Ghana

*Address all correspondence to: elizabethaddy160@gmail.com

IntechOpen

© 2022 The Author(s). Licensee IntechOpen. This chapter is distributed under the terms of the Creative Commons Attribution License (http://creativecommons.org/licenses/by/3.0), which permits unrestricted use, distribution, and reproduction in any medium, provided the original work is properly cited. (cc) BY

References

[1] Bass BM, Riggio RE. Transformational Leadership. New York: Psychology Press; 2006

[2] Iddrisu S, Alhassan E, Kinder T. Polytechnic education in Ghana: Management delivery and challenges. The International Journal of Social Sciences and Humanities Invention. 2014;1(6):2349-2031

[3] Leiber T, Stensaker B, Harvey LC. Bridging theory and practice of impact evaluation of quality management in higher education institutions: A SWOT analysis. European Journal of Higher Education. 2018;8(3):351-365

[4] Owusu-Agyeman Y. Transformational leadership and innovation in higher education: A participative process approach. International Journal of Leadership in Education. 2021;24(5):694-716

[5] Peng J, Li M, Wang Z, Lin Y. Transformational leadership and employees' reactions to organizational change: Evidence from a meta-analysis. The Journal of Applied Behavioral Science. 2021;57(3):369-397

[6] Kinicki A, Kreitner R. Organizational Behavior: Key Concepts, Skills & Best Practices. New York, NY: McGraw-Hill Irwin; 2012

[7] Korejan MM, Shahbazi H. An analysis of the transformational leadership theory. Journal of Fundamental and Applied Sciences. 2016;8(3):452-461

[8] Novitasari D, Supiana N, Supriatna H, Fikri MA, Asbari M. The role of leadership on innovation performance: Transactional versus transformational style. JIMFE (Jurnal Ilmiah Manajemen Fakultas Ekonomi). 2021;7(1):27-36

[9] Lin CS, Huang PC, Chen SJ, Huang LC. Pseudo-transformational leadership is in the eyes of the subordinates. Journal of Business Ethics. 2017;141(1):179-190

[10] Oppermann B, Nault W. Transformational leadership in the navy—Cultivating a learning-organization culture. Naval War College Review. 2021;74(1):10

[11] Thompson G, Glasø L. Situational leadership theory: A test from a leader-follower congruence approach. Leadership and Organization Development Journal. 2018;39(5):574-591

[12] Acquah PC, Frimpong EB, Borkloe JK. The competency based training (CBT) concept of teaching and learning in the technical universities in Ghana: Challenges and the way forward. Asia Pacific Journal of Contemporary Education and Communication Technology. 2017;3(2):172-182

[13] Nsiah-Gyabaah K. Polytechnic education in Ghana: The past, the present and the future. In: Kick-off Conference: NPT/UCC Project on Building Management and Leadership Capacity in Polytechnics. University of Cape Coast; 2005

[14] Callistus T, Clinton A. Conceptual framework for enhancing engineering education in Ghana's polytechnics

[15] Ministry of Education (MOE). Report of the Technical Committee on Conversion of the Polytechnics in Ghana to Technical Universities [Online]. 2014. Available from: www.moe.gov.gh/assets/media/docs [Accessed: 14 October 2021]

[16] Bass BM. Leadership: Good, better, best. Organizational Dynamics. 1985;13(3):26-40

[17] Bass BM. From transactional to transformational leadership: Learning

to share the vision. Organizational Dynamics. 1990;**18**(3):19-31

[18] Bass BM, Avolio BJ. Multifactor Leadership Questionnaire. Palo Alto, CA: Consulting Psychologists Press; 1990

[19] Northouse PG. Transformational leadership. In: Leadership: Theory and Practice. Vol. 4. Thousand Oaks: SAGE Publications; 2007. pp. 175-206

[20] Yukl G. An evaluation of conceptual weaknesses in transformational and charismatic leadership theories. The Leadership Quarterly. 1999;**10**(2):285-305

[21] Bass BM. Two decades of research and development in transformational leadership. European Journal of Work and Organizational Psychology. 1999;**8**(1):9-32

[22] Mouton N. A literary perspective on the limits of leadership: Tolstoy's critique of the great man theory. Leadership. 2019;**15**(1):81-102

[23] Siangchokyoo N, Klinger RL, Campion ED. Follower transformation as the linchpin of transformational leadership theory: A systematic review and future research agenda. The Leadership Quarterly. 2020;**31**(1):101341

[24] Derue DS, Nahrgang JD, Wellman NE, Humphrey SE. Trait and behavioral theories of leadership: An integration and meta-analytic test of their relative validity. Personnel Psychology. 2011;**64**(1):7-52

[25] Nawaz ZA, Khan I. Leadership theories and styles: A literature review. Leadership. 2016;**16**(1):1-7

[26] Benmira S, Agboola M. Evolution of leadership theory. BMJ Leader. 2021;**5**(1):3-5

[27] Northouse PG. Leadership: Theory and Practice. 3rd ed. London: SAGE Publications; 2004

[28] Spector BA. Carlyle, Freud, and the great man theory more fully considered. Leadership. 2016;**12**(2): 250-260

[29] Buch R, Thompson G, Kuvaas B. Transactional leader–member exchange relationships and followers' work performance: The moderating role of leaders' political skill. Journal of Leadership and Organizational Studies. 2016;**23**(4):456-466

[30] Odumeru JA, Ogbonna IG. Transformational vs. transactional leadership theories: Evidence in literature. International Review of Management and Business Research. 2013;**2**(2):355

[31] Avolio BJ, Sosik JJ, Kahai SS, Baker B. E-leadership: Re-examining transformations in leadership source and transmission. The Leadership Quarterly. 2014;**25**(1):105-131

[32] Lajoie D, Boudrias JS, Rousseau V, Brunelle É. Value congruence and tenure as moderators of transformational leadership effects. Leadership and Organization Development Journal. 2017;**38**(2):254-269

[33] Podsakoff PM, MacKenzie SB, Moorman RH, Fetter R. Transformational leader behaviors and their effects on followers' trust in leader, satisfaction, and organizational citizenship behaviors. The Leadership Quarterly. 1990;**1**(2):107-142

[34] Hill CWL, McShane SL. Principles of Management. Boston: McGraw-Hill Irwin; 2008

[35] Bass BM. Does the transactional–transformational leadership paradigm transcend organizational and national boundaries? The American Psychologist. 1997;**52**(2):130

[36] Burns JM. Leadership. New York, NY: Harper & Row; 1978

[37] Burns DM. Human resources in academe: Challenge for leadership. Journal of the College and University Personnel Association. 1978;**29**(3):6-10

[38] Namugenyi C, Nimmagadda SL, Reiners T. Design of a SWOT analysis model and its evaluation in diverse digital business ecosystem contexts. Procedia Computer Science. 2019;**159**: 1145-1154

[39] Yang CL, Hwang M. Personality traits and simultaneous reciprocal influences between job performance and job satisfaction. Chinese Management Studies. 2014;**8**(1):6-26

[40] Mirkamali M, Shateri K, Uzbashi A. Explaining the role of transformational leadership in the field of organizational creativity. Journal of Innovation and Value Creation. 2013;**2**:23

[41] Northouse PG. Leadership: Theory and Practice. Thousand Oaks, CA: SAGE Publications; 2021

[42] Afsar B, Masood M, Umrani WA. The role of job crafting and knowledge sharing on the effect of transformational leadership on innovative work behavior. Personnel Review. 2019;**48**(5):1186-1208

[43] Asbari M, Prasetya AB, Santoso PB, Purwanto A. From creativity to innovation: The role of female employees' psychological capital. International Journal of Social and Management Studies. 2021;**2**(2):66-77

[44] Hu H, Gu Q, Chen J. How and when does transformational leadership affect organizational creativity and innovation? Critical review and future directions. Nankai Business Review International. 2013;**4**:147-161

[45] Shin SJ, Zhou J. Transformational leadership, conservation, and creativity: Evidence from Korea. Academy of Management Journal. 2003;**46**(6): 703-714

[46] Anderson N, Potočnik K, Zhou J. Innovation and creativity in organizations: A state-of-the-science review, prospective commentary, and guiding framework. Journal of Management. 2014;**40**(5):1297-1333

[47] Anderson M. Transformational leadership in education: A review of existing literature. International Social Science Review. 2017;**93**(1):4

[48] Moss SA, Ritossa DA. The impact of goal orientation on the association between leadership style and follower performance, creativity and work attitudes. Leadership. 2007;**3**(4):433-456

[49] Sadeghi A, Pihie ZA. Transformational leadership and its predictive effects on leadership effectiveness. International Journal of Business and Social Science. 2012;**3**(7)

[50] Hannah ST, Schaubroeck JM, Peng AC. Transforming followers' value internalization and role self-efficacy: Dual processes promoting performance and peer norm-enforcement. The Journal of Applied Psychology. 2016;**101**(2):252

[51] Moradi Korejan M, Shahbazi H. An analysis of the transformational leadership theory. Journal of Fundamental and Applied Sciences. 2016;**8**(3S):452-461

[52] Yukl G et al. An improved measure of ethical leadership. Journal of Leadership & Organizational Studies. 2013;**20**(1):38-48

[53] Bass BM, Avolio BJ. The implications of transactional and transformational leadership for individual, team, and organizational development. Research in Organizational Change and Development. 1990;**4**(1):231-272

[54] Karadag E. The effect of educational leadership on students' achievement: A cross-cultural meta-analysis research on

studies between 2008 and 2018. Asia Pacific Education Review. 2020;**21**(1):49-64

[55] Asbari M. Is transformational leadership suitable for future organizational needs? International Journal of Social, Policy and Law. 2020;**1**(1):51-55

[56] Ramalingam T, Piaralal SK, Osman Z, Arokiasamy L. Effect of transformational leadership and creativity and innovation on organizational performance: A conceptual model. Electronic Journal of Business and Management. 2021;**6**(1): 20-31

[57] Meindl JR, Ehrlich SB, Dukerich JM. The romance of leadership. Administrative Science Quarterly. 1985;**30**(1):78-102

[58] Charbonnier-Voirin A, El Akremi A, Vandenberghe C. A multilevel model of transformational leadership and adaptive performance and the moderating role of climate for innovation. Group & Organization Management. 2010;**35**(6):699-726

[59] Kark R, Shamir B, Chen G. The two faces of transformational leadership: Empowerment and dependency. The Journal of Applied Psychology. 2003;**88**(2):246

[60] Yin RK. Case Study Research: Design and Methods. Los Angeles, London, New Delhi: SAGE; 2009

[61] Bell GG, Rochford L. Rediscovering SWOT's integrative nature: A new understanding of an old framework. The International Journal of Management Education. 2016;**14**(3): 310-326

[62] Helms MM, Nixon J. Exploring SWOT analysis—Where are we now? A review of academic research from the last decade. Journal of Strategy and Management. 2010;**3**(3):215-251

Chapter 5

Leadership Values and Understandings from an Islamic Perspective

Hailan Salamun and Asyraf Ab Rahman

Abstract

This writing proposes the life of the Prophet Muhammad (peace be upon him) as a leadership framework for developing the concept of Rabbani's leadership. The development of the leadership framework begins with the spiritual aspect, which is very closely related to the faith. Rabbani's character in the leadership shown by Prophet Muhammad (PBUH) so emphasizes the spiritual aspect with a different approach from ordinary spiritual values. The faith generates Rabbani's characteristics that influence the leadership framework that emphasizes two principles, namely the vision of leadership and the impact of leadership practice. The impact of leadership as a predictor has the potential to influence leadership practices related to the appreciation of divinity, humanity, and the development of life. The Rabbani characteristics that develop in a leader will influence his vision of leadership as a manifestation of the appreciation of religious life based on faith. Both of these principles act as key factors in the creation of an organizational leadership framework that demonstrates the relationship between faith and spirituality.

Keywords: Rabbani leadership, vision of leadership, impact of leadership, upholding the vision, social justice and humanity, sustainable development

1. Introduction

Over the last few years, there are organizations put the primary concern on some components of leadership values. Over 150 studies show that spiritual values, practices, and effective leadership have interconnected. Values such as integrity, honesty, responsibility, temperance, justice, courage, and wisdom have been demonstrated to influence leadership success. All the following practices have been emphasized in many spiritual teachings, and they have also been found to be crucial leadership skills.

A proposed conceptual model postulates spiritual belief (e.g., hope and faith in God) as a causal factor in the formation of Rabbani leaders' values and behaviors. Furthermore, the model posits those spiritual practices (temperance, wisdom, justice, and courage) are a moderating variable of Islamic leadership behavior and the outcome variable, leadership effectiveness, as perceived by followers.

In Islam, the concept of leadership must act only to implement Allah's laws on earth as the essence and primary responsibility of leaders. Leadership in Islam, as a trust (Amanah), and a sacred position that can solve the problems of humanity and guide them to the eternal betterment of here and hereafter. Although developments of several leadership models are just to solve the problem. On the other hand, leadership in Islam must think about humanity and the satisfaction of Allah the Almighty. The results of the field study indicate that there is a significant relationship between the spiritual values of leadership with Rabbani's leadership practices. The results suggest that organizational direction requires divine or spiritual-based leadership.

2. Islam and leadership

Leadership is the position of a person responsible for showing how to determine group decisions towards the right goals. Therefore, the leader must work hard to influence others to accept the decisions and instructions determined to achieve the goals of the group or organization. This means that leaders have a very close relationship with followers so that they can contribute energy and work together to realize the organization's goals are achieved.

In Islam, leadership describes a person or a group of people who guide and lead followers or mankind from the brink of destruction to the path of Allah. The Qur'an (the Holy Book) and the Sunnah (the actions of the Prophet Muhammad (PBUH) are the sources that determine the complete code of life for Muslims, including matters related to leadership. The leadership framework in the West is bound by rules and conditions, which are considered official duties to implement. But Islam regards leadership as a responsibility entrusted to be exercised to the followers or mankind. God's rules and commandments are carried out with the cooperation of leaders and followers.

Chaston and Lips-Wiersma [1] argue that spirituality-based leadership is still in the early stages of study maturity. Thus, most studies of spirituality-based leadership require findings based on in-depth follower perspectives in addition to leader perspectives that highlight a two-sided leadership approach. One question arises, how to combine these two effective leader codes of conduct based on leadership principles in a holistic framework? More importantly, a holistic approach in leadership aims to transform organizations where leaders and the spirituality of their employees can be developed as human beings capable of meeting their physical, mental, emotional, and spiritual needs. In this regard, Rabbani's leadership opens space for leadership practitioners to adhere to Shariah-compliant leadership especially to Muslims who are not interested in dealing with conventional leadership models because of religious beliefs.

The main objective of this study is to lay the foundation of Rabbani's conceptual leadership model from an Islamic perspective based on the life of the Prophet Muhammad PBUH and his approach. The construction of Rabbani's leadership framework not only discusses aspects related to Shariah but also an understanding of Islamic values and principles that govern the practice of leadership in general.

3. Rabbani conceptual framework

In general, the Qur'an and the sunnah left by the Prophet when leading the Muslims became a reference to the construction of the conceptual framework of Rabbani's leadership.

> *"It is not for a human (prophet) that Allah should give him the Scripture and authority and prophethood and then he would say to the people," "Be servants to me rather*

Leadership Values and Understandings from an Islamic Perspective
DOI: http://dx.doi.org/10.5772/intechopen.101989

> *than Allah," but (instead, he would say), "Be pious scholars of the Lord because of*
> *what you have taught of the Scripture and because of what you have studied." (3:79)*

The word "Rabbani" is an Arabic word derived from the word "rabb" and adds the letter "Alif" and the letter "Nunn" is pronounced with Rabbani which refers to the most gracious God. When the word Islam is associated with Rabbani, it carries the meaning that Islam has a relationship with the rights possessed by Allah almighty. In this case, the framework of rules and laws derived from Islam is based on the principles of values derived from Allah almighty. Many Tafsir scholars such as Tafsir al-Baidhowi [2], and Al-Alusi [3], interpret Rabbani's words as a person of knowledge and wisdom in managing human rule who has a close relationship with leadership.

Ibn Hisham (213H) describes Ibn Abbas's (3 SH–68 H) interpretation of the events that took place in verse 79, surah Ali Imran. He explained that Prophet Muhammad (peace be upon him) was not sent to invite Jews and Christians to worship him. This explanation proves that the call of Prophet PBUH is to guide mankind to the generation of Rabbani. In this case, Rabbani's words are closely related to human beings who use their understanding and superiority to invite others to worship Allah.

Rabbani's leadership is focused on the effort to invite goodness by doing the things God has commanded, and abandoning the things God has forbidden. The measuring stick of good and bad is referred to the Book of Allah and the Hadith of the Prophet. In this case, the honesty of the leader is inviting his followers to carry out God's commands sincerely can be translated through a fair and just relationship.

The strength of Rabbani's characteristics of a leader is linked to what the leader does and the personality of the leader. Someone who is deeply concerned about the leader's behavior and its relationship to the well-being of his followers. In any decision-making situation, the issue of religion is implicitly involved. The choices made by leaders and the way they respond in each situation reflect the strength of their Rabbani characteristics.

The nature of Rabbani is part of the nature of Islamic leadership that colors the pattern of leadership in organizations that have strong paradoxical and practical values. Despite its novels and paradoxes, Rabbani's basic ideas, and prescriptions of leadership can contribute to the development of an Islamic approach in leadership to determine the direction of a group or organization. Praise for Rabbani's conceptual framework came from a variety of well-known writers, including Al-Baidhowi [2], Alusi [3], and Al-Haj Maulana Fazlul-Karim [4].

A study of the life of the Prophet Muhammad saw during the events of the migration from Mecca to Medina reveals how the behavior of the Rabbani leader was translated into the responsibilities and practices of effective leadership. Rabbani leadership reveals a framework of leadership practice that has a close relationship with leadership character. The behavior and decisions of the leader will have a direct impact on the system and work culture of the organization being led. Rabbani's leadership model has three main characteristics, a relationship with divinity; humanity; and human development.

The Rabbani leader is not only a person who is able to lead, knowledgeable, and wise to adapt to the demands and needs of life in this world and the hereafter. The Rabbani leader is also able to share responsibility with his followers by giving full responsibility to carry out the trust that is driven by the spiritual aspect. By doing so, Rabbani leaders are able to cultivate noble values (Ihsan) which are fundamental principles while promoting follower capacity building, group unity, cross-cultural knowledge, and natural resource development.

Rabbani's leadership specifically reveals a framework of ideas about the role of leaders to determine the true direction and morals of an organization based on shariah-compliant. Iehsan [5] explains that the methodology of Rabbani education delivered must be based on an understanding of the real role of human beings living in the world to be servants of Allah (al-Zariat: 56), human beings as caliphs (al-Baqarah: 30), and human beings living will through a test given by Allah (al-Mulk: 2) [6]. Man is responsible for undergoing a philosophical framework (Hablum minAllah wa hablun min al-Nas) in his life based on surah Ali Imran (3: 112) as the basis of happiness in this world and the hereafter [7]. Adibah Rahim [8] explains that behavior in Islam has a good relationship between Khaliq (Creator) and makhluq (creatures), and between humans and other creatures.

Thus, Rabbani's leadership is in two broad domains namely the concept of leader behavior and the concept of leader character. Al-Ghazali [9] explained that human beings consist of two forms, behavior, and character. Behavior refers to the physical form of man while character refers to the spiritual form of man. Thus, Islamic ethics from Al-Ghazali's point of view is rooted in the soul and manifests itself through human actions. Such character can be acquired through practice and training. Adibah Rahim [8] combines both the domains of behavior and character in one word, referred to as Islamic ethics.

Rabbani's concepts related to leader behavior is further divided into two types: concepts that emphasize the consequences of a leader's actions and those that emphasize the vision and mission that govern the actions of leaders. In assessing the consequences, there are three different approaches to making decisions about the conduct of Rabbani leadership: Divinity, Humanity, and the Development of human life [10].

4. The vision of leadership

A leader who leads an organization certainly has a vision that must be fulfilled. Leaders will share their dreams and determine the direction of the organization to drive the goals and actions of employees or followers. Islam provides a complete framework of life; Therefore, it introduces the two main sources of the Qur'an (Holy Book) and the Sunnah (the actions of the Prophet Muhammad (peace be upon him)) as the life principles of an individual as well as society [11].

Rabbani's leadership begins with a natural feeling (fitrah) that one wants to cultivate goodness among his followers through charming communication to transform the purpose of the individual into the goal of the ummah. Rabbani leaders always strive to increase piety, where they act without disregarding sharia and ethics, regardless of the expectations of other individuals. A person with full awareness always aspired to lead others to obey all the commands of Allah so that it becomes the highest priority in accordance with the principles of Maqasid Shariah. Thus, Rabbani's leadership is a framework for elevating oneself and his followers to the highest level of moral development because leadership behaviors reflect a personality that can adapt to the development of life in this world and the hereafter. This approach would show that Rabbani leaders tend to move towards superior development, which involves held personal values and standards (e.g., integrity, justice, and caring for the good of society). To clarify Rabbani's leadership for practitioners, there is something important in the development of spiritual values.

4.1 Devinity: courage and justice

Courage refers to an individual's ability to be a visionary leader for an organization, sharing an explanation of his or her mission and leadership direction. This

Leadership Values and Understandings from an Islamic Perspective
DOI: http://dx.doi.org/10.5772/intechopen.101989

approach goes beyond thinking to deal with daily activities because it focuses on the "big picture." The courage of revelation-based leaders will emphasize the value of justice that equips Rabbani leaders to respond to complex organizational problems in creative ways, enabling them to address the intricacies of the organization in relation to its long-term goals.

Hence, a leader must be seen as someone who was not afraid to face danger when he delivered *Tawhid* and revelation to the community. The leader involved articulating, communicating, and inspiring a vision to his followers in the organization. He was showing courage and the ability to take calculated risks were essential attributes of a leader. These attributes describe Rabbani behavior, which promoted the concept of Tawhid by cooperation, creativity, and innovation through informal and formal sharing of divinity (al-Qur'an). The Rabbani leader employed divine teaching to reshape the culture and climate of humanity. The Rabbani's teachings addressed the soul that was the most important component of humanity.

4.2 Humanity: temperance and justice

A common theme that occurs through Rabbani's leader perspective is the sense of simplicity of the leader-follower relationship as emphasized in ethical leadership. In addition, this perspective emphasizes the need for leaders to pay attention to the diverse needs of followers. Temperance a state that is naturally inclined morality to do what is right within the right way shows the balance of the faculty of appetite by reason and law. In an Islamic perspective, the actions of leaders are morally correct if they express concern in protecting followers who have been known to need help and hope for well-being. Caring ethics is very important in organizations because it is a key element in building trust and collaborative relationships.

Thus, good communication between leaders and followers is an interactive process that includes the transmission and reception of messages such as speaking and listening. The decency of a revelation-based leader will be accompanied by a feature of justice that complements Rabbani's leader "standing in the place" of others and striving to see the world from that person's point of view. The empathetic Rabbani leaders show that they truly understand what their followers think and feel. When a Rabbani leader shows empathy, it affirms and confirms his followers. In addition, Rabbani leaders were concerned with the personal well-being of their followers. They support followers by helping them overcome personal problems. Rabbani's leaders are committed to helping everyone in the organization grow personally and professionally.

4.3 Human life: wisdom and justice

Wisdom is an award that qualifies a person to know in-depth to produce precise and balanced actions when making conscious decisions. This action will generate the confidence to have high motivation, inner strength, and enthusiasm to interact and speak convincingly. The qualities in Rabbani leaders make them very familiar and accepting of their physical, social, and political environment. This includes understanding oneself and one's impact on others. With divinely controlled wisdom, it will be accompanied by justice that equips Rabbani leaders who can step out and see their own views and their own perspectives in the context of a larger situation. The knowledgeable person inherits the wisdom that will use his skills in dealing with challenging situations and strive to unravel each problem with his knowledge, beliefs, and skills shared with his followers in the organization.

Hence, the leader has persistent communication that convinces others to change. As opposed to coercion, which utilizes positional authority to force compliance, persuasion creates change using gentle nonjudgmental arguments. The advantage of a Rabbani leader is the ability to know the future based on what has happened in the present and what has happened in the past. A high sense of responsibility can engender a far-sighted view by a leader because of the willingness to take risks on every decision and action that can lead to failure that can be reasonably expected.

5. The impact of Rabbani's leadership

Based on the framework of this writing will describe the practical dimensions of Rabbani's leadership which include the behavior of leaders such as the divine aspects that produce the values of courage and justice; aspects of humanity that produce the values of decency and justice; aspects of human life that prioritize the values of wisdom and justice; and its consequences on leadership responsibilities. There are three important responsibilities that every leader can fulfill throughout their tenure of leadership, and make decisions that have consequences.

5.1 Upholding the vision (Tawhid)

Al-Tauhid is a key element in the concept of the Islamic worldview. Muslims are very monotheistic and vehemently reject any attempt to make God visible or human. Islam rejects all forms of idolatry, even if the purpose is to "get closer" to God and reject the Trinity or any attempt to make God human. The teachings are based on the holy book of religion which is the holy book of the Qur'an and sunnah. It compresses the seen and the unseen world. Tauhid or the doctrine of tauhid shows that only He (Allah) is worthy of worship. An obedient person is a human being who lives a life to surrender his soul and body as a servant of Allah [12].

Discussions on the concept of Islamic leadership are rooted in the life of the Prophet Muhammad PBUH. Rabbani is an attribute shown by Prophet as a leader and bestowed on a person who claims to be a servant. In fact, the way a person emerges as a leader is by first becoming a servant of God. Leaders should begin the move by setting a direction to drive their followers to work fulfilling the vision of the organization. In addition, a leader must have the courage to defend the truth for the sake of the survival of the organization. The vision of the organization is actually very important to be shared with all employees in order to inspire followers to make improvements in the organization. A leader who dares to defend and fight for idealism is embodied in the skills of speaking, communicating, inspiring all his followers to make improvements. Courage accompanied by justice can have such a profound effect on followers that they are willing to sacrifice time and energy to perfect the vision of the organization. This spirit was actually inspired by the example set by the Prophet when he called on the people of Mecca and Medina to make changes in all areas of life.

The qualities highlighted by Prophet Muhammad (peace be upon him) leading the companions to maintain their beliefs, implement religious teachings, and build a nation reflect Rabbani's behavior. All decisions to determine the goals and actions of defending and fighting for religious life are based on monotheistic beliefs that emphasize God and glorify him. These attributes with cooperation, creativity, and innovation through informal and formal sharing of divinity (the Qur'an). The Prophet (peace be upon him) used divine teachings to reshape the culture and climate of mankind. The teachings of the Prophet touch the soul which is the most important component of mankind. He taught with wisdom and changed the souls of individuals among the companions like Umar bin Khatab.

Leadership Values and Understandings from an Islamic Perspective
DOI: http://dx.doi.org/10.5772/intechopen.101989

Therefore, the process of learning gradually so as to be able to develop a culture of knowledge in the Muslim community is a reflection of Rabbani's leadership. This approach contributed to changes in the lives of his followers and as a result, they have stopped doing things that are forbidden in Islam such as stopping drinking alcohol, killing, civil war, etc. [13].

5.2 Social justice and humanity

In Islam, the leader is entrusted to guide his people to surrender their entire lives to gain the pleasure of Allah by carrying out all of his commands and abandoning all of his prohibitions. Islam introduces a framework of life that connects the soul of the servant to Allah in every action to meet the necessities of life. The freedom of action of a human being to live the life of the world must be bound in scope as a slave who has a relationship of life in the hereafter.

In matters related to efforts to uphold universal justice, Rabbani leaders must be able to emphasize justice in the governance of the organization. If there is a problem or conflict and reconciliation, a leader should refer to the guiding principles given in the Qur'an and Sunnah (the actions of the Prophet Muhammad) on contemporary world issues [11]. A leader can spend his leadership time teaching and guiding his followers in the virtues and values of Islam. In this case, the leader should be able to help his followers to see something beyond their self-interest, and he himself strives to emphasize universal brotherhood, prioritizes virtue, goodness, justice, and strives against the influence of selfishness in himself.

Accordingly, Rabbani's leadership can guide and control change to achieve the stated contextual objectives. Empowerment is the willingness to enable people with the skills and knowledge to use their talents and energy to be more effective. When people are empowered, they are able to solve job-related problems and make decisions, preferably as a team unit. Rabbani's leaders constantly encouraged his followers to practice what they believed in. He urged his followers to practice Islam even when situations are contrary to personal desire and gain [13].

Rabbani leaders are able to teach followers about the concept of love and brotherhood, which is the value of caring while dealing with each other in their daily lives. Rabbani leaders strive to unite followers of the values of togetherness, starting from the individual, family, and community levels. He clarified the rights for each category and ensured that carrying out joint duties should be upheld in society. Followers are able to sacrifice their wealth to others for the sake of Allah and work together as believers to achieve the goals of the Ummah [13].

Islam aims to build an organization or society based on religion, morality, and social justice [14]. The Rabbani leader is actually a leadership framework for realizing social justice through the teachings of revelation. Rabbani's leaders built the foundation of developing society with the guidance of revelation to be able to face the challenges of finding solutions. Rabbani's characteristics become more apparent when a leader enthusiastically invites his followers to appreciate the teachings of the Qur'an. This leader does not consider himself to have an advantage over others but always considers his followers as brothers so willing to work together to help advance the organization. Social justice is strengthened through the concept of brotherhood to create a sense of belonging. This spirit of brotherhood makes a follower responsible for fulfilling the trust given and cooperating with each other. This commitment develops by itself to be seen as a key element that can evoke a spirit of helping each other and caring for the basic needs of those in need [15].

5.3 Sustainable development

Prophet Muhammad PBUH provided an example of community and national life while laying the foundation stone for the construction of the state of Madinah. The Prophet PBUH gave an example to his ummah on how to deal with various backgrounds such as religion and race to create the spirit of patriotism referred to as ummah. The Prophet saw made a fair decision when granting minority rights to different religious groups through treaties. This treaty is considered an important document that binds the diversity of ethnic and religious groups to live together to defend the homeland from being invaded and damaged. This attachment also opens space for all parties to contribute energy, thoughts, and strength to contribute towards the development of the country. The leadership of the Prophet succeeded in creating a new system that could manage balanced development to meet both the spiritual and material growth of the different religious groups that were able to survive under Islamic rule. The framework of state life shown by Prophet Muhammad PBUH is recognized by many historians as a method that can deal with the lives of people of different backgrounds in order to live together under the auspices of the Islamic State of Madinah [16].

The wisdom of Rabbani's leadership shown by the Prophet has been able to formulate a good strategy. Prophet Muhammad managed to choose among the companions to contribute their expertise to help develop a nation. In this regard, a Rabbani-characterized leader should have the advantage of managing by mobilizing his followers to contribute expertise to develop an organization. A knowledgeable person inherits wisdom that may describe his skills in dealing with situations he faces because of his knowledge, beliefs, and skills. Many hadiths suggest the importance of knowledge and skills. These changes describe determination, the people who aspired to a civilized society. Every single follower plays an important role in managing natural resources and developing them for the benefit of their lives. Human development approaches to addressing religion and spirituality at work and its surrounding.

The word Adl in the Arabic language defines as developed and excellence. The word Adl in Arabic is defined as advanced and growing. Justice brings the principle of balance to produce the inner motivation of the self that contributes to the production of quality and excellence shrouded in moral values. Islam encourages its people to be committed to contributing energy towards development without neglecting the ethical elements that can affect the development of individuals and society. A good individual will give birth to a good society in general [17].

Islam teaches human beings to value good relations among human beings and their environment. This sense of responsibility will cultivate a sense of always accepting and protecting all life in the world as a good value. This attitude can cultivate a passion for preserving and conserving the environment that contributes to the ecological balance of nature. A good environment can be utilized to meet the economic and social needs of human life. The right to use and utilize natural resources, which God has bestowed on human beings necessarily involves an obligation on the part of human beings to conserve them quantitatively and qualitatively. In this case, the leader should be able to inspire his followers or his community to be responsible for preserving and conserving the environment for the sake of survival [15].

Adibah Rahim [8] argues that most people see ethics as a less important part and rarely combined with other sciences, such as law, politics, science, economics, and others. This situation has an impact on modern science-based knowledge that is seen as empty and soulless. Therefore, ethics should be a basic principle in every development of values such as justice, freedom, equality, and rights and should be ensured to exist and be used in all disciplines. Without ethics, every evolving

Leadership Values and Understandings from an Islamic Perspective
DOI: http://dx.doi.org/10.5772/intechopen.101989

discipline of knowledge will face various problems and ultimately affect the harmony of human life and its environment. Similarly, skills are seen to have a certain importance in every discipline of knowledge that contributes to quality and prosperous life. The balance of disciplines of knowledge accompanied by values, and skills is actually an important element that contributed to the life of the Prophet, especially during the migration from the city of Mecca to the city of Medina.

Accordingly, of course, knowledge, skills accompanied by ethics and values have a positive impact on efforts to manage and develop natural resources. Zulkifli Mohamad [18] pointed out that in fact many hadiths and verses of the Qur'an that touch on the importance of knowledge, skills, and values as human capital to manage all forms of human life needs. The man should always refer to the code of ethics to monitor his relationship with God, with family, with fellow human beings in society so that his life finds happiness and goodness.

Accordingly, human beings should not neglect the code of ethics in the affairs of life when making decisions or actions. In terms of human relations, it is clearly mentioned in the Qur'an that Muslims are brothers. Therefore, one should have ethics in association, such as being helpful, kind, generous, and polite to each other. The forgetfulness of a person who is willing to release the bonds of self and life from the code of ethics can affect the well-being of life. This condition can upset the balance of life which will eventually plunge a person towards ruin and stray from the religious life [19].

6. Core principles of effective leadership (Maqasid Shariah)

Hence, Rabbani concept has inspired the objective of the organization's policy that emphasizes certain divinity thinking derived from religion. Rabbani leadership may inspire the practicing Islamic teaching for selecting and producing quality human capital.

6.1 Cultivating benevolence (Deen)

The notion of religious belief as a source of knowledge and guidance is well-known as the basis of the Islamic worldview. The concept of Tawhid or belief in the oneness of God is at the core of the Islamic worldview. The Islamic faith of oneness of God (tawhid) promotes the spirit of integration and inseparability in man and nature, and of a human fraternity, which concerns of unity for the mutual good in guiding individual action. The challenges with the current idea from other religions are behind the growing relevance of secularism when dealing with individuals, and theology is only one part of identity. Muslims are strictly monotheistic and fiercely reject any idea to make God visible. The obedient person whose life is governed by the principles of *Tawhid* that lead a divinely inspired life.

According to the Islamic view, leadership position has a relationship with trust and responsibility, rather than as a privilege [10, 20]. Leaders must uphold the principles of leadership that is virtuous based on faith or belief. The values of trust and responsibility will motivate employees or their followers to emulate the nature of a leader and work with a full sense of responsibility. A leader who devotes himself to guiding his followers will produce obedient workers. Leaders not only determine the direction of the organization but are also able to protect and deal with followers fairly. In this case, the leader always communicates directly with his followers in matters relating to work affairs and also in relation to God. This approach will encourage employees to always be concerned about matters related to the affairs of worldly life and the hereafter.

71

The leadership of the Prophet Muhammad (peace be upon him) proves some of the leadership practices shown involve example, good speech, guidance by inspiring his followers (the companions). His courage in carrying the message of God had to be paid for with the sacrifice of his whole soul and body, as well as the lives of his followers. Successful leaders are those who are willing to take risks to achieve their vision and mission. Leaders not only instruct followers to perform tasks but at the same time help their followers by setting direction, good guidance as well as being role models who can inspire their followers [21].

An organization that has a clear vision, can help every member of the organization to learn and understand the assigned task better. A good understanding can smooth the work entrusted to be carried out according to the given guidelines. If all members of the organization feel valued for having been involved together in determining the vision or mission of the organization. Of course, the trust given by the organization will be seen as a responsibility that must be fulfilled with good and quality results.

6.2 Empowerment (livelihood)

The approaches of humanitarian relationships may offer a viable solution that empowerment is one of a mechanism to encourage employee commitment in any organization. In the Islamic view, empowerment signifies a form of discussion which is known as Syuratic. This discussion aims to make decisions that are applied at all levels, both in the administration and management of the organization collectively. While leaders play a major role in articulating a vision, the emergence of a vision comes from both the leader and the follower. This means they build a framework that can develop an identity of attachment to the organization. These leaders deliver a direction that can develop their organizational values and norms.

In Islam, a way of life is defined as religious life. People who are religious are those who have a system of beliefs and laws that affect life have a relationship with God. Religious life does not set aside material demands from spiritual demands or vice versa. However, the religious life is to drive the desire for materialism which is accompanied by a spirituality that has to do with the teachings of religion. Accordingly, thoughts or ideologies that do not associate religion with the way of life are actually contrary to the notion of religion itself. They may reject ideological doctrines that isolate religion in matters of life such as secularism, humanism, and liberalism because they contradict Islamic beliefs.

The position of a leader is different referring to the hierarchy in an organization that has many areas of duties and responsibilities. Worldly missions emphasize that leadership can place commitment in fulfilling responsibilities. A leader can determine certain needs to be implemented collectively for the welfare of an organization by doing good ('Amr Bil Maroof) and preventing evil (Nahi-Al-Munkar). Accordingly, the Islamic leadership model should provide a vision that can be shared with followers. Each follower will work according to a set task to fulfill a shared vision in the organization. The vision of ideal leadership in any organization certainly wants the existence of a developed society to be able to provide welfare and prosperity. At the same time, a leader will ensure that the well-being of society is not affected by elements of discrimination, oppression, and exploitation.

Leaders should be able to guide their followers or people to know and understand Islam as a whole. Leaders should be prepared to serve Muslims by providing comprehensive guidelines on the management of personal and professional affairs. Leaders are willing to establish good and unique relationships with trusted followers through family activities ("usrah"). In this regard, Islam sees good work as a virtue and a form of worship. Every job or trust given is a responsibility that must be fulfilled and it is obligatory for every Muslim to complete the task. Satisfaction will

Leadership Values and Understandings from an Islamic Perspective
DOI: http://dx.doi.org/10.5772/intechopen.101989

be born after every trust and work entrusted can be completed perfectly. This effort can actually cultivate the blessings of life.

6.3 Brotherhood (offspring)

Brotherhood in Islam is like a human being with a perfect body. If one limb is sick, then the whole body will be sick. Therefore, there needs to be a bond between individuals with one another in a team. Cooperation, consideration, solidarity may strengthen the bond of brotherhood. There must be a high determination in each member of the organization to express the meaning of commitment in the organization. An understanding of religious life, with an emphasis on morality and fighting for social justice, is the main spice for developing a competitive socio-economy society [22].

In the view of Islam, the development will be born when human needs, natural and social resources can be preserved from the elements of lust that only pursue the pleasures of life to boast of wealth and luxury. The spirit of brotherhood built in a society will be able to guard against greed. Members of the community can live a life that prioritizes a spirit of cooperation, consideration, and even solidarity with other less fortunate members of the community. Charity and knowledge become an added value to human life that binds progress and the pursuit of happiness as part of the human responsibility of living on earth. Community life on the principle of brotherhood will actually be able to develop a society that lives in harmony [23].

Rabbani leadership designed the framework of social justice to bring harmonies life through his moral teachings [14]. The effort led to restructure the resources to settle down the problem faced during the administration period. The only reliable way to do by launching the concept of Islamic brotherhood so that they started to think of every follower as their brother regardless of the color, caste, and clan. This notable policy showed Rabbani leader is a successful leader, undoubtedly. The notion of Islamic brotherhood is an optimal solution for this problem that unity is the foundation for the harmonious life of society. This work provided proof that binding the humanitarian relationship between multi followers' social backgrounds may grow up a positive way as a progressive society.

Rabbani leaders do the pervasiveness of coalitions or set alliances with any agencies as mechanisms of upgrading the organization's influence, by convincing peers, subordinates, superiors, and outsiders to join forces to pursue their common interests. This approach shows a move that officially marked the start of the development collaboration between the followers and outsider agencies.

6.4 Knowledge management culture change

Knowledge management culture change that stimulates followers to be creative and innovative Aqal (*intellect*) is regarded as the starting point of knowledge. Islam forbids the practice of drinking alcohol because it can damage the mind that can affect its function to acquire knowledge. This type of leadership supports followers as they try new approaches and develop innovative ways of dealing with organizational issues. It encourages followers to think things out on their own and engage in careful problem-solving.

In this regard, preservation of the mind may avoid things that can impair the function of the mind which can disrupt the harmony of social life. The preservation of the intellect must be accompanied by faith that provides the direction of the reason for the truth. Faith requires the mind to adjust to a shariah understanding of the current context and environment. In general, Islam guides its people to preserve the main source of human intellectual development capable of knowing Allah Almighty.

Leaders should have a philosophy of monotheistic values to be translated through leadership practices. This confidence will be able to give birth to the basic principles for handling all human affairs and organizational development efforts. Leaders will always set an example by showing a good example of personal life to their followers. Leaders always keep promises and give high commitment when in social activities with their followers. This practice will strengthen the identity and bonding relationship between leaders and followers in an organization. Rabbani leaders encourage others and celebrate their accomplishments and lead followers' feel better about themselves and their contributions to the greater common good.

The preservation of the intellect is not limited to the avoidance of harmful acts, but also to the development of the faculties of the intellect that contribute to the cultivation of knowledge. The exploration of knowledge should be encouraged by providing for all the needs of knowledge development and identifying factors that may hinder its smoothness. Rabbani leadership can contribute elements of the knowledge management culture change that are in line with common sense goals. In this case, political leaders should be willing to harness the power to shed light on the importance of knowledge in life. In addition, political leaders can also organize programs that stimulate the community's desire to gain knowledge. The sensible mind can accept the facts of truth without being influenced by emotion and bigotry. The sensible mind also readily accepts the rules and laws set by Allah Almighty. On the other hand, unhealthy minds cannot accept the good or prevent the damage described from the sources of the Qur'an and the Sunnah of the Prophet PBUH.

6.5 Management (resources)

Islam sees natural resources as the greatest gift from God to all human beings. Natural resources are sources of sustenance allocated to human beings to be utilized. Thus, part of the objective of the development of an economic-social system is to emphasize the collective responsibility in utilizing, allocating, and preserving this whole universe. Islam emphasizes efforts towards environmental protection, taking and utilizing natural resources for business purposes, and the importance of social sustainability. Therefore, the leader is responsible for guiding the followers or the people to utilize the natural resources they have for the needs of life and maintain the balance of the environment. The categories of human needs are many, and they are classified in terms of variance of goods, individual and social services related to health, employment, education, housing training, building relationships, and including the environment to ensure an acceptable standard of living for all (Khalfan, 2002).

The creation of man is a combination of spiritual and physical elements. Both of these elements actually influence the hopes, desires, and needs of human life. Humans always need something to meet the demands of a member's life. At the same time, human beings also need spiritual elements to meet the needs of internal elements such as intellect, lust, and even spirit. All three internal elements feel empty if one has not yet discovered or known God [15, 24]. In this case, the leader should be able to take care of all the living needs of his followers or his people well. Good management will produce the equipment needed fairly and equitably. This agenda can cause followers to appreciate the leader's efforts by highlighting positive self-expression. This situation will be able to bind the relationship of leaders and followers who are guided to fulfill the vision of the organization. Good management opens up space for leaders to express high expectations to followers and help them gain confidence and self-efficacy. In short, Rabbani's leadership works because it binds followers and their self-concepts to organizational identity.

Leadership Values and Understandings from an Islamic Perspective
DOI: http://dx.doi.org/10.5772/intechopen.101989

7. Conclusion

In summary, Rabbani's leadership model produces three components that influence the perspective of the leadership framework: The vision of leadership, The impact of leadership, and the core principles of effective leadership (Maqasid Shariah). The main focus of the approach is the impact of leadership that nurtures Rabbani's leadership: Upholding the vision (Tauhid); Uphold social justice and humanity; and Sustainable Development. Certain cultures and contexts, the nature of the leader, and the followers 'acceptance of leadership can influence the degree of ups and downs of Rabbani characteristics in leadership. Leaders who have Rabbani characteristics, it is likely to contribute to increased outcomes at the individual, organizational, and community levels.

The Rabbani leadership approach works differently than many of the prior theories we have discussed. Rabbani leadership focuses on the behaviors leaders should exhibit to put followers concerned the faith and shariah's compliance for the mutual good in guiding individual action to support followers' personal development. It is concerned with how leaders treat subordinates and the outcomes that are likely to emerge. It begins when a leader begins to focus on the development of spiritual values by exhibiting honesty when interacting with them, and treating them fairly. The leader of Rabbani prioritizes his followers to obey the commands of Allah and abandon all prohibitions when dealing with any party. Leaders can realize the importance of maintaining a religious life to build good relationships among human beings and the environment throughout life. A good relationship built between a leader and a follower allows the leader to understand the abilities, needs, and goals of the follower. This information is very important, as the main source to motivate followers to strive to the maximum extent of developing the potential of followers. When many leaders in an organization adopt Rabbani's leadership orientation, work culture of harmonizing others inside and outside the organization is created.

Finally, Rabbani's leadership actually has the opportunity to make a difference to individuals, followers, and employees in an organization. Leaders who care about individuals and groups will inspire employees to be more committed in developing organizations that care about their needs. Organizations that practice a Rabbani leadership culture are committed to helping those in need while operating outside the organization.

Acknowledgements

This study is part of the project under a research grant (FRGS-59280) funded by the Ministry of Higher Education (KPT). The authors are grateful to the Ministry of Higher Education, Malaysia, for the financial support granted towards the success of the research project.

Leadership in a Changing World - A Multidimensional Perspective

Author details

Hailan Salamun* and Asyraf Ab Rahman
Center for Fundamental and Continuing Education (PPAL), UMT,
Kuala Terengganu, Terengganu, Malaysia

*Address all correspondence to: hailan@umt.edu.my

IntechOpen

© 2022 The Author(s). Licensee IntechOpen. This chapter is distributed under the terms of the Creative Commons Attribution License (http://creativecommons.org/licenses/by/3.0), which permits unrestricted use, distribution, and reproduction in any medium, provided the original work is properly cited.

References

[1] Chaston J, Lips-Wiersma M. When spirituality meets hierarchy: Leader spirituality as a double-edged sword. Journal of Management, Spirituality & Religion. 2014;**12**(2):111-128

[2] Al-Baidhowi, Nasruddin Abi Said Abdullah bin Umar bin Muhamad Syirazi al-Baidhowi. Tafsir Baidhowi. Beirut: Daril Jil; 1968

[3] Al-Alusi, Alamah abi al-Fadl Syihabudin as-Sayid Mahmud al-Alusi al-Baghdadi. Tafsir ruh al-maani. Beirut: Dar al-Fikr; 1987

[4] Al-Haj Maulana Fazlul-Karim. Imam Ghazzali's Ihya ulum-din. New Delhi: Adbdul Naeem for Islamic Book Service; 2005

[5] Iehsan MH. Al-manhaj al-rabbani fi bina "wa tarbiat al-mujtama" al-insani wa athar al-taqaddum al-ilmi fih. Kertas disertasi Doktor Falsafah Pengajian Islam. Bangi: Universiti Kebangsaan Malaysia; 2003

[6] Din H. Manusia dan Islam. Kuala Lumpur: Percetakan Watan Sdn. Bhd; 1988

[7] Othman F. "Pendidikan Islam: Konsep dan Realiti" dlm. Ismail Ab. Rahman (peny.) Pendidikan Islam Malaysia. Bangi: Penerbit Universiti Kebangsaan Malaysia; 1993

[8] Rahim ABA. Understanding Islamic ethics and its significance on the character building. International Journal of Social Science and Humanity. 2013;**3**(6):508-513

[9] Ghazali I. Keajaiban hati. Terjemahan Nurhickmah. Singapura: Pustaka Nasional Pte. Ltd; 1988

[10] Salamun H, Shah S. An Islamic perspective on educational leadership. Al-SHAJARAH. 2013;**18**:103-130

[11] Salma N. The Role of Prophet of Islam Muhammad's (P.B.U.H.) Strategy of Dialogue in Conflict Management and Peace Building in the New Millennium. 2018. Available from: http://ptsm.edu.pl/wp-content/uploads/2018/01/salma-naz.pdf

[12] Al-Faruqi IR. Islamisasi Pengetahuan. Terjemahan. Bandung: Penerbit Pustaka; 1995

[13] Farooq M, Ssekamanya SA. The role of education in the development of spirituality and community empowerment: Lessons from the approach of Prophet Muhammad (pbuh). Interdisciplinary Journal of Education. 2018;**1**(2):239-249

[14] Hasan A. Social justice in Islam. Islamic Studies. 1971;**10**(3):209-219

[15] Muwazir MR, Muhamad R, Noordin K. Corporate social responsibility disclosure: A Tawhidic approach. Jurnal Syariah. 2006;**14**(1):125-142

[16] Emon A. Reflections on the "Constitution of Medina": An essay on methodology and ideology in islamic legal history. UCLA Journal of Islamic and Near Eastern Law (JINEL). 2001;**1**(103):103-133

[17] Rahman AA, Said S, Salamun H, Aziz H, Adam F, Ibrahim WAW. Sustainable development from islamic perspective. International Journal of Civil Engineering and Technology. 2018;**9**(4):985-992

[18] Zulkifli Mohamad al-Bakri. Himpunan Hadis Modal Insan. Kuala Lumpur: Telaga Biru Sdn. Bhd; 2007

[19] Seferta YHR. The doctrine of prophethood in the writings of Muhammad 'Abduh and Rashīd Riḍā. Islamic Studies. 1985;**24**(2):139-165

[20] Beekun RI, Badawi J. Leadership: An Islamic Perspective. Beltsville, MD: Amana; 1999

[21] Salamun H, Rahman AA, Aziz H, Rashid R. Malay leadership pattern in Malaysian politics. The Journal of Social Sciences Research. 2018;4(12):451-458

[22] Krstić N, Dinić J, Gavrilović D. Religiosity and informal economic practices in Southeastern European societies. Religions. 2018;9(10):295

[23] Markom R. The role of law and *Shariah* governance in islamic finance towards social justice in diversity. Diponegoro Law Review. 2018;3(2): 142-153

[24] Tanyi RA. Towards clarification of the meaning of spirituality. Journal of Advanced Nursing. 2002;39(5):500-509

Chapter 6

E-Leadership: Lessons Learned from Teleworking in the COVID-19 Pandemic

Luciana Mourão, Gardênia da Silva Abbad and Juliana Legentil

Abstract

During the pandemic crisis, teleworking was compulsory for many workers, without the time and conditions to organize themselves for this transition. Therefore, the leadership needs to respond quickly to changes that occur in times of crisis—such as the current pandemic—adjusting its competencies to prioritize the well-being of employees, define performance goals, follow-up on these goals, provide guidance and support teleworkers, and improve feedback processes. The present study aims to propose an e-leadership theoretical model based on lessons learned from the coronavirus pandemic. To that end, we describe and discuss a survey on the perceptions of support received from managers during the initial 3 months of the pandemic. For this purpose, we collected data with 7608 workers distributed to 95 public service organizations in Brazil. In addition, we also reviewed several empirical studies that assessed the role of leadership in the proper functioning of telework. The support of leaders is directly associated with the theory of organizational support. In moments of crisis like the current one, this focus on leadership is even more critical. Thus, we present a theoretical model for e-leadership that should expand from the telework experiences during the coronavirus pandemic.

Keywords: e-leadership model, managerial support, leadership role, teleworking, COVID-19 pandemic

1. Introduction

The COVID-19 pandemic changed the world and how people work, creating challenges for the needs, and need for adaptation for workers [1, 2]. Before the pandemic, with the advancement of technologies, telework was already being discussed and adopted as a strategy considered advantageous by some public and private organizations [1, 3]. However, with the social distancing protocols to face the pandemic, some discussions about telework gained prominence in the surveys. One of them focuses on the studies of workers' physical and mental health, with isolation and lack of social contact being factors that can affect workers' health and well-being. Leadership support in this context can improve relationship levels and increase the chances of teleworkers staying healthy [4]. Therefore, the COVID-19 pandemic, compulsory teleworking reached workers in several countries, raising concern about managerial support. Before the pandemic, studies on teleworking already showed a need for more significant support from the leadership for this type of work.

Thus, the pandemic context instigated the discussion of electronic leadership, which promotes the adaptability of companies and workers. A set of challenges about telework and e-leadership started to be studied. Telework is often seen as an opportunity, with gains for the productivity of companies and for people who work remotely [1, 5]. However, a good part of telework results depends on leadership performance, which cannot be conventional. On the one hand, organizational structures need to be less hierarchical. On the other hand, leadership must establish a solid and trustworthy relationship with its employees, maintaining a genuine concern for their well-being [1, 3, 6].

Research indicates that in uncertain contexts, such as the pandemic, support for workers oriented toward management practices can increase employee engagement and reduce worker burnout [7]. In this pandemic context, interactions between management and the team become remote, requiring a set of coping strategies from workers [2, 8]. Leaders had to review the distribution and execution of goals and deadlines and establish shared goals. Leaders also had to monitor resource consumption and anticipate potential problems and track the progress of work by each member of their team [9].

Thus, the role of leaders in this challenging context gained even greater centrality [6] since the stressful situations experienced by workers [10] required more outstanding organizational and supervisory support. Positive results in the teleworking method require mechanisms that favor establishing a trust relationship [9]. Leadership encouragement was already considered decisive for the professional development of their subordinates [11], but in times of pandemic, the role of leadership became even more evident [6, 8–10]. However, excessive control by managers—with constant verification of employees or their performance—signals a feeling of distrust that affects the psychological safety of workers and the bond they establish with the organization [8].

Faced with mandatory work on the pandemic, leaders must be able to (i) improve communication processes in the team; (ii) ensure employee access to technology; (iii) prioritize the emotional stability of employees; (iv) maintain attention to the organization's goals and financial health; and (v) promote organizational resilience [6]. This supportive action by leaders is associated with the theory of organizational support discussed in this chapter.

So, the present study aims to propose an e-leadership theoretical model based on lessons learned from the coronavirus pandemic. To that end, we describe and discuss a survey on the perceptions of support received from managers during the initial 3 months of the pandemic. In other words, we propose to present a theoretical model of e-leadership, based on a broad study of how teleworkers perceived the support that received from their leaders during the compulsory telework carried out in the COVID-19 pandemic.

In addition to this broad empirical study, we also consider important lessons learned about leadership from the recent literature on the subject to consider e-leadership based on the lessons learned from the pandemic. Thus, after the section on the empirical study, we complement it with other studies in the literature, culminating with the proposition of the e-leadership theoretical model.

2. Role of leadership in organizational support

The perception of organizational support stems from a view that employees have the organization's support. This perception is formed from the treatment that the employee receives in the organization. Thus, if the leader takes care of social welfare and values subordinates' contributions, they tend to perceive organizational support positively. This positive perception can affect work motivation, employees' effort to perform well, and their intention to remain in the organization [12, 13]. This is a chain process. Furthermore, the way leaders are treated also affects the organizational support perceived by subordinates since leaders who feel supported by the organization tend to treat their associates well [14].

The organizational support theory is based on the social exchange theory [15], whose central principle is that the interaction between individuals relates to attempts to maximize rewards and reduce costs. This social psychology perspective establishes that people maintain interactions because they perceive some benefit/reward in material or nonmaterial terms.

In the organizational support theory, employees' beliefs about the support that they receive from the organization are evaluated [13]. Perceived support would be positive when they present a consistent assessment that organizational actions demonstrate concern for their well-being. This theory is based on the theory of social reciprocity. The norm of reciprocity is taught as a moral obligation and describes the development of exchange mechanisms for what is seen as mutually beneficial [16]. Thus, organizational support theory indicates a social exchange and reciprocity—employees' commitment to the organization increases as they perceive the organization's commitment to them.

According to this theory, social support from coworkers and leadership is perceived as social support. Leadership plays a significant role in coaching, providing care, and feedback to subordinates regarding their work tasks [9, 17]. This leadership support plays a vital role in workers' psychological safety and commitment [18]. As discussed in organizational support theory, treating employees well makes a difference in workers' returns to the organization [13].

In teleworking, the support of managers becomes even more relevant, whether due to the moment of crisis in the pandemic scenario or due to the difficulty of self-management of performance by workers, with processes of learning new skills and renegotiating work goals [2, 10]. Managers in such a context had to be dynamic, reorganizing work routines and adapting to the unique demands of workers and the organization [6]. The exchange of resources between leaders and subordinates in the context of the COVID-19 pandemic included several elements, such as tasks, information, open communication, shared goals, flexibility, feedback, and sharing of ideas and decisions [8]. Positive interactions and exchanges based on reciprocal relationships are associated with more favorable perceptions of psychological security at work [8].

Leaders have a relevant role in the development of their subordinates and in supporting them so that they can adequately perform their activities at work [11]. In this sense, we understand that the role of leadership needs to act on two simultaneous fronts—focus on results and focus on people. Therefore, bosses need to provide the necessary support to their subordinates in terms of return on performance and showing concern with the fulfillment of work tasks and, at the same time, act to promote the well-being of associates [19].

During the COVID-19 pandemic, a study with teleworkers showed that social support, autonomy, monitoring, and work overload are directly related to well-being at work performed in the home environment [20]. The results show that the workers' social support and autonomy acted as a work resource that contributes to telework management. However, monitoring and work overload served as demands that negatively affected the teleworker's well-being.

These results show the importance of leadership support, as leaders are directly responsible for the degree of autonomy assigned to workers and monitoring the fulfillment of tasks and goals [9, 19]. It is also up to the leaders to define the goals that may or may not generate overload [9]. This set of studies presented here shows a need to think about a different role on the part of leaders in the telework scenario. In this sense, the term e-leadership has been used, discussed in the next section.

3. E-leadership and its elements

The digital revolution has led to an intensification of telework that has become more prominent from the experiences of millions of workers during home-based work in pandemic. This expressive expansion of telework brought about the need to discuss the role of leaders in this new work context. Thus, the discussion of e-leadership became relevant, as it is a different form of management.

E-leadership or electronic leadership involves management carried out through information and communication technologies. Given the challenges faced in teleworking during the COVID-19 pandemic crisis, some researchers have carried out studies to discuss the concepts and characteristics of this e-leadership. Although researching different contexts and countries, these authors have some points in common. One of them is the understanding that the demands and competencies to meet these demands are different in traditional and electronic leadership. Some of the points raised in this e-leadership discussion are summarized below.

Based on an exploratory case study, [21] proposed an operational definition based on six factors for e-leadership, also called e-competencies for leaders. According to these authors, these six skills are e-communication, e-social skills, e-team building skills, e-change management, e-technological skills, and e-trustworthiness.

According to [21], e-communications skills involve three specific skills—communication clarity, lack of miscommunication, and management of communication flow. E-social skills, in turn, refer to good leader support, that is, ensuring that all teleworkers are provided with customized communication from time to time, with robust interaction methods. E-team building skill comprises three specific skills of virtual team leaders—team motivation, team accountability, and team and team member recognition. E-change management skill contemplates change management techniques by preplanning transitions, monitoring implementation, and refining technology practice with experience. E-technological skills are related to four elements—currency with relevant ICTs, blending traditional and virtual methods, basic technological savvy, and technical security. Finally, e-trustworthiness contemplates three central aspects—trustworthiness in a virtual environment, work-life balance, and diversity management [21].

In a similar vein, [22] surveyed education industry leaders and highlighted three of the best leadership practices for dealing with adaptive challenges as presented by the COVID-19 pandemic. A first point would be, considering the type of servant leadership, to emphasize the empowerment, involvement, and collaboration of leaders, putting the interests of others above their own. A second point would be for leaders to distribute leadership responsibilities to a network of teams across the organization, to improve the quality of decisions and crisis resolution. Finally, the third point would be for leaders to communicate clearly and frequently with all stakeholders by using various communication channels. In summary, the study by [22] suggests a leadership style called "allostatic leader," which would describe leaders with flexibility and adaptability to learn and evolve in crisis management, to respond more effectively and with less effort to future challenges.

Another study, of an exploratory and qualitative nature, was carried out by [23], who investigated electronic leadership in the context of the Lithuanian public sector. The authors highlight four central roles of e-leadership—instructing employees to use electronic tools, collecting, and sharing information, monitoring and reviewing the division of roles and tasks. The authors compared e-leadership with the leadership that they had before the COVID-19 pandemic crisis, considering three criteria—(i) communication mode, channels, and tools, (ii) time management, and (iii) delivering tasks [23].

According to [23], in the first criterion, communication mode, channels, and tools, there would be a demand that e-leadership act with multilateral communication dominates, main communication channels (audio, video, written mode) and main ICT tools (phone, Zoom, Email, Facebook groups, "Hive," teams). In the time management criterion, the main demands for e-leadership to manage would be— flexible work schedule, short-term and irregular on-demand meetings, the number of sessions sharply increases, reduced meeting time to avoid "redundant" talks, lunch break at the same time in all public sector organizations, and using ICT tools (Google calendar, Zoom, or Teams calendars). Finally, the delivering tasks criterion comprises challenges for e-leadership, such as explicit attention given to the clarity of the requestor of the tasks via email to assure the quality of their performance, and explicit norms of urgent responses, for example, establishing a maximum deadline for reply.

The study by [24] also discusses the need for an effective e-leadership to promote companies' adaptability, so telework can be understood as an advantageous opportunity for the productivity of companies, the environment, and people who work remotely. For the authors, the prosperity of telework depends on an e-leadership model that makes the structure of companies less hierarchical and simultaneously develops skills to establish a solid and trustworthy relationship with employees. Thus, a central role of e-leadership would be to consolidate the performance of virtual teams so that they can have an effective implementation and be capable of meeting organizational goals. But [24] consider that electronic or e-leadership is not just an extension of traditional leadership; it requires a crucial change in how leaders and their virtual teams report within the organizations and with stakeholders. Moreover, e-leadership implies the development of specific skills, as discussed by [21–23].

Although e-leadership can benefit from previous models on leadership, some adaptations are necessary for the leaders to act electronically. In addition, virtual teams have different demands from face-to-face groups, requiring work redesign [25]. In this sense, authors such as [26] suggest the construction of a new theory and the conduct of more empirical research that support organizations to design, structure and manage more effectively virtual work teams. The following section presents the empirical and exploratory study on the perception of leadership support to teleworkers during the pandemic. This empirical study, together with several other studies revisited and briefly presented here, served as inspiration for the proposition of the theoretical model shown at the end of this chapter.

4. Empirical study on leadership support for telework in the COVID-19 pandemic

Assessing leadership support for teleworking in pandemic times is relevant, as this reconciliation between productivity and workers' mental health depends on leaders. Furthermore, even after the pandemic, it is expected that many of the remote practices will be continued and expanded [2, 6].

Considering what was previously exposed, the present study proposes an e-leadership model based on lessons learned from the coronavirus pandemic.

To that end, we describe and discuss a survey on the perceptions of support received from managers during the initial 3 months of the pandemic. We propose to present a theoretical model of e-leadership, based on a broad study of how teleworkers perceived the support received from their leaders during the compulsory telework carried out in the COVID-19 pandemic. In addition to this comprehensive study, we also consider important lessons learned about leadership from the recent literature on the subject to consider e-leadership based on the lessons learned from the pandemic.

The research carried out had a quantitative approach, with an online questionnaire to an extensive sample of workers from Brazilian public institutions who were teleworking. One of the differentials of this work was that data collection was carried out from April to June 2020, that is, in the first months of the pandemic that began in Brazil in mid-March 2020. Therefore, this study was exploratory but allowed the construction of an overview of how teleworkers realized the support received from their leaders to carry out compulsory telework during the COVID-19 pandemic.

4.1 Participants

A total of 7608 public servants in Brazil, spread over 22 states, took part in this study, but with a greater concentration in the capital Brasília. Participation in the research was previously authorized by the 95 public organizations to which these participants are linked. Most of these organizations already worked telework before the pandemic, but they expanded this type of work due to social distancing protocols.

The sample was mainly composed of female participants (59.3%), aged between 38 and 47 years (34.2%) and between 28 and 37 years (29.8%), and married/in a stable relationship (63.5%). Almost the entire sample (93.4%) had completed higher education, and 60.5% had graduate degrees. However, only 6.6% of the sample were workers with high school education. Regarding the previous experience with telework, most participants (58.1%) had no prior experience with this type of work. Of that 41.9% who had previous experience with telework, 93.7% rated that the incidents had been positive, and 6.3% negatively evaluated their previous experience with telework.

4.2 Instruments

The items were built from the literature analysis on challenges, difficulties, demands, benefits, and barriers associated with teleworking at home and on the supportive role of leadership at that time. This work resulted in the construction of six items, and for each of them, the theoretical and empirical framework that supported it was analyzed. The central concepts considered for the construction of the items were—feedback, goal (attribution and monitoring), support, guidance, well-being, and infrastructure.

After choosing the items, an analysis of the judges was performed. Human resources professionals from two public institutions with previous experience in telework participated in this stage, as well as masters and doctors in psychology, linked to three postgraduate courses in Brazil. The judges assessed that the items adequately represented the main aspects of leadership support for telework performed from home.

The items included in the survey were—(i) I receive constructive feedback from my manager about my performance in remote activities, indicating opportunities for improvement; (ii) the remote work goals assigned to me by my manager are

E-Leadership: Lessons Learned from Teleworking in the COVID-19 Pandemic
DOI: http://dx.doi.org/10.5772/intechopen.100634

compatible with the workload from my sector; (iii) I receive support from my manager when I ask for directions to perform tasks remotely; (iv) my manager monitors the achievement of my work goals; (v) my manager is concerned about the adequacy of my infrastructure to work remotely (computer, internet, and furniture); and (vi) my manager demonstrates that he cares about my health and well-being. All these items were answered on a Likert scale of agreement, ranging from 1 (I totally disagree) to 5 (I totally agree). In addition, in the instructions for answering the questionnaire, participants were asked to answer the items considering their experiences during the pandemic period, linked to telework performed from home.

4.3 Data collection and analysis procedures

Data collection took place online, from links generated by researchers and forwarded by organizations to their teleworkers. The release of the questionnaire was subject to acceptance, by the participants, of an informed consent form. This form presented the research objectives and the responsible researchers and ensured the confidentiality of individual responses and the freedom to interrupt their participation in any research phase.

For data analysis, we used the Statistical Package for Social Sciences (SPSS) software, version 25. We performed descriptive and inferential analyses to identify differences between the average scores of perceptions of leadership support. The tests used were the Student's t test to identify differences in means as a function of gender, Spearman's correlation to identify a possible relationship between the scores and age groups of the participants. We also performed Pearson's correlation to identify a correlation between the items that assessed the perception of support from leaders to teleworkers.

4.4 Main results of the empirical study

The survey included some fundamental concepts for e-leadership, including feedback from leaders to their subordinates. Feedback can be understood as information about the difference between the actual and desired levels of performance, which allows the implementation of corrective actions capable of eliminating this difference [27]. Feedback is even more prominent regarding telework, especially that carried out compulsorily in the pandemic period [9, 25, 28]. Leaders need to establish exchanges with subordinates in the COVID-19 pandemic—feedback, the sharing of ideas and decisions [8].

The survey results showed that most teleworkers (69.8%) received constructive feedback on their performance in remote activities, indicating opportunities for improvement. However, those who did not realize that their leaders were giving constructive feedback in the telework period in the COVID-19 pandemic totaled 11.7%. In addition, there were also 18.5% who had difficulty in giving their opinion about receiving constructive feedback from leaders about their performance in remote activities.

About goals, they gained greater relevance with the goal orientation theory, which goes beyond the content of what people are trying to achieve (goals, specific standards). The theoretical emphasis here is on why and how people try to achieve goals, thus referring to broader goals of achievement behavior [29]. This theory comprises both the process of assigning goals and monitoring them.

The lack of monitoring or improper monitoring of the subordinates' performance and goals are configured as forms of destructive leadership. In the study of [30], researchers tested 658 team members out of 149 teams to compare abusive supervision and laissez-faire leadership effects from a Bayesian multilevel analysis. Abusive supervision lowered team trust and subsequent organizational citizenship behavior at the individual and team level, whereas laissez-faire was not related to team trust on the team level. The results indicated that laissez-faire was more harmful to organizational citizenship than abusive supervision on both groups.

In the context of telework, leaders must review the distribution and execution of goals, considering the workers' conditions to avoid overload [9] and organizational needs [6, 24]. In this sense, it is sometimes necessary to renegotiate deadlines and establish shared goals [2, 9, 10]. In addition, a careful process of monitoring tasks and goals must be carried out by leaders to monitor the progress of each member of their team, reassessing the degree of autonomy attributed to each worker [9, 19].

In the survey with teleworkers, we observed a positive perception of the establishment of compatible goals by the leadership. For example, we observed that 85% agreed with the statement, "The remote work goals assigned to me by my manager are compatible with the workload from my sector." In a complementary way, 90.5% agreed with the sentence "My manager monitors the achievement of my work goals." In this sense, the positive performance of e-leadership in the Brazilian public service during teleworking in the COVID-19 pandemic was evident. These results are consistent with several studies that pointed out the importance of having feasible and agreed goals in telework and monitoring the leader concerning these goals.

In addition to feedback and goals, it is also necessary to consider as an essential attribution of e-leadership the support and guidance given by leaders to their subordinates. Such support and guidance are theoretically linked to the supervisor's support, which concerns contributions and guidelines from the head and those influencing behaviors in the work context [13, 17]. But excessive guidance and monitoring by managers characterize micromanagement, which causes psychological insecurity in the worker [31].

During the COVID-19 pandemic, e-leadership needed to be aware of the workers' new demands for learning and the guidelines and guidelines they needed to receive. Compulsory telework added to pre-existing learning demands, a set of new directions, and leaders' care in observing and surveying such needs [25]. Supporting the performance of teleworkers is directly related to this survey of conditions and the availability of opportunities for new learning, in addition to the leader's ability to direct the performance of their virtual team.

In the survey conducted with teleworkers, we observed that few (3%) disagreed that they receive support from their leadership when they request directions to perform their remote tasks. On the other hand, most respondents (91.1%) rated satisfactorily the support that they received from their leaders when they asked for guidance. Several authors associate this ability to provide advice and support to subordinates as a central element of e-leadership [9, 25, 30].

Another aspect investigated in the survey with teleworkers was the infrastructure they must work remotely from their homes. These structural elements relate to the physical working conditions present in the production locus that characterize the physical environment, instruments, equipment, raw material, and institutional support. For example, for a home office to be ergonomically efficient, healthy, and safe, there must be a workspace and designated tools, including a computer, desk, chair, telephone, and internet connection [32].

With the tendency of teleworking to remain in many organizations after the end of the COVID-19 pandemic, e-leadership must actively seek to promote adequate infrastructure conditions for the work of its virtual team. In this new context of home-based work, workers need to have furniture, a computer, internet access, and easier access to the organizations' work platforms.

E-Leadership: Lessons Learned from Teleworking in the COVID-19 Pandemic
DOI: http://dx.doi.org/10.5772/intechopen.100634

It is worth noting that home-based work can affect the physical health of workers for several reasons. One is the configuration of home workstations that are not ergonomically designed and can result in poor posture and musculoskeletal disorders [33]. A study by [34] showed that 41.2% of participants experienced low back pain, and 23.5% experienced neck pain and other pain while teleworking in the pandemic. These percentages increased over time and reduced levels of job satisfaction.

In this sense, [25] consider that e-leadership needs to dialog about the ergonomic and technological conditions of the home office, additionally preventing stress and injuries. The authors argue that leaders should seek to provide multi-functionality tools (synchronous and asynchronous collaborative work, video calls, and repository of documents). The use of asynchronous work tools (wikis, database shared on the cloud, messaging tools, and work management) and synchronous work tools (technology-mediated virtual meetings) are crucial to coordinate the interdependence of tasks with demands, goals, and work schedules and conditions in home-based work [25].

In the survey carried out with teleworkers, we observed that providing adequate ergonomic conditions for teleworking was the item with the worst evaluation. Only 21.3% of teleworkers fully agree that their leaders are concerned about the adequacy of the infrastructure for the remote work of virtual teams. The percentage of teleworkers who agreed or totally agreed with the statement "My manager is concerned about the adequacy of my infrastructure to work remotely (computer, internet, furniture)" was 55.4%. However, it is worrying that 44.6% of teleworkers do not realize that their leaders are concerned about their physical working conditions.

Finally, the last item in the survey referred to how much teleworkers realized, during the COVID-19 pandemic, that their leaders were concerned about their health and well-being. Well-being at work, in turn, can be understood as a multidimensional psychological construct, integrated by positive affective bonds with work and with the organization [4] and with a clear association with the health of the worker.

Studies on telework have investigated how remote work can be related to the worker's well-being, which can be considered a source of stress due to possible role conflicts between work and personal life tasks. In this sense, an e-leadership can contribute to the realization of telework to be effective and reduce the risks of this modality of telework, such as social isolation and increased work–family conflict [24].

The e-leadership needs to prevent work from invading the times and spaces of family life, resulting in a breach of the psychological contract, which can be harmful to both teleworkers and organizations. The work-family and family–work conflict are among the principal risks of telework [24, 35] and, therefore, should deserve attention from the e-leadership in managing their virtual teams. Research on the JD-R theory during the pandemic found a mediating effect of job stress between the breach of psychological contract and the well-being of those who are only working at home [36].

In the empirical study carried out with teleworkers in the public sector in Brazil, we observed that 74% of respondents agreed with the statement, "My manager demonstrates that he cares about my health and well-being." This result indicates that most e-leadership manifested behavior of attention to the health and well-being of their workers. However, it is worrisome that, amid a pandemic such as that of COVID-19, one in four workers did not realize that their leaders showed concern for taking care of the health and well-being of their team members. Therefore, it needs to be reinforced with those who will act with electronic leadership.

Taken together, the results of this empirical study show that leaders also need to develop to act in the context of telework (**Figure 1**). However, in the view of the surveyed teleworkers, most leaders are already able to meet central aspects of e-leadership, such as providing feedback, setting, or renegotiating goals, monitoring goals, providing support/orientation, provision of infrastructure for teleworking, and demonstrating care for the health and well-being of members of their virtual teams.

The results indicate that two of the most favorable e-leadership performances aim to provide support to their team when they request guidelines for the performance of their tasks in the remote context and monitor the achievement of members' work goals of your team. Furthermore, these items had higher means in their scores (4.4 and 4.3, respectively) and were the only ones whose most frequent value (mode) was 5.0, that is, the highest point of the scale. At the same time, these items were also the ones with the lowest coefficient of variation, signaling a greater homogeneity in the assessment that the 7608 teleworkers made of their leaders.

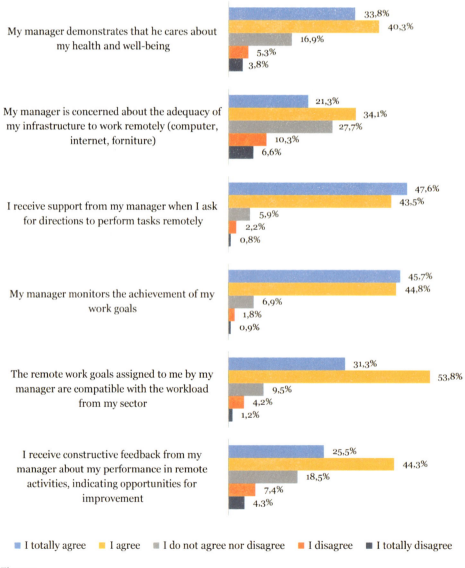

Figure 1.
Perception of e-leadership support during teleworking in the COVID-19 pandemic.

E-Leadership: Lessons Learned from Teleworking in the COVID-19 Pandemic
DOI: http://dx.doi.org/10.5772/intechopen.100634

At the opposite extreme, there is the item related to the demonstration of concern with the adequacy of the infrastructure for remote work and the item associated with receiving constructive feedback from leaders about performance in remote activities. In both cases, the mean scores (3.5 and 3.8, respectively) were lower than those of the other items. Furthermore, these items have the highest coefficient of variation, which indicates greater heterogeneity in the responses. Thus, while some respondents positively assess the support received from their leaders in terms of concern with providing physical conditions for remote work and constructive feedback for the virtual team, other respondents negatively assess their leaders in these two aspects. **Table 1** summarizes the perceptions of leadership support for teleworkers during the COVID-19 pandemic. It is possible to verify that the evaluation tended to be positive in all items, although the average scores varied.

Student's t tests to identify differences in means as a function of the gender indicated that the only item with significantly different means ($p < 0.01$) was "I receive support from my manager when I ask for directions to perform tasks remotely." However, the female average (4.38) was slightly above the male average (4.31), and the size of Cohen's $d = 0.09$) indicated an effect of shallow magnitude. In this sense, there is no need to talk about differences between genders regarding the perception of support arising from e-leadership.

As for the results of Spearman's correlation to identify a possible relationship between the age groups of the participants and the scores of items supporting leadership for teleworkers, the results did not indicate significant relationships. The only significant correlation ($p < 0.05$) was with the item "I receive support from my manager when I ask for directions to perform tasks remotely." However, the large sample size influenced the indication of significance, as the magnitude of the correlation was only 0.03, that is, relatively insignificant. In conclusion, the age group of teleworkers does not correlate with their perception of the support they receive from their leaders.

Finally, the Pearson's correlation matrix analysis showed that the items correlated significantly with each other ($p < 0.001$), with bivariate correlations generally above 0.50. On the one hand, the strongest correlations occurred between the

Leadership support items for teleworkers during the Pandemic	Mean	Mode	Standard deviation	Coef. of variation (%)
I receive support from my manager when I ask for directions to perform tasks remotely	4.4	5.0	0.76	17.4
My manager monitors the achievement of my work goals	4.3	5.0	0.75	17.4
The remote work goals assigned to me by my manager are compatible with the workload from my sector	4.1	4.0	0.82	20.1
My manager demonstrates that he cares about my health and well-being	4.0	4.0	1.03	26.0
I receive constructive feedback from my manager about my performance in remote activities, indicating opportunities for	3.8	4.0	1.04	27.4
My manager is concerned about the adequacy of my infrastructure to work remotely (computer, internet, furniture)	3.5	4.0	1.13	32.0

Note. For all items Median = 4.0.

Table 1.
Summary of perceptions of leadership support for teleworkers during the COVID-19 pandemic (n = 7608).

Leadership in a Changing World - A Multidimensional Perspective

Leadership support items for teleworkers during the Pandemic	(1)	(2)	(3)	(4)	(5)	(6)
(1) I receive constructive feedback from my manager about my performance in remote activities, indicating opportunities for improvement	—	0.46	0.55	0.56	0.55	0.56
(2) The remote work goals assigned to me by my manager are compatible with the workload from my sector		—	0.50	0.47	0.40	0.42
(3) I receive support from my manager when I ask for directions to perform tasks remotely			—	0.66	0.48	0.54
(4) My manager monitors the achievement of my work goals				—	0.50	0.50
(5) My manager is concerned about the adequacy of my infrastructure to work remotely (computer, internet, furniture)					—	0.67
(6) My manager demonstrates that he cares about my health and well-being						—

Note. $p < 0.01$.

Table 2.
Correlations of perceptions of leadership support to teleworkers during the COVID-19 Pandemic (n = 7608).

following pairs of items—leadership support for infrastructure and leaders' concern for the health and well-being of teleworkers (0.67); and leadership support in directing a compelling performance of remote tasks monitoring the achievement of teleworkers' goals. On the other hand, the weakest correlations involved the item of the establishment of compatible goals by the leadership, either with the perception of support from managers for the well-being of subordinates (0.42) or with the concern with adequate infrastructure for telework (0.40). **Table 2** details the correlations of perceptions of leadership support for teleworkers during the COVID-19 pandemic.

5. E-leadership: lessons from telework in the pandemic

Despite the benefits of teleworking, this modality also presents risks for workers, such as reduced interpersonal contact and increased sense of social isolation and distance from the organizational culture [21, 24]. The role of leaders is fundamental in providing social support and reducing risks related to the well-being of teleworkers. It is also up to them to think of strategies to promote the professional development of their subordinates [11]. As we have seen in the revised literature, the attributions of e-leadership are diverse, such as (i) the transfer of goals, objectives, and expectations of the organization, (ii) delegation of responsibilities, (iii) maintenance of fluid and frequent communication with team members and encouragement of communication between team members, and (iv) monitoring of appropriate work behaviors and conflict reduction [9, 21, 25].

Self-discipline is also indicated in the literature as a critical competence for working virtually, with the potential to affect work motivation, effective performance, and the well-being of teleworkers [20]. In this sense, e-leadership must encourage self-discipline and autonomy so that teleworkers can simultaneously achieve better results in their work and greater well-being at work.

E-Leadership: Lessons Learned from Teleworking in the COVID-19 Pandemic
DOI: http://dx.doi.org/10.5772/intechopen.100634

It is also worth considering that studies by [20] indicate that monitoring and control had less resistance from teleworkers in the context of a pandemic, as these mechanisms helped to deal effectively with procrastination and work demands in the home environment [20]. In this sense, many workers tended to positively evaluate the actions of e-leadership in terms of monitoring and control.

Another important point highlighted in the literature is that workers without experience with telework before the pandemic expressed more negative opinions about telework than experienced workers. For those who were experiencing telework for the first time during the COVID-19 pandemic, there were reports of adverse experiences. They complain about the lack of face-to-face interaction with the leader, the difficulty of accessing work-related information, the lack of feedback, the distractions caused by others in the home environment, the inability of leaders to estimate the workload, the concern about the possibility of information loss, the delay in decision-making processes, and the expense of asynchronous communications [28]. All these points point to the importance of e-leadership having an effective action with teleworkers, especially in times of crisis.

In the discussion about the role of e-leadership, it is also necessary to consider the results of several studies that show that telework has produced benefits to personal life (decrease in time spent commuting from home to work, organization of free time, the balance between work and family, improvement in social life,) and professional life (reduction of interference from colleagues, increased flexibility of timetables, greater autonomy to organize and plan the performance of tasks, greater job satisfaction, and reduced stress). In this sense, an e-leadership can contribute to the realization of teleworking to be effective and to reduce the risks of this modality of telework, such as social isolation, increased work-family conflict, and reduced social learning with coworkers [24].

Thus, an effective e-leadership should be able to contribute to minimizing the risks for teleworkers. In addition, e-leadership would also be expected to generate positive impacts for organizations. In the study of [25], the authors present an extensive set of competencies for e-leadership and consider that telework requires a redesign of work. In this sense, electronic leadership should be able to (i) negotiate achievable goals and monitor them through indicators; (ii) dialog about the ergonomic and technological conditions of the home office, preventing additional stress and conflicts; (iii) provide multi-functionality tools (synchronous and asynchronous collaborative work, video calls, repository of documents) to coordinate the interdependence of tasks with demands, goals, and work schedules and conditions in remote work at home; (iv) schedule virtual meetings to times suitable for workers engaged in activities; (v) learn new ways to manage time, and to balance work-family; (vi) develop new skills to provide emotional support to coworkers; (vii) develop new skills of social support; and (viii) provide constructive feedback [25].

It is essential to understand that teleworking during the Covid-19 pandemic period occurred in a specific context that involved compulsory telework, amid a pandemic crisis that led to isolation and lack of social contact [9, 24, 26, 28]. Furthermore, there was a lack of experience with telework on the part of many workers and leading leaders. In addition to the specific issues of the pandemic, the telework experience occurred in a context marked by a changing and uncertain environment, advancement of digital technologies, and in a context of more congested cities [2, 24, 26, 28, 34].

The results of these experiences with telework also depend on procedures adopted by organizations, covering different types of resources (material, financial, procedural, technological, resources, and human resources) [5, 20, 21, 26, 33, 34]. In addition to organizational inputs, several studies show that much of the success of telework experiences depends on an e-leadership's supportive activities and skills. The importance of e-leadership support was highlighted in the study reported in this chapter and is also widely explored in telework literature, before or during the pandemic [2, 3, 5–8, 20–26, 28, 36]. These e-leadership skills can turn to hard skills (more focused on technological and tool aspects) and soft skills. The soft one involves skills to provide emotional support to coworkers, in addition to other factors related to dialog, constructive feedback guidance, team confidence, and time management [25, 28, 33].

The results of telework can be very positive, including a reduction in travel time, increased work autonomy and well-being, reduced worker burnout risks, and improved workers' sense of psychological security. Other positive results from remote work are solid and trustworthy relationships with employees, higher effort

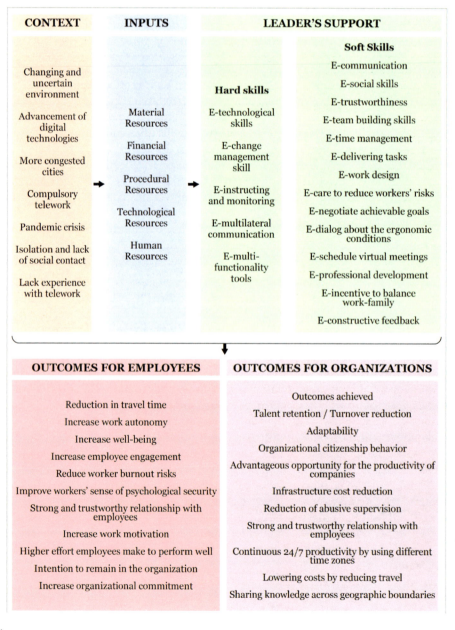

Figure 2.
E-leadership theoretical model.

E-Leadership: Lessons Learned from Teleworking in the COVID-19 Pandemic
DOI: http://dx.doi.org/10.5772/intechopen.100634

employees make to perform well, and intention to remain in the organization [2, 7, 20, 22–25, 28, 33, 34]. Likewise, telecommuting can also bring many positive results for organizations. These outcomes include talent retention, increased organizational citizenship behavior, higher productivity levels, infrastructure cost diminution, abusive supervision reduction, and continuous 24/7 productivity by using different time zones [6, 8, 20, 24–26].

Given so much research on e-leadership that gained greater prominence during the COVID-19 pandemic, we present below a model of e-leadership based on lessons learned during the academic period. The model shown in **Figure 2** is supported by the empirical study presented here and in the revised literature, as presented above. It does not intend to replace theoretical leadership models but to present specificities that characterize e-leadership and its performance in virtual teams.

6. Conclusions

Millions of professionals worked remotely during the pandemic, mediated by technologies, modifying traditional communication, monitoring, and managing teams. It is the e-leadership's role to identify the activities that require adjustments in telework, including surveying the resource demands of each subordinate. Thus, telework success depends on leaders mapping out which support routines need to be developed for remote work [9]. The present study aims to propose an e-leadership theoretical model based on lessons learned from the coronavirus pandemic. To that end, we describe and discuss a survey on the perceptions of support received from managers during the initial 3 months of the pandemic. For this purpose, we collected data with 7608 workers distributed to 95 public service organizations in Brazil.

Therefore, this paper presents a theoretical research and intervention model on the effectiveness of e-leadership, which assumes relationships between context variables, inputs, processes, and outcomes. The model includes context variables (changing and uncertain environment, advances of digital technologies, more congested cities, lack of experience with telework), which have led organizations to adopt telework in its most varied forms. For example, full-time or part-time telework, in fixed locations (work from home or in satellite offices) or different spaces (mobile work, work anywhere and anytime), for a fixed or indefinite period with or without flexible working hours. Furthermore, the health crisis generated by the COVID-19 pandemic added to these situations, social distancing, the lack of face-to-face social contacts, and the sudden change in the design of the work to the compulsory remote modality in a fixed location (at home). This situation highlighted the importance of leadership support to teleworkers, previously evidenced by telework literature.

In addition to these context variables, the model includes inputs or resources (material, financial, technological, and human), which need to be considered in studies on the effectiveness of e-leadership since they are antecedents of the leader's supportive behaviors for the teleworkers. The e-leadership actions comprise e-hard and e-soft skills, which characterize the effective conduct of leadership, associated with valuable outcomes for employees and organizations. In summary, the theoretical model proposed in this work can be used to plan and conduct research on relationships between antecedent variables (context, inputs), e-leadership processes, and their effects on essential criterion variables (outcomes for teleworkers and organizations).

The leadership theoretical model also contributes to the improvement of telework management, indicating variables that need to be considered by organizations to enable leadership support actions for teleworkers. These actions increase the chances of achieving positive results for teleworkers and organizations. Before implementing telework, the organization, according to the proposed model, should analyze the following resources—technological support (management and monitoring systems for deliveries, digital information, and communication technologies); material and financial support for the acquisition and maintenance of equipment, internet access necessary for teleworking; characteristics of work processes eligible for telework (description of activities, measurement of work volume and flow, the interdependence of tasks between members of the same team and between different groups and organizational units, optimization of work processes) and the characteristics of human resources with motivation and good profile for telework (professional experience, autonomy, and self-discipline).

It is essential to point out that despite the many positive results presented in the e-leadership model, telework also poses many risks for workers and organizations [4, 5, 21, 24–26]. Without the proper performance of e-leadership, especially in terms of support for teleworkers, the demands (overload, difficulty in reconciling work and nonwork, feelings of loneliness, and social isolation) are likely to increase the risk of exhaustion, stress, and burnout. Likewise, without a compelling performance of e-leadership, telework can also be harmful to organizational results. From these preliminary analyses, organizations need to provide the resources necessary to exercise effective leadership and provide training and e-leadership skills development programs. In addition, we recommended defining in advance the expected results (outcomes) for teleworkers and the organization, aiming to choose teleworking arrangements compatible with the organization's work, people, and culture. After the implementation of teleworking, we suggested monitoring and evaluating resources, e-leadership processes (considering hard and soft skills), and their effects on the behavior (outcomes) of teleworkers and the organization to achieve adjustments and improvements in each component of the model.

An important warning—the e-leadership theoretical model does not intend to replace all leadership models but to present specificities that characterize e-leadership and its performance in virtual teams. Thus, even though it is based on empirical studies found in the literature and on reviews about telework, the e-leadership model presented in this chapter lacks further testing. But it can be helpful for organizations that intend to maintain telecommuting or a hybrid system with face-to-face workers and remote workers. We also hope that the model can contribute to those already involved in e-leadership or who intend to move to this new management format.

It is worth considering the generalization of the results to the Brazilian context and other countries. Despite the convenience sample, its breadth and the heterogeneity of respondents encourage more extensive use of the findings. However, although comprising 95 organizations, the sample was aimed at public servants, and there may be differences for workers from private organizations. As for the model's generalization to other countries, we consider it possible and indicate empirical tests since it is a theoretical model. What leads us to believe in more global use of this model is that it was based not only on the extensive research carried out in Brazil but also on an expressive set of studies carried out in different countries during the pandemic.

Regarding this generalization to other countries, it is worth mentioning that the e-leadership theoretical model is in tune with the practical guide prepared by the International Labor Organization [37]. This guide indicates that teleworking policies can be planned as part of a continuity plan to keep operational organizations and people safe in their homes in contexts of unforeseen events, such as extreme weather conditions, natural disasters, terrorist actions, and pandemics. The analysis presented is that the experience arising from the measures of social distancing

E-Leadership: Lessons Learned from Teleworking in the COVID-19 Pandemic
DOI: http://dx.doi.org/10.5772/intechopen.100634

necessary to contain the COVID-19 pandemic marked the beginning of a new era of telework, which tends to be a labor modality adopted by some organizations even in "normal time."

But to ensure the well-being and maintenance of productivity in telecommuting, whether in "new normal" or contingency periods (such as pandemics and other unexpected events), attention is needed in some aspects. Thus, with illustrations of situations or legislation from different countries, eight focuses are listed to ensure well-being and productivity in telework, these are—focus on time and work organization, focus on performance management, focus on digitization, focus on communication, focus on safety and health at work, focus on legal and contractual implications, focus on training, and focus on reconciling professional and personal life. In addition to these eight focal points, the ILO's practical guide also presents reflections in two other directions—gender equity and trust and organizational culture. Thus, it is considered that teleworking should not become a setback to previous achievements in terms of equality between men and women, nor should it hinder the efforts of diversity and inclusion by companies. Finally, there are also recommendations to strengthen trust as a value and a practice in the organizational culture. Therefore, we recommend avoiding, for example, the use of tools and software for control and surveillance of employees, which in addition to ethical issues can impact the relationship between the worker and the employing organization, leading to negative attitudes and counterproductive behavior [37].

Considering the set of these recommendations for the future of teleworking after the pandemic, we observe that the e-leadership theoretical model can be applied in contingency periods and in new normal or "normal time." Moreover, the scope of this theoretical model shows that the lessons learned from the coronavirus pandemic made it possible to advance on reflections on telework and propose strategies that simultaneously ensure organizational productivity and workers' well-being. About expectations for the future of teleworking after the pandemic, one of the basic premises is that teleworking should result from a voluntary agreement between employers and workers, establishing working hours or hours worked, communication tools, tasks to be performed, supervision procedures, systematic recording of tasks performed, and workplace which can be at the workers' homes or elsewhere [37].

The expectation is that after the pandemic we have a new era of telework, with many lessons learned during this period [2, 20, 24, 25, 37]. Unlike the pandemic phase, there are predictions that hybrid models of telework will be adopted, with variability in terms of full-time or part-time, fixed or flexible hours, workplaces [at home, satellite offices or mobile, and ubiquitous work (anytime and from anywhere)]. A study that projected the potential of telecommuting in Brazil and worldwide confirms a growing relationship between the proportion of jobs that can be performed at home. The level of economic development among 86 countries, Brazil occupied the 45th position, with 25.7% of teleworking. Considering the 12 Latin American countries that made up the study, Brazil occupies the third position, approaching Chile (25.8%) and Uruguay (27.3%). Directors, managers, and professionals in science and intellectuals had a high percentage of occupations subject to telework (between 61% and 65%) [38].

The large sample of the research reported in this study, made up of professionals with a high level of education, suggests that the results are generalizable to developing countries and may be helpful for organizations and workers in developed countries. Moreover, the usefulness of this survey and others carried out during the pandemic period is even greater if we consider that the potential for telecommuting was little explored globally, as only 2.9% of workers worked from home before the COVID-19 pandemic [39].

Additional evidence is reported by the International Labor Organization, signaling those workers from developed countries are more likely to work from home. They also add that many workers from developing countries carry out activities that do not allow for adopting the modality, such as civil construction, or work informally. Suppose the structure of labor occupations and available technologies are considered. In that case, the estimated difference between developed and developing countries reaches 15%, and there may be regional differences in each country [38]. Depending on the level of social inequality, it is possible to find realities similar to those in Brazil, even in developed countries, which increases the generalization of the results.

Acknowledgements

The authors wish to thank the Brazilian National Council for Scientific and Technological Development (CNPq) Carlos Chagas Filho Foundation for Research Support of Rio de Janeiro State (FAPERJ) for their support. We would also like to thank the Aprimora—Nucleus for Studies in Trajectory and Professional Development members and the E-Work Group—Research Group on Telework in the Public Service.

Author details

Luciana Mourão[1,2]*, Gardênia da Silva Abbad[3] and Juliana Legentil[3]

1 Salgado de Oliveira University, Niterói, RJ, Brazil

2 State University of Rio de Janeiro, Rio de Janeiro, RJ, Brazil

3 University of Brasília, Brasília, DF, Brazil

*Address all correspondence to: mourao.luciana@gmail.com

IntechOpen

© 2021 The Author(s). Licensee IntechOpen. This chapter is distributed under the terms of the Creative Commons Attribution License (http://creativecommons.org/licenses/by/3.0), which permits unrestricted use, distribution, and reproduction in any medium, provided the original work is properly cited. (cc) BY

References

[1] Allen TD, Golden TD, Shockley KM. How effective is telecommuting? Assessing the status of our scientific findings. Psychological Science in the Public Interest. 2015;**16**:40-68. DOI: 10.1177/1529100615593273

[2] Kniffin KM, Narayanan J, Anseel F, Antonakis J, Ashford SP, Bakker AB, et al. COVID-19 and the workplace: Implications, issues, and insights for future research and action. American Psychologist. 2021;**76**(1):63-77. DOI: 10.1037/amp0000716

[3] Abbad GDS, Legentil J, Damascena M, Miranda L, Feital C, Neiva ER. Percepções de teletrabalhadores e trabalhadores presenciais sobre desenho do trabalho. Revista Psicologia Organizações e Trabalho. 2019;**19**(4):772-780. DOI: 10.17652/rpot/2019.4.17501

[4] Mishima-Santos V, Renier F, Sticca M. Teletrabalho e impactos na saúde e bem-estar do teletrabalhador: Revisão sistemática. Psicologia, Saúde & Doenças. 2020;**21**(3):865-877. DOI: 10.15309/20psd210327

[5] Hau F, Todescat M. Teleworking in the perception of teleworkers and their managers: Advantages and disadvantages in a case study. Navus—Revista de Gestão e Tecnologia. 2018;**8**(3):37-52

[6] Dirani KM, Abadi M, Alizadeh A, Barhate B, Garza RC, Gunasekara N, et al. Leadership competencies and the essential role of human resource development in times of crisis: A response to COVID-19 Pandemic. Human Resource Development International. 2020;**23**(4):380-394. DOI: 10.1080/13678868.2020.1780078

[7] Acuña-Hormazabal Á, Mendoza-Llanos R, Pons-Peregort O. Burnout, engagement y la percepción sobre prácticas de gestión en pandemia por COVID-19 que tienen trabajadores del centro sur de Chile. Estudios Gerenciales. 2021;**37**(158):104-112. DOI: 10.18046/j.estger.2021.158.4364

[8] Lee H. Changes in workplace practices during the COVID-19 pandemic: The roles of emotion, psychological safety and organisation support. Journal of Organizational Effectiveness: People and Performance. 2021;**29**(1):97-128. Available from: https://www.emerald.com/insight/2051-6614.htm

[9] Sandall H, Mourão L. Job performance: Challenges for workers and managers. In: Queiroga F, editor. Work and Containment Measures for COVID-19: Contributions from Work and Organizational Psychology in the pandemic Context, Home Office Guidelines in the COVID-19 Pandemic. Vol. 1. Porto Alegre: Artmed; 2020. pp. 19-25

[10] International Labour Organization [ILO]. COVID-19 and the world of work: Impact and policy responses (ILO Monitor Number 1). 2020. pp. 1-15. Available from: https://bit.ly/3xMo1iw [Accessed: 2020-06-10]

[11] Mourão L. The role of leadership in the professional development of subordinates. In: Göker SD, editor. Leadership. London: InTech; 2018. DOI: 10.5772/intechopen.76056

[12] Kurtessis JN, Eisenberger R, Ford MT, Buffardi LC, Stewart KA, Adis CS. Perceived organizational support: A meta-analytic evaluation of Organizational Support Theory. Journal of Management. 2017;**43**(6):1854-1884. DOI: 10.1177/0149206315575554

[13] Eisenberger R, Huntington R, Hutchison S, Sowa D. Perceived organizational support. Journal of

Applied Psychology. 1986;**71**(3):500-507. DOI: 10.1037/0021-9010.71.3.500

[14] Shanock LR, Eisenberger R, Heggestad ED, Malone G, Clark L, Dunn AM, et al. Treating employees well: The value of organizational support theory in human resource management. The Psychologist-Manager Journal. 2019;**22**(3-4):168-191

[15] Blau P. Exchange and Power in Social Life. New York: Wiley; 1964

[16] Gouldner AW. The norm of reciprocity: A preliminary statement. American Sociological Review. 1960;**25**(2):161. DOI: 10.2307/2092623

[17] Eisenberger R, Stinglhamber F, Vandenberghe C, Sucharski IL, Rhoades L. Perceived supervisor support: Contributions to perceived organizational support and employee retention. Journal of Applied Psychology. 2002;**87**(3):565-573. DOI: 10.1037/0021-9010.87.3.565

[18] Singh B, Shaffer MA, Selvarajan TT. Antecedents of organizational and community embeddedness: The roles of support, psychological safety, and need to belong. Journal of Organizational Behavior. 2018;**39**(3):339-354. DOI: 10.1002/job.2223

[19] Mourão L, Faiad C, Coelho Junior FA. Análise psicométrica da escala de heteroavaliação de estilos de liderança. Estudos de Psicologia. 2016;**21**(3):293-304. DOI: 10.5935/1678-4669.20160028

[20] Wang B, Liu Y, Qian J, Parker SK. Achieving effective remote working during the COVID-19 pandemic: A work design perspective. Applied Psychology. 2021;**70**(1):16-59. DOI: 10.1111/apps.12290

[21] Van Wart M, Roman A, Wang X, Liu C. Operationalizing the definition of E-Leadership: Identifying the elements of E-Leadership. International Review of Administrative Sciences. 2019;**85**(1):80-97. DOI: 10.1177/0020852316681446

[22] Fernandez AA, Shaw GP. Academic leadership in a time of crisis: The coronavirus and COVID-19. Journal of Leadership Studies. 2020;**14**(1):39-45. DOI: 10.1002/jls.21684

[23] Toleikienė R, Rybnikova I, Juknevičienė V. Whether and how does the crisis-induced situation change e-leadership in the public sector? Evidence from Lithuanian public administration. Transylvanian Review of Administrative Sciences. 2020;**16** (SI):149-166. DOI: 10.24193/tras.SI2020.9

[24] Contreras F, Baykal E, Abid G. E-Leadership and teleworking in times of COVID-19 and beyond: What we know and where do we go. Frontiers in Psychology. 2020;**11**:3484. DOI: 10.3389/fpsyg.2020.590271

[25] Abbad, G. S., Legentil, J. Workers' New Learning Demands due to the COVID-19 Pandemic. In M.M. de Moraes Work and Containment Measures for COVID-19: Contributions from Work and Organizational Psychology in the Pandemic Context. 2 The Impacts of the Pandemic on Workers and their Work Relationship SBPOT Publications. Brasília. 2020. p. 38-47.

[26] Dulebohn JH, Hoch JE. Virtual teams in organizations. Human Resource Management Review. 2017;**27**:569-574. DOI: 10.1016/j.hrmr.2016.12.004

[27] Ramaprasad A. On the definition of feedback. Behavioral Science. 1983;**28**(1):4-13. DOI: 10.1002/bs.3830280103

[28] Raišienė AG, Rapuano V, Varkulevičiūtė K, Stachová K. Working

from home—Who is happy? A survey of Lithuania's employees during the COVID-19 quarantine period. Sustainability. 2020;**12**(13):5332. DOI: 10.3390/su12135332

[29] Kaplan A, Maehr ML. The contributions and prospects of goal orientation theory. Educational Psychology Review. 2007;**19**(2):141-184. DOI: 10.1007/s10648-006-9012-5

[30] Klasmeier KN, Schleu JE, Millhoff C, Poethke U, Bormann KC. On the destructiveness of laissez-faire versus abusive supervision: A comparative, multilevel investigation of destructive forms of leadership. European Journal of Work and Organizational Psychology. 2021:1-15. DOI: 10.1080/1359432X.2021.1968375

[31] Richardson J. Managing flex workers: Holding on and letting go. Journal of Management Development. 2010;**29**(2):137-147. DOI: 10.1108/02621711011019279

[32] Thatcher A. Green ergonomics: Definition and scope. Ergonomics. 2013;**56**(3):389-398. DOI: 10.1080/00140139.2012.718371

[33] Reznik J, Hungerford C, Kornhaber R, Cleary M. Home-based work and ergonomics: Physical and psychosocial considerations. Issues in Mental Health Nursing. 2021:1-5. DOI: 10.1080/01612840.2021.1875276

[34] Moretti A, Menna F, Aulicino M, Paoletta M, Liguori S, Iolascon G. Characterization of home working population during COVID-19 emergency: A cross-sectional analysis. International Journal of Environmental Research and Public Health. 2020;**17**(17):6284. DOI: 10.3390/ijerph17176284

[35] Solís M. Moderators of telework effects on the work-family conflict and on worker performance. European Journal of Management and Business Economics. 2017;**26**(1):21-34. DOI: 10.1108/EJMBE-07-2017-002

[36] Karani A, Deshpande R, Mall S, Jayswal M. Testing the link between psychological contract, innovative behavior and multidimensional well-being during the COVID-19 pandemic. International Journal of Sociology and Social Policy. 2021:1-17. DOI: 10.1108/IJSSP-02-2021-0032

[37] International Labour Organization [ILO]. Practical Guide on Teleworking during the COVID-19 Pandemic and Beyond. 2020. Available from: https://www.ilo.org/ankara/areas-of-work/covid-19/WCMS_751232/lang--en/index.htm [Accessed: 2021-09-06]

[38] Goes EF, Ramos DO, Ferreira AJF. Desigualdades raciais em saúde e a pandemia da Covid-19. Trabalho, Educação e Saúde. 2020;**18**(3):e00278110. DOI: 10.1590/1981-7746-sol00278

[39] International Labour Organization [ILO]. Working from Home: Estimating the Worldwide Potential (ILO Policy Brief. 2020. pp. 1-10. Available from: https://www.ilo.org/global/topics/non-standard-employment/publications/WCMS_743447/lang--en/index.htm [Accessed: 2021-9-21]

Chapter 7

The New Institutional Approach as a Lens on Local Network Leadership

Anna Uster

Abstract

This chapter derives from an overview of key research findings and core concepts on network leadership, focusing on leading purpose-oriented networks. These are increasingly viewed as prominent modes of local service delivery as local government transitions to "local governance" and where local government mostly follows a lead organization format. The literature encompassing local leadership emphasizes the context of structures and processes for any leader's action. This chapter treats the importance of the institutional factors in the era of local network governance, using the New Institutional approach, focusing especially on discursive institutionalism, together with and network governance theory. As public managers are increasingly relying on inter-organizational networks providing public services, the manner they lead them is of great importance. The following chapter presents vital factors that may assist their effective leadership in an era of local network governance.

Keywords: local networks, network leadership, new institutionalism, purpose-oriented networks, local government

1. Introduction

The past three decades have witnessed changes in the structure, function, and leadership modes of public organizations, both at the local and national levels. These changes are captured in the literature by the Post New Public Governance (NPG) approach [1], a holistic view of government in which citizens and non-governmental actors become partners in the public management process [2–4]. "Focus on governance involves the use of institutions and structures of authority and collaboration to allocate resources and to coordinate and control joint action across the network as a whole" [5]. The literature describes these changes using various terms, such as collaborative governance, collaborative leadership and management, new public governance, co-governance, and meta-governance [1, 6–13]. Ansell and Gash [9] define governance as both the structure of "laws and rules that pertain to the provision of public goods" and as the process of "collective decision making that includes both public and private actors" (p. 545). The move toward a collaborative mode of governance derives from the phenomenon known as the hollow state, "...a metaphor for the increasing use of third parties, often non-profits, to deliver social services and generally act in the name of the state" ([14], p. 360).

IntechOpen

Leadership in a Changing World - A Multidimensional Perspective

At the local level, this condition occurs due to the lack of local government (LG) capacity to provide multiple services to meet the needs and demands of the citizenry. Consequently, local government is growing increasingly conscious of the potential of working as a collaborative network to provide these services in the municipal arena [15, 16]. Collaboration enables external organizations such as non-profits, non-local public, private organizations, and citizens to share knowledge and experience to initiate novel solutions to different social, educational, and environmental wicked problems [17, 18].

Local authorities now employ network modes of governance to include people and organizations which play a greater role in the provision of local services, generally organized as a purpose-oriented network, defined as "a network comprised of three or more autonomous actors who participate in a joint effort based on a common purpose" ([19], p. 210). Berthod and Segato [20] and Lemaire et al. [21] proposed the term "purpose-oriented" networks to extend the well-known term of art "goal-directed networks". According to this line of research goal-directed refers to network members who have identified and agreed on a set of goals that guide the work of the network, which is not necessarily reality-based [22]. "Purpose-oriented networks' (PONs) highlight the collective purpose that is "translated into actionable goals whose achievement can be monitored" (Carboni et al., p. 15), thus encompassing the complex reciprocity between the network members as well as the environment in which they operate. Such networks are understood to solve the wicked problems which characterize service delivery in local authorities.

The idea underpinning PON's is that by combining actors' differing capabilities, skills, and resources the network's outcomes will be improved [23]. In the local arena, these networks are generally headed by one lead organization, e.g., the local authority, which selects the other network partners, while coordinating decisions and activities [5]. This organization usually possesses sufficient resources and legitimacy to lead together with the capacity to take on most of the responsibilities of running and coordinating the network's activities. Given local policy makers' increasing reliance on networks to achieve the provision of public goods and services, leadership constitutes a paramount challenge facing contemporary local governance. Thus, changes in leadership style and form are required [24, 25], and these, in turn, affect the establishment and coordination of these networks [26].

2. Major challenges to local leadership in era of purpose-oriented networks

Synchronizing collaboration activity and enhancing informational flow presents a primary challenge, due to the multiplicity of opinions and interests of the various network actors [27, 28]. Moreover, even with a strong lead-organization, network organizations are dynamic, not static [29, 30], often including and excluding certain actors or adapting to changing needs by altering the form of network governance [5]. Networks create numerous managerial dilemmas by diminishing the lead actor's degree of control over adherence to public policy. Monitoring and coordinating public policy implementation, for example, while at the same time permitting autonomy to network actors concerning the delivery of the public service requires constant attention [1, 10, 31–33]. There is always a risk of poor coordination and of defection by one or more partners [34]. Furthermore, in certain cases, an action can increase conflict and create tension in a network. These tensions might lead to misunderstanding and a reluctance to engage with the lead organization in the future [35]. Different cultural characteristics may cause friction, diminishing a commitment from different management levels: the internal world of the organization employing the participants and the external world of the network in which their organization is involved [36]. Cultural tensions may include different approaches to decision-making, levels of professionalism, and methods of providing service. When individual parties within the network expect different outcomes from the collaboration because of different norms or have different ways of communicating cultural friction is almost inevitable. In sum, these tensions create coordination fatigue, with the result that the coordination of network activities requires considerable time and effort. In addition, unequal distribution of power between network members can create cases in which powerful stakeholders influence network decision-making to favor certain interests, resulting in harm to the public interest and potential corruption [37]. Naturally, these types of tensions may impair the local network's ability to produce high-quality local services and perform effectively.

Therefore, leading autonomous organizations, not directly subject to local authorities, raise questions about accountability, cost-effectiveness, and the ability to shape, implement, and monitor local policies reducing the quality of local services [38]. To overcome these tensions and affect the overall local network, network leaders should possess the capacity to make decisions and mobilize the resources required to implement their policies [39]. As a result, considerable effort has been taken in the public administration literature on this issue, focusing on diverse coordinative, facilitative, and mobilizing leadership skills and behaviors required for effective local network leadership [28, 40–48]. The main thrust of this research holds that lead organization managerial and leadership behaviors exerted by the local authority with the aim of enhancing network collaboration may help minimize the mentioned these above-mentioned risks, thus adapting to complex and dynamic environments [49].

However, while most literature draws attention to leadership skills, less attention has been paid to the characteristics of the specific local context as a crucial factor. Local government literature thus calls for a new local leadership style concentrating more on agenda-setting and network brokering in creating a vision, but less focused on policy implementation [50, 51]. This entrepreneurial model concentrates on context to mobilize and attract resources, generating new policies which establish collaborative networks with other governmental or non-governmental actors [25, 52–54].

Consideration of context is important because local leaders do not act in a homogeneous local environment and because various features distinguish local authorities from each other. Local government does not operate in a vacuum; it is embedded in the external political the environment within the local context [55–61]. This situation is quite evident in the local contexts where, in addition to structural characteristics, there is a cultural difference in the local authority. Together these factors shape the leadership environment influencing the leaders and their ability to govern [25].

3. The new-institutional approach to local leadership: discursive and sociological and environmental factors

> *"Political institutions do not determine the behavior of political actors, but provide the framework of understandings within which actors identify, compare and select courses of action." Lowndes and Leach ([59], p. 560).*

The new-institutional perspective's premise is that to understand the causes and consequences of different forms of leadership we should consider whether the institution has constraining or enabling effects on the leadership behavior (in terms of formal and informal rules), and judge their level of effectiveness as well as the extent of their activity [50, 62]. Accordingly, different leaders respond differently to the same situation, depending on their environment. This environment includes structural factors, such as legislative rules and regulations, intra- and inter-organizational interactions. Thus, leaders behave contingent upon the locality's context including local authority size, socio-economic status, central-local relationship as well as leaders' structural position in various networks [53, 55].

Further, cultural identity and norms are important factors influencing a leader's ability to govern. This captures the new-sociological institutionalism which has become particularly important in research on norms and legitimacy, focusing on an understanding of the importance of how and why norms, formal rules and culture in institutions [63–65] to shape their leaders' actions of the leaders.

Parallel to this stream of new institutionalism, a discursive perspective on leadership arises. Discursive institutionalism emphasizes the role of ideas and discourse to dynamic reality. Discourse is considered the interactive process of conveying ideas. Therefore, discourse does not only consist of ideas or what is said but includes the context in which we map why and by whom a particular message is delivered. Applying the two forms of discourse (coordinative and communicative discourse) to leadership research enables us to argue that the first form, coordinative discourse, refers to the communication among the network actors themselves, focusing on central actors' coordinative ability to lead the networks. The latter term refers to communicative discourse, that is, the communication and messages delivered from network actors and their leaders to the external stakeholders.

4. Discursive factors in network leadership research

> *"This shift in governance structure often necessitates that public managers not only lead the agency in which they are employed, but also work within, and often lead, a network. These two different contexts in which public managers operate require different managerial and leadership approaches"* [66].

Scholars propose that leadership in the network governance era be characterized by certain specific skills and behaviors. Network management and network leadership study mostly emphasize the importance of facilitation behaviors, which increase cooperation and coordination between network members and thus change both the network's rules and structure [9, 67–70]. Most studies focus on leadership skills as facilitating [48], framing and synthesizing [45], and bridging [43], and these capture the idea of coordinative discourse within the network. For example, Agranoff and McGuire [45] grouped network leadership behaviors into four categories based on their operational differences: activation, framing, mobilization, and synthesizing. Framing involves behaviors designed to establish work rules. Examples include ensuring individual roles are understood by all network members, asking network members to follow standard rules and regulations, and sharing the leadership role. Synthesizing regards behaviors promoting productive interactions among network participants by looking out for the personal welfare of network members, fostering trust, brainstorming, encouraging network members to use their own judgment in solving problems, and setting expectations for network members. Williams [71] noted several necessary leadership behaviors which promote communication inside the network: understanding of and empathy with the partners, trust-building, developing sustainable interpersonal relationships,

The New Institutional Approach as a Lens on Local Network Leadership
DOI: http://dx.doi.org/10.5772/intechopen.101988

and communication aimed at establishing shared meanings and resolving conflicts. Bass [72] defined such behaviors as structuring work relationships utilizing encouragement and rewards on one hand and sanctions on the other.

The literature on collaborative leadership distinguishes between three facilitating roles of collaborative leaders: that of convener (or steward), mediator, and catalyst [73]. Conveners facilitate and safeguard collaboration while maintaining project integrity. Mediators facilitate collaboration by managing conflict and arbitrating exchange between stakeholders. Catalyzers facilitate, help identify and realize value-creating opportunities. According to Ansell and Gash [73], "facilitative leadership will typically require leaders to play all three of these roles" (18–19). Piatak, Romzek, LeRoux, and Johnston [74] examined the management of goal conflicts in public service delivery networks and found that the lead organization should play the dual role of both network manager and member. Their data suggested that network managers should exert formal, vertical authority, combining it with informal, horizontal interactions which build goal consensus, thus relieving goal conflict. They also underscore the important use of rewards and sanctions when leading successful networks [75].

Provan and Kenis [5] proposed three modes of network governance which capture discursive coordinative communication in institutions: the network leader, or Participant-Governed Networks (participatory and internal coordination); Lead Organization-Governed Networks, featuring centralized and internal coordination, and; Network Administrative Organizations, emphasizing centralized and external coordination. In Participant-Governed Networks, for example, control and reflexive coordination of activities occur through direct collaboration in participatory decision-making. By contrast, coordination in Lead Organization-Governed Networks one central leader coordinates, often drawing its power from resource dependencies or other types of obligation. The final mode, Network Administrative Organizations (NAO) is coordinated via a separate, neutral administrative body, acting as a central broker for the activities of the entire network and bridging between diverse actors Berthod et al. [76].

Coordinative and communicative discourse is well-manifested in the literature on internal and external legitimacy. Leading the networks requires maintaining both two types of legitimacies [44]. The former, the internal legitimacy of the network, is concentrated on the communication inside the network, developing trust-based ties between members, resolving conflicts to everyone's satisfaction, and building communication mechanisms emphasizing the leader's coordinative and facilitative ability.

By contrast, building external legitimacy consists of seeking new members, promoting the network and its activities to outsiders, and mobilizing outside resources to achieve network goals matching the activating, mobilizing, and abilities of the leadership [43, 45]. These capture in communicative form the "discourse" in discursive institutionalism.

Reviewing the literature we may conclude that a network leader should invest the effort to develop both forms of discourse: promoting the coordinative abilities inside the network and communicative abilities from the network outward toward external actors and the environment.

5. Environmental factors in network leadership research: the local authority context

> *Contexts are the circumstances that form the setting for an event, statement, or idea, and in terms of which it can be fully understood ([77], p. 75).*

As network collaborations are embedded in a specific context their functioning is logically dependent on that context [11, 75]. More specifically, an effective local network in one context may not be successful in another, even when they have a similar purpose [78].

Virtanen [79] distinguished between two types of scientific knowledge in the context of public administration: *conceptual* and *factual*. The former relates to frameworks and theories through which certain phenomena in public administration are explained. The latter maintains that public administration is part of social reality and refers to such factors as actor and place, sector, culture, and institution. Public administration scholars study various contexts according to the research topic. For example, context is prominent where institutional embeddedness, environment, background, and settings are concerned [80–82], or administrative tradition and government capacity [83], and the network characteristics of decision-making [84]. In team leadership studies, context plays an important role in the relationship between shared leadership and performance [85–87].

Public administration scholars note that structures and processes define the context in which leaders act [88]. According to Provan and Milward's [89] networks framework any change in the network's environment originating outside, such as financial stability, challenges the network's overall effectiveness [89–91]. Researchers have established that an integrated structure through network centralization and direct mechanisms of external control has a positive effect on network effectiveness. However, these relationships are moderated by contextual conditions, such as stability and the availability of abundant resources.

According to the contingency approach, the tasks and goals of collaborations affect a leader's ability to collaborate successfully and promote collaborative innovation. For example, in their research on workforce development, Ansell and Gash [9] identified four contextual conditions influencing the efficacy of a collaboration leader: (1) access to resources; (2) the strength of the relationships with current and potential partners; (3) regional, state and local governance and service delivery infrastructures, and; (4) historical perceptions of workforce development shared by industry and economic development stakeholders. They found that local autonomy and conditions for economic competitiveness were the most important contextual characteristics for leading successful collaborations.

Contextual factors may include environmental complexities under government regulation, legal constraints, or a combination of organizational culture, norms, and management practices [92]. Local government studies bestow great importance to community characteristics in context [93–96]. In fact, research has shown that a community's socio-economic status affects the local leader's capacity to govern [97], and studies have supported the argument that local efficiency is positively related to the level of education in the community; more educated residents tend to select more capable leaders and have a better understanding of the issues on which they vote [47, 93, 94], tend to be actively involved in local affairs [98] and press the leaders for more accountability and have better evaluative tools to cause the standard of service to conform to their expectations [99].

In his comparative project on local political leadership in Europe, Steyvers [55] focused on mayoral business orientation as an aspect of external networking to show that institutional form affects leadership behaviors while being highly contingent upon leadership context. The indicators of leadership context include the municipalities' size and institutional position of municipalities in the intergovernmental arena.

Further, the *cultural context* of the community where the network operates can be crucial for leading effective networks [100–102]. More broadly, Klijn et al. [84] found that effective meso- (changes in the relationship between network organizations) and micro-level characteristics of network management (the level of decision-making and implementation) highly depend on the cultural context. Uster Beeri and Vashdi [103] continue this line of thought, focusing on the importance of such contextual issues as socio-economic status and ethnicity in a local authority to the relationship between network leadership and effectiveness. They found that the manner in which the local authority leads the local network derives from network structure, which in turn impinges on effectiveness. A sample of 586 participants from 68 networks indicated that this association is contingent on the politico-cultural characteristics of the local authority and its socio-economic status in which the network exists.

In general, local government research points to the differences in local authorities based on their size, economic stability, and type of population [25, 59, 94, 104]. Local authorities differ enormously in their structural, political, cultural, and socio-economic indicators, not just cross-nationally, but also within a specific country, and these factors influence local leaders' ability to govern [61, 95, 105, 106]. In sum, both the local political and cultural systems and the intergovernmental context within which the local networks are situated are crucial explanatory factors for local leaders` behaviors.

6. Structural factors: a leader's position in the network

Mouritzen and Svara [53] classified legislative-executive relations in terms of a combination of factors encompassing the acquisition and maintenance of the leadership position, the degree of control leaders has over appointment responsibilities, and the integration of leadership functions in the institutional position.

Some studies propose that leaders in a central position (when network is integrated through a central organization, and all members connect to a principal actor) better coordinate with other organizations to achieve network goals [107], using this central position to prevent free-riders while monitoring and controlling other network members [89, 107]. Further, they have an advantage over decentralized systems (with their multiplicity of players and linkages) in their ability to facilitate both integration and coordination [89, 108]. This is crucial to local purpose-oriented networks, which require better coordinative skills to achieve the network-level goal. Additionally, leaders holding central positions may more efficiently promote systems and integrate services [89] through an organized exchange of information and the coordination of collective action [109, 110].

The "brokerage" is still another structural position that could be a crucial factor for a network leader. While the leader may play a role of a broker, connecting disparate groups, he or she can more easily identify opportunities for creating new knowledge or products [111, 112], thus facilitating communication among diverse actors [113]. The position of broker plays a substantial and influential role in leadership ability, enabling governance by controlling access to resources and information across differing set of actors [114–118] while reducing the costs of interlocal cooperation [119]. According to Paquin and Howard-Grenville [120], brokers influence the network by "developing common goals, spurring actor interest and engagement, and/or defining norms of action" (p. 1625).

More recent conceptualizations of brokerage regard this role not as a mediator between two actors, but as a function that improves the quality of the relationship between these actors [121]. For example, leaders holding a brokerage role tend to resolve conflicts between organizations better, increase the network's social capital, and find resources to support collaboration [122]. Thus, the brokerage position enables leaders to act as a catalyst enhancing cooperation that builds and sustains connections in the network.

Leadership in a Changing World - A Multidimensional Perspective

Therefore, an organization's position in a network is essential to affecting its ability to lead effectively, enhancing its cooperative and coordinative skills.

7. Conclusions

This chapter aimed at providing an overview of current thinking on network leadership and related factors affecting local governance. The study focused on the leadership of local purpose-oriented service delivery networks, as these are prevalent in the local arena. To reiterate, the leadership of inter-organizational networks is concerns more than organizational leadership [123]. Such leadership requires organizational ability to achieve goals through collaboration with other organizations, and as a result, challenges emerge and evolve, necessitating the autonomous organization to be reconstituted in network form. The question then arises: How can local leaders administer networks so as to provide improved local services? The literature as reviewed above proposes many factors which affect the ability to lead those networks. The focus here has drawn on the New Institutional lens which encompasses the whole cycle of factors unique to local government and considered relevant to local leaders' ability to administer the networks. By combining the literature on network leadership in public administration with local governance the chapter offered insights on the structural, discursive, and environmental factors affecting a local lead organization's ability to run the networks.

These factors include the local lead organization's coordinative skills with the network itself. Such communicative abilities act as a bridge between the network and external stakeholders, thus enhancing its external legitimacy. Further, certain structural factors regarding a lead organization's position in a network were shown to be essential in leading the network. Finally, examining network leadership in the local arena, attention was directed to local environmental factors. These environmental factors refer to locality characteristics such as the intergovernmental context, political, cultural features of the specific municipality in which the network runs, alongside its size and socio-economic status of its community, and are crucial for the local lead organization. Future research might examine the combination of the factors discussed here in the context of conditions under which local lead organizations could bring about better functioning of local networks.

Author details

Anna Uster
Department of Political Science, The Max Stern Academic College of Emek Yezreel, Jezreel Valley, Israel

*Address all correspondence to: annau@yvc.ac.il

IntechOpen

© 2022 The Author(s). Licensee IntechOpen. This chapter is distributed under the terms of the Creative Commons Attribution License (http://creativecommons.org/licenses/by/3.0), which permits unrestricted use, distribution, and reproduction in any medium, provided the original work is properly cited. (cc) BY

The New Institutional Approach as a Lens on Local Network Leadership
DOI: http://dx.doi.org/10.5772/intechopen.101988

References

[1] Osborne SP. The New Public Governance?: Emerging Perspectives on the Theory and Practice of Public Governance. London: Routledge; 2010

[2] Goldfinch S, Wallis J. Two myths of convergence in public management reform. Public Administration. 2010;**88**(4):1099-1115

[3] Lodge M, Gill D. Toward a new era of administrative reform? The myth of post-NPM in New Zealand. Governance. 2011;**24**(1):141-166

[4] Christensen T, Lægreid P. The whole-of-government approach to public sector reform. Public Administration Review. 2007;**67**(6):1059-1066

[5] Provan KG, Kenis P. Modes of network governance: Structure, management, and effectiveness. Journal of Public Administration Research and Theory. 2008;**18**(2):229-252

[6] Johnson C, Osborne SP. Local strategic partnerships, neighbourhood renewal, and the limits to co-governance. Public Money and Management. 2003;**23**(3):147-154

[7] Kim Y. Can alternative service delivery save cities after the great recession? Barriers to privatisation and cooperation. Null. 2018;**44**(1):44-63

[8] McGuire M, Agranoff R, Silvia C. Collaborative public administration. The Foundations of Public Administration Series. 2010;**61**(6):671-681

[9] Ansell C, Gash A. Collaborative governance in theory and practice. Journal of Public Administration Research and Theory. 2008;**18**(4):543-571

[10] Sørensen E, Torfing J. Making governance networks effective and democratic through metagovernance. Public Administration. 2009;**87**(2):234-258

[11] Emerson K, Nabatchi T, Balogh S. An integrative framework for collaborative governance. Journal of Public Administration Research and Theory. 2012;**22**(1):1-29

[12] O'Leary R, Gerard C, Bingham LB. Introduction to the symposium on collaborative public management. Public Administration Review. 2006;**66**:6-9

[13] Torfing J. Rethinking path dependence in public policy research. Critical Policy Studies. 2009;**3**(1):70-83

[14] Milward HB, Provan KG. Governing the hollow state. Journal of Public Administration Research and Theory. 2000;**10**(2):359-380

[15] Tibbs CD, Layne D, Bryant B, Carr M, Ruhe M, Keitt S, et al. Youth violence prevention: local public health approach. Journal of Public Health Management and Practice. 2017;**23**(6):641-643

[16] Palinkas LA, Fuentes D, Finno M, Garcia AR, Holloway IW, Chamberlain P. Inter-organizational collaboration in the implementation of evidence-based practices among public agencies serving abused and neglected youth. Administration and Policy in Mental Health and Mental Health Services Research. 2014;**41**(1):74-85

[17] Mitra A. Terms of Trade and Class Relations: An Essay in Political Economy. Hyderabad: Orient Blackswan; 2005

[18] Cashmore J. The link between child maltreatment and adolescent offending: Systems neglect of adolescents. Family Matters. 2011;**89**:31-41

[19] Carboni JL, Saz-Carranza A, Raab J, Isett KR. Taking dimensions of

purpose-oriented networks seriously. Perspectives on Public Management and Governance. 2019;**2**(3):187-201

[20] Berthod O, Segato F. Developing purpose-oriented networks: A process view. Perspectives on Public Management and Governance. 2019;**2**(3):203-212

[21] Lemaire RH, Mannak RS, Ospina SM, Groenleer M. Striving for state of the art with paradigm interplay and meta-synthesis: Purpose-oriented network research challenges and good research practices as a way forward. Perspectives on Public Management and Governance. 2019;**2**(3):175-186

[22] Nowell BL, Kenis P. Purpose-oriented networks: The architecture of complexity. Perspectives on Public Management and Governance. 2019;**2**(3):169-173

[23] Krishnan CPM. The New Age of Innovation. New York: Tata McGraw-Hill Education; 2008

[24] Cole A, John P. Governing education in england and france. Public Policy and Administration. 2001;**16**:106-125

[25] Yáñez CJN, Magnier A, Ramírez MA. Local governance as government–business cooperation in western democracies: Analysing local and intergovernmental effects by multi-level comparison. International Journal of Urban and Regional Research. 2008;**32**(3):531-547

[26] Borraz O, John P. The transformation of urban political leadership in Western Europe. International Journal of Urban and Regional Research. 2004;**28**(1):107-120

[27] O'Leary R, Bingham LB. Conclusion: Conflict and collaboration in networks. International Public Management Journal. 2007;**10**(1):103-109

[28] Russell JL, Meredith J, Childs J, Stein MK, Prine DW. Designing

inter-organizational networks to implement education reform: An analysis of state race to the top applications. Educational Evaluation and Policy Analysis. 2015;**37**(1):92-112

[29] Kapucu N. Interorganizational coordination in dynamic contexts: Networks in emergency management. Connect. 2005;**26**(2):33-48

[30] Whelan C. Managing dynamic public sector networks: Effectiveness, performance, and a methodological framework in the field of national security. International Public Management Journal. 2015;**18**(4):536-567

[31] Stewart J. The meaning of strategy in the public sector. Australian Journal of Public Administration. 2004;**63**(4): 16-21

[32] Stoker G. Public Value Management and Network Governance: A New Resolution of the Democracy/Efficiency Tradeoff. Manchester, UK: University of Manchester; 2003

[33] Huxham C, Vangen S. Managing to Collaborate: The Theory and Practice of Collaborative Advantage. London: Routledge; 2005

[34] Feiock RC. The institutional collective action framework. Policy Studies Journal. 2013;**41**(3):397-425

[35] Vangen S, Winchester N. Managing cultural diversity in collaborations: A focus on management tensions. Public Management Review. 2014;**16**(5): 686-707

[36] Agranoff R. Managing Within Networks: Adding Value to Public Organizations. Washington, DC: Georgetown University Press; 2007

[37] O'Toole LJ. Networks and networking: The public administrative agendas. Public Administration Review. 2015;**75**(3):361-371

[38] Üster H, Wang X, Yates JT. Strategic evacuation network design (SEND) under cost and time considerations. Transportation Research Part B: Methodological. 2018;**107**:124-145

[39] Stone CN. Urban regimes and the capacity to govern: A political economy approach. Journal of Urban Affairs. 1993;**15**(1):1-28

[40] Klijn EH. Analyzing and managing policy processes in complex networks: A theoretical examination of the concept policy network and its problems. Administration & Society. 1996;**28**(1):90-119

[41] Klijn E, Teisman GR. Strategies and games in networks. Managing Complex Networks: Strategies for the Public Sector. 1997;**98**:118

[42] Kenis P, Provan KG. Towards an exogenous theory of public network performance. Public Administration. 2009;**87**(3):440-456

[43] Saz-Carranza A, Ospina SM. The behavioral dimension of governing interorganizational goal-directed networks—Managing the unity-diversity tension. Journal of Public Administration Research and Theory. 2011;**21**(2):327-365

[44] Human SE, Provan KG. Legitimacy building in the evolution of small-firm multilateral networks: A comparative study of success and demise. Administrative Science Quarterly. 2000;**45**(2):327-365

[45] Agranoff R, McGuire M. Big questions in public network management research. Journal of Public Administration Research and Theory. 2001;**11**(3):295-326

[46] Davies S. Third Sector Provision of Local Government and Health Services: A Report for UNISON. Unison: Cardiff School of Social Sciences; 2007

[47] Crosby BC, Bryson JM. A leadership framework for cross-sector collaboration. Public Management Review. 2005;**7**(2):177-201

[48] Kickert WJ, Klijn E, Koppenjan JF. Managing Complex Networks: Strategies for the Public Sector. Thousand Oaks, CA: Sage; 1997

[49] Uster A, Beeri I, Vashdi D. Don't push too hard. Examining the managerial behaviours of local authorities in collaborative networks with nonprofit organisations. Local Government Studies. 2019;**45**(1): 124-145

[50] Greasley S, Stoker G. Urban political leadership. Theories of Urban Politics. 2009;**2**:125-136

[51] Magnier A. Strong mayors? on direct election and political entrepreneurship. In: The European Mayor. Berlin: Springer; 2006. pp. 353-376

[52] Clarke L. Acceptable Risk? Making Decisions in a Toxic Environment. New York: Univ of California Press; 1989

[53] Mouritzen PE, Svara JH. Leadership at the Apex: Politicians and Administrators in Western Local Governments. Pittsburgh, Pennsylvania: University of Pittsburgh; 2002

[54] Steyvers K, Reynaert H, Delwit P, Pilet J. Comparing local political leadership in transformation. In: Local political leadership across europe. Town chief, city boss or Loco President? Belgium: Vanden Broele & Nomos; 2009. pp. 9-28

[55] Steyvers K. A knight in white satin armour? New institutionalism and mayoral leadership in the era of governance1. European Urban and Regional Studies. 2016;**23**(3):289-305

[56] Clark TN, Ferguson LC. City money. Political processes, fiscal strain, and

Retrenchment. New York: Columbia University Press; 1983

[57] Kantor P. The dependent city: The changing political economy of urban economic development in the United States. Urban Affairs Quarterly. 1988;22(4):493-520

[58] Kantor P, Savitch HV, Haddock SV. The political economy of urban regimes: A comparative perspective. Urban Affairs Review. 1997;32(3):348-377

[59] Lowndes V, Leach S. Understanding local political leadership: Constitutions, contexts and capabilities. Local Government Studies. 2004;30(4):557-575

[60] Ramírez E. Political institutions and conservation by local governments. Urban Affairs Review. 2005;40(6): 706-729

[61] Savitch HV, Kantor P. Cities in the International Marketplace. Princeton: Princeton University Press; 2002

[62] Scharpf FW. Introduction: The problem-solving capacity of multi-level governance. Journal of European Public Policy. 1997;4(4):520-538

[63] Katzenstein PJ. Regionalism in comparative perspective. Cooperation and Conflict. 1996;31(2):123-159

[64] Richards JC, Schmidt RW. Longman Dictionary of Language Teaching and Applied Linguistics. London: Routledge; 2013

[65] Finnemore M. International organizations as teachers of norms: The United Nations Educational, Scientific, and Cutural Organization and science policy. International Organization. 1993;47(4):565-597

[66] Silvia C. Collaborative governance concepts for successful network leadership. State and Local Government Review. 2011;43(1):66-71

[67] Klijn E, Edelenbos J. Meta-governance as network management. In: Theories of Democratic Network Governance. Berlin: Springer; 2007. pp. 199-214

[68] Maron A, Benish A. Power and conflict in network governance: Exclusive and inclusive forms of network administrative organizations. Public Management Review. 2021;2021(May):1-21

[69] Klijn EH, Koppenjan J. The impact of contract characteristics on the performance of public–private partnerships (PPPs). Public Money & Management. 2016;36(6):455-462

[70] Edelenbos J. Water as connective current. On Water Governance and the Importance of Dynamic Water Management. 2010

[71] Williams-Boyd P. Educational Leadership: A Reference Handbook. Santa Barbara, California: Abc-Clio; 2002

[72] Bass BM. The Bass Handbook of Leadership: Theory, Research, and Managerial Applications. New York: Simon and Schuster; 2008

[73] Ansell C, Gash A. Stewards, mediators, and catalysts: Toward a model of collaborative leadership. The Innovation Journal. 2012;17(1):2

[74] Piatak J, Romzek B, LeRoux K, Johnston J. Managing goal conflict in public service delivery networks: Does accountability move up and down, or side to side? Public Performance & Management Review. 2018;41(1):152-176

[75] Romzek B, LeRoux K, Johnston J, Kempf RJ, Piatak JS. Informal accountability in multisector service delivery collaborations. Journal of Public Administration Research and Theory. 2014;24(4):813-842

[76] Berthod O, Grothe-Hammer M, Müller-Seitz G, Raab J, Sydow J. From high-reliability organizations to high-reliability networks: The dynamics of network governance in the face of emergency. Journal of Public Administration Research and Theory. 2017;27(2):352-371

[77] Bouckaert G. Reflections and challenges for the public administration community. Teaching Public Administration. 2013;31(2):226-229

[78] Isett KR, Mergel IA, LeRoux K, Mischen PA, Rethemeyer RK. Networks in public administration scholarship: Understanding where we are and where we need to go. Journal of Public Administration Research and Theory. 2011;21(suppl_1):i157-i173

[79] Virtanen I. In search for a theoretically firmer epistemological foundation for the relationship between tacit and explicit knowledge. Electronic Journal of Knowledge Management. 2013;11(2):118-126

[80] Lonsdale J. The right tools for the job? methods, choice and context. In: Performance Auditing. Cheltenham, UK: Edward Elgar Publishing; 2011

[81] Peters BG. Reform begets reform: How governments have responded to the new public management. In: Innovations in Public Governance. Amsterdam, Netherlands: IOS Press; 2011. pp. 110-121

[82] Rugge F. The intransigent context: Glimpses at the history of a problem. In: Context in Public Policy and Management. Cheltenham, UK: Edward Elgar Publishing; 2013

[83] Halligan J. A comparative perspective on canadian public administration within an anglophone tradition. In: Dwivedi OP, Mau TA, Sheldrick B, editors. The Evolving Physiology of Government: Canadian Public Administration in Transition. Ottawa, Cananda: University of Ottawa Press; 2009. pp. 292-311

[84] Klijn E, Sierra V, Ysa T, Berman EM, Edelenbos J, Chen D. Context in governance networks: Complex interactions between macro, meso and micro. A theoretical exploration and some empirical evidence on the impact of context factors in Taiwan, Spain and the Netherlands. In: Context in Public Policy and Management. Cheltenham, United Kingdom: Edward Elgar Publishing; 2013

[85] Pearce CL, Manz CC. The New Silver Bullets of Leadership: The Importance of Self-and Shared Leadership in Knowledge Work. 2005.

[86] D'Innocenzo L, Mathieu JE, Kukenberger MR. A meta-analysis of different forms of shared leadership–team performance relations. Journal of Management. 2016;42(7):1964-1991

[87] Pearce CL, Manz CC, Sims HP Jr. The roles of vertical and shared leadership in the enactment of executive corruption: Implications for research and practice. The Leadership Quarterly. 2008;19(3):353-359

[88] Huxham C, Vangen S. Leadership in the shaping and implementation of collaboration agendas: How things happen in a (not quite) joined-up world. Academy of Management Journal. 2000;43(6):1159-1175

[89] Provan KG, Milward HB. A preliminary theory of interorganizational network effectiveness: A comparative study of four community mental health systems. Administrative Science Quarterly. 1995;40(1):1

[90] Provan KG, Milward HB. Do networks really work? A framework for evaluating public-sector organizational networks. Public Administration Review. 2001;61(4):414-423

[91] Milward HB, Provan KG. Managing networks effectively. In: National Public Management Research Conference. Georgetown University, Washington, DC; 2003

[92] O'leary R, Vij N. Collaborative public management: Where have we been and where are we going? The American Review of Public Administration. 2012;**42**(5):507-522

[93] Loikkanen HA, Susiluoto I. Cost Efficiency of Finnish Municipalities in Basic Service Provision 1994-2002. In: 45th Congress of the European Regional Science Association: "Land Use and Water Management in a Sustainable Network Society", 23-27 August 2005. Amsterdam, The Netherlands: European Regional Science Association (ERSA), Louvain-la-Neuve; 2005

[94] Milligan K, Moretti E, Oreopoulos P. Does education improve citizenship? Evidence from the united states and the united kingdom. Journal of Public Economics. 2004;**88**(9-10):1667-1695

[95] Beeri I, Uster A, Vigoda-Gadot E. Does performance management relate to good governance? A study of its relationship with citizens' satisfaction with and trust in Israeli local government. Public Performance & Management Review. 2018:1-39

[96] De Borger B, Kerstens K. Cost efficiency of Belgian local governments: A comparative analysis of FDH, DEA, and econometric approaches. Regional Science and Urban Economics. 1996;**26**(2):145-170

[97] Wu X, Ramesh M, Howlett M. Policy capacity: A conceptual framework for understanding policy competences and capabilities. Policy and Society. 2015;**34**(3-4):165-171

[98] Vetter A, Kersting N. Democracy Versus Efficiency? Comparing Local Government Reforms Across Europe.

Reforming Local Government in Europe. Berlin: Springer; 2003. pp. 11-28

[99] Boyne GA. Sources of public service improvement: A critical review and research agenda. Journal of Public Administration Research and Theory. 2003;**13**(3):367-394

[100] Mitchell RK, Smith B, Seawright KW, Morse EA. Cross-cultural cognitions and the venture creation decision. Academy of Management Journal. 2000;**43**(5): 974-993

[101] Zakocs RC, Edwards EM. What explains community coalition effectiveness?: A review of the literature. American Journal of Preventive Medicine. 2006;**30**(4): 351-361

[102] Hasnain-Wynia R, Shoshanna S, Bazzoli GJ, Alexander JA, Shortell SM, Cconrad DA, et al. Members' perceptions of community care network partnerships' effectiveness. Community Partnerships and Collaboration. 2003;**60**(4):40S

[103] Uster A, Beeri I, Vashdi D. Enhancing local service effectiveness through purpose-oriented networks: The role of network leadership and structure. American Review of Public Administration. Forthcoming

[104] Hamilton JD. Oil and the macroeconomy since world war II. Journal of Political Economy. 1983;**91**(2):228-248

[105] Sellers JM. Governing from Below: Urban Regions and the Global Economy. Cambridge, UK: Cambridge University Press; 2002

[106] DiGaetano A, Klemanski JS. Power and City Governance. Minnesota: University of Minnesota Press; 1999

[107] Raab J, Mannak RS, Cambré B. Combining Structure, Governance, and

The New Institutional Approach as a Lens on Local Network Leadership
DOI: http://dx.doi.org/10.5772/intechopen.101988

Context: A Configurational Approach to Network Effectiveness. 2013.

[108] Hollenbeck K, Erickcek GA, Timmeney B. An Assessment of the BC CAREERS Employer Resource Network: Its Contributions to the ERN Model. 2011.

[109] Huang K, Provan KG. Structural embeddedness and organizational social outcomes in a centrally governed mental health services network. Public Management Review. 2007;**9**(2):169-189

[110] Bryk AS, Gomez LM, Grunow A. Getting ideas into action: Building networked improvement communities in education. Frontiers in Sociology of Education: Springer. 2011:127-162

[111] Shipilov AV. Network strategies and performance of Canadian investment banks. The Academy of Management Journal. 2006;**49**(3):590

[112] Burt RS. Structural holes and good ideas. American Journal of Sociology. 2004;**110**(2):349-399

[113] Wukich C, Hu Q, Siciliano MD. Cross-sector emergency information networks on social media: Online bridging and bonding communication patterns. The American Review of Public Administration. 2019;**49**(7): 825-839

[114] Andrew SA, Carr JB. Mitigating uncertainty and risk in planning for regional preparedness: The role of bonding and bridging relationships. Urban Studies. 2013;**50**(4):709-724

[115] Faas A, Velez A, FitzGerald C, Nowell B, Steelman T. Patterns of preference and practice: Bridging actors in wildfire response networks in the american northwest. Disasters. 2017;**41**:527-548

[116] Sandström A, Carlsson L. The performance of policy networks: The

relation between network structure and network performance. Policy Studies Journal. 2008;**36**(4):497-524

[117] Aldrich DP. Building Resilience: Social Capital in Post-Disaster Recovery. Chicago, IL: University of Chicago Press; 2012

[118] Lee Y. Impact fees decision mechanism: Growth management decisions in local political market. International Review of Public Administration. 2010;**15**(2):59-72

[119] Feiock RC, Lee IW, Park HJ, Lee KH. Collaboration networks among local elected officials: Information, commitment, and risk aversion. Urban Affairs Review. 2010;**46**(2):241-262

[120] Paquin RL, Howard-Grenville J. Blind dates and arranged marriages: Longitudinal processes of network orchestration. Organization Studies. 2013;**34**(11):1623-1653

[121] Collins-Dogrul J. Tertius iungens brokerage and transnational intersectoral cooperation. Organization Studies. 2012;**33**(8):989-1014

[122] Lemaire RH, Provan KG. Managing collaborative effort: How Simmelian ties advance public sector networks. The American Review of Public Administration. 2018;**48**(5):379-394

[123] Uster A, Vashdi D, Beeri I. From organizational leadership to lead-organizations—The future of leadership in interorganizational networks. Journal of Leadership Studies. 2019;**12**(4):79-81

Chapter 8

Leadership Challenges among Undergraduate Students: Case Study of Dominion University, Ibadan

Afatakpa Fortune and Okedare David Olubunkunmi

Abstract

Student leadership is critical too for the smooth running of the University. Unlike other areas of human endeavor, leadership challenges among undergraduate students are a phenomenon. It is against this background; this chapter examined the leadership challenges among students of Dominion University, Ibadan, Nigeria. It is an empirical study. It is a qualitative study. Data; were gathered through in-depth interviews, key informant interviews, and focus group discussions. The study also made use of non-participant observation. Data; were gathered from 100 L, 200 L, 300 L students and staff of the University. Data were zanalyzed using content analyzed and using the narrative style. Findings show that Dominion University has the mandate of producing; value-based education. Leadership challenges undergraduate students include lack of support for selected leaders, lack of respect, and the wrong perception. The chapter concludes that with the right kind of training, Dominion University leadership skills acquisition can transform the plethora of challenges facing undergraduate leaders in Dominion University.

Keywords: leadership, challenges, dominion university, undergraduate

1. Introduction

The management of a university system is a tripod stand: The University Management led by the Vice-Chancellor, the lecturers, and organized student body. But, this chapter focuses on the leadership challenges among undergraduate students. According to Kunz and Garner [1], excellence in the students can empower others while managing themselves. Consequently, leadership is critical to undergraduate students in our contemporary world. It entails the development of student leadership teams and helping the University Management team to implement the decisions of management. Aymoldanovnaa et al. [2] acknowledge the active participation of students in corporate governance. It is a crucial element needed for a university to thrive. Aymoldanovnaa et al. [2]; maintain that engaging students as part of the governance structure would open spaces to develop their leadership skills, increase management skills, take responsibility, and manage competitiveness. These are relevant skills needed to thrive and survive; in the global market. Universities have their traditions and characteristics; they are critical to determining how undergraduate students can manage and govern themselves. This chapter provides an exploratory insight into the leadership challenges among the undergraduate students of Dominion University. The chapter has six sections. Section one is the introduction; it gives the background to the study. Section two deals with reviews of extant studies to identify the gap(s) to fill. The methodology is in section three. Section four focuses on the findings and, section five will discuss and analyze. While section six concludes the study.

2. Literature review

Student leadership among undergraduates has attracted attention of scholars. Zuokemefa and Sese [3] focus attention on the challenges of student union leadership in Nigeria's polytechnics, colleges of education, and universities. They contend that the insensitivity of the authorities to the needs of students is a trigger of conflict between them and the student's leadership. The article speaks to the importance of university authorities lending listening ears to other layers of leadership; to forestall conflict. Ezekwem [4] believes that conflict emanates in a University system when the Authorities do not respect the opinions of student leaders. The submission of Ezekwem establishes the cultural idiosyncrasy that youths should be seen but should not be heard. Rachel and Odey [5] uncovered that there is; a high level of conflict emanating from undergraduate students in their leadership pursuit. Furthermore, conflict among undergraduate leadership is a result of the accruable financial and material benefits. They maintain that as long as a leadership position among undergraduate students is economically lucrative, the conflict will be rife. Leadership challenges among undergraduate students are often by the University Authorities. They provide financial and material resources to students' leadership to tame their fellow students. Accordingly, the extravagant lifestyles of student leaders on campus is a critical challenge to undergraduate leadership in Nigerian universities [6]. Rachel and Odey [5] and Usman [6] establish the effects of elite conspiracy in creating toxicity among students. Olaniyi [7] believes that leadership challenges among undergraduate students are traceable to the high level of corruption in the university system. He explained that some students do not respect student leadership because of their connection with lecturers. Equally, students tagged as "lecturers' boys" are known to display flagrant disrespect to their fellow students occupying leadership positions. Also, student leadership challenges are traceable to the inability of University Authorities to provide enabling environment for them to thrive. Where a platform is for students' leadership, they micromanage them. It is a cause of friction between student leadership and the University Authorities in Nigeria [8]. It speaks to the thesis that constituted authority manipulate because of their hidden agenda. Leadership challenges among undergraduate leaders are traceable to the lack of leadership skills. The leadership challenges among students are attributed; to the failure of the Nigerian Universities to equip them with the relevant skills. According to Anunobi [8], twenty-first century students must develop leadership skills that can enable them to engage their fellow students. Twenty-first century leadership skills such as critical thinking, emotional intelligence, and financial intelligence; should be developed in students. She believes the failure to incorporate these skills will lead to contentions between students and leaders. Muftahu [9] opines that leadership challenges are endemic when institutional leaders (including student leaders) because many are untrained. It is sacrosanct to integrate leadership training in the learning management of tertiary institutions in Nigeria. As important as these studies, they offer no insight on leadership challenges among undergraduate students in Dominion University, Ibadan, Nigeria. This chapter fills the gap.

3. Methodology

It is empirical. It is also a qualitative study that engages case study research design. The study was at Dominion University, Ibadan, Nigeria. It is a seven (7) month research; conducted between January and July 2021. It relied on primary data collected from the students, lecturers, and management of the University. The students' population of Dominion as at the time of writing this chapter is three hundred and fifty-four (354) comprising 100 L, 200 L, and 300 L students. The staff population of the University is sixty (60). A total of Ninety (90) interviews were carried out; In-depth with Lecturers (14). Key informants' interviews with Course Representatives (20); Students Female Hall Residence 1 Representatives (5); Student Female Hall of Residence 2 Representatives (5); Male Hall of Residence Representatives (10). Dean of Students Affairs (1). Female Hall Wardens (3); Male Hall Warden (1); Presiding Bishop of Victory International Church. Three Focus Group Discussion (FGD) comprising 10 participants were for; 100 L, 200 L, and 300 L students. The study also made use of non-participant observation. The respondents were purposively selected. The interviews are in the English Language. Data collected were content analyzed using the narrative method.

4. Leadership in the context of this study

The new Oxford Dictionary of English explains that leadership is "the action of leading a group of people or an organization, the state or position of being a leader". Merriam-Webster Dictionary believes that leadership is "the office or position of a leader, the capacity to lead, and the act or instance of leading" [10]. However, among the numerous synonyms proposed by Merriam-Webster, the following should be taken note of administration, direction, shepherding, care, and steward-ship. This definition shall apply to this chapter.

5. Findings and discussion

5.1 Brief history of Dominion University, Ibadan

The proprietor of Dominion University is Rehoboth Cathedral, Victory International Church. The Church is well experienced in the management of educational institutions. Rehoboth Cathedral, Victory International Church, has two other institutions performing excellently. The schools are the; Victory Christian Academy and the Victory Christian College. The Presiding Bishop of Rehoboth Cathedral, Bishop Taiwo Adelakun affirms that the idea of providing access to university education was conceived by the Church out of its desire to contribute to the promotion of academic standards of university education in Nigeria. He explained that providing access to university education was conceived by the Church. It was born out of the desire to add value to the eroding standards of tertiary education in Nigeria. His explanation substantiates Bowman [11] that corporate goals are; enhanced through vision. It dictates change by inspiring moti-vation and galvanizing an integrated corporate pursuit. In the words of Bishop Taiwo Adelakun:

Leadership in a Changing World - A Multidimensional Perspective

> *The desire to establish a university started some twelve years ago when as the Visioner, I was praying for the Nation, Nigeria. I was burdened by the vices bedeviling the Nation's tertiary institutions. I then received a vision from the Lord asking me to take positive steps in curbing the menace. I was told to take a child from birth into the Daycare Center, then through Nursery and Primary School up to the Secondary and University, instilling the fear of God into them while training their souls academically [12].*

The above statement corroborates Bowman [11] vision helps to clarify purpose. According to Bowman, vision; enhances the clarity of the bigger picture. The "take a child from birth into the Daycare Centre, then through Nursery and Primary School up to the Secondary and University, instilling the fear of God into them while training their souls academically" speaks to submission of Bowman [11] that dreams and passions are driven; by vision. It goes beyond the setting and attainment of goals. It provides the vigor and energy for the generation of results.

Bishop Adelakun attested that Dominion University is raising generational leaders in all fields of endeavor. It also boils down to the power of vision providing meaning to life. Fishman [13] espouses that vision propels a meaningful life. It is the compass that dictates the pathway of the choices we make. Thus, every life's pursuit should be guided; by the vision. Bishop Adelakun contends that Africa is the most endowed continent. In terms of resources, one of the poorest continents on earth hence, the need for a university that will address leadership deficiency in the African Continent.

> *The motto of Dominion University is "Raising Generational Leaders" who are morally upright and passionate about their nation. It is an institution of excellence both in infrastructure as well as educational delivery. Dominion University is our humble contribution to the development of our nation (Nigeria) and our blessed continent (Africa) [12].*

This first line of the above statement strengthens the advocacy for value-based education. Patil [14] discusses the importance of value-based education as an integral part of the educational curriculum. Since the youths in most societies are carried away with the vagaries of technology, coupled with exposure to violence, value-based education; must be given attention. Many undergraduates in Nigeria are confused. To raise generational leaders with strong value-based orientation would require establishing a University that would initiate and implant value-based spiritual learning to the younger generation [14]. It exposes the mind of Bishop Taiwo Adelakun that Dominion University would instill the fear of God into her students while training their souls academically.

Currently, Dominion University has two faculties: The Faculty of Computing and Applied Sciences and Faculty of Arts Social and Management Sciences. As at the time of writing this chapter, Dominion University does not have a Student Union Government. So, it does not have a formal leadership governance structure for the students. The student leadership is adhoc. Few students were selected to help manage some aspects of the campus. And departments based on recommendations. It is a unique feature of the university. Therefore, the findings are on the informal student leadership governance structure.

6. Leadership challenges among students of Dominion University

6.1 Lack of support

One of the leadership challenges among the undergraduate of Dominion University is the lack of support from the student population. According to

Respondent 1, a 300 L student in the Department of Mass Communication, "we are not enjoying support and cooperation from our fellow students. It is a great challenge because it makes tasks given to us laborious [15]". Another respondent admitted that "presently, we do not have a formal self-governing system as students. Some of us were hand-picked by the school authorities to take off some issues. But I discovered that some of our colleagues do not want to cooperate with us [16]". Participants in the three Focus Group Discussion concur that most of the students' leaders are not enjoying the cooperation of their fellow students. As a result, the student leaders always run to the University Management to rally their support. A respondent in 200 L remarked that "we only listen to them out of fear of being sanctioned by the University Management. They are fond of reporting those not cooperating with them [17]". Some of the leaders confirmed utter defiance of some students to instruction. In the words of a Course Representative, "the majority of the student only comply when we threaten to report them to a higher authority [18]".

6.2 Lack of respect

Disrespect among students to their fellow leaders is a leadership challenge. According to a 200 L student, "they see us as peers. Consequent on this perception we are not respected. It makes it difficult for us to get compliance [19]". Rudolph et al. [20] maintained that respect is crucial for leadership. The leadership cannot properly galvanize group members when there is a lack of respect. It also validates Rudolph et al. [20] that respect is the assessment of the leadership status of the group. It is one of the factors that can engender the influence of the leaders in the exertion of authority. Respect reflects one's evaluation of their status within the workgroup, and voice can engender respect. A member of the Sanitation Committee cited this example "I saw a fellow 200 L student throwing a bottle Coca-Cola on the floor after exhausting the liquid content. When I confronted him, he asked me what authority I have to challenge him. He said, after all, we are both in 200 L [21]. It coheres with the concept of particularized respect espoused by Rogers and Ashforth [22]. Particularized respect in leadership; is the worth a person deserves based on attributes, achievements, and behavior. Analyzing the statement indicates that there is nothing to offer for the fellow peer.

The Dean of Students Affairs made these observations "because they are peers, most of the same age bracket, the tendency is to take their leadership for granted [23]". It corroborates Pont et al. [24] that leading other peers is a challenge because of the possibility of taking each other for granted. A 300 L student detailed that "how can they place a junior student as a leader over me and you expect me to give such a person respect? How can I be taking instructions from a lower-level student in the name of leadership? [25]". Lack of respect for some of the students chosen to lead resonated among the participants in the three FGDs. Lecturer also acknowledged "our university is unique. Most of our students know themselves right from their high school days. Even our new 100 L students are familiar with many of our 200 L and 300 L students. It is, therefore, not out of place to find them handling their leaders with a certain level of levity [26]. Literature that were reviewed such as Sashkin [27], Siddaway et al. [28], The Neuroscience of Respectful Leadership [29], Van Quaquebeke and Felps [30], did not capture junior undergraduate students dishing orders to senior undergraduate students as a leadership challenge among undergraduates. This finding is unique to this study.

7. Wrong perception of leadership

Leadership challenges among the undergraduate students of Dominion are traceable to the wrong perception. One Hall Warden said that "they think leadership is all about the title. They do not understand that leadership is sacrifice. It validates Helms [31]. He posits that the perception of followers about their leaders is critical to leadership any outcome. The wrong perception creates the "we" versus the, "they" dichotomy. A Lecturer posits that "many of the students only look at the privileges. They forget the responsibility attached to the work of leadership [32]". The FGDs are unanimous in their responses that the wrong perception is instrumental to the lack of cooperation. Helms [31] argues that leadership can produce positive effects; based on how they are perceived. The positive perception of leaders in the heart of those they lead can help to promote cooperation and collaboration. Where there is the wrong perception, dissonance will be the order. Helms also affirm that wrong; perception of leadership by the followers also reduces the effectiveness and accomplishments of leaders.

A female Hall Warden attested that "the result of the wrong perception is jealousy. You hear them make remarks like, if not for the higher authority that some of them are close to, can they ever smell leadership? [33]". The dominant narrative among respondents is that some students believe that their leaders will always be subjective to those who appointed them. As a result, they seem not to be enjoying the cooperation of their fellow students. It verifies the claims of Thompson et al. [34] that negative perceptions can produce jealousy. They affirm that the presence of jealousy in the system paralyzes leadership effectiveness. Jealousy from followers leads to resistance to leadership. They believe that social loafing by followers is closely associated with; jealousy. It is also counterproductive to leadership effectiveness. Another lecturer stated that "it is the general trend among students that their leaders are stooges of management. This perception is a major challenge facing our student leaders [35]. It resonated among the three FGDs that students are careful of the presence of their student leaders in some gatherings. Students believe that leaders are informants to the university management. The researcher observed that students are suspicious when they see appointed leaders in their midst. They are also not trusted by their peers. They even change the subject of their discussion for fear of being quoted by a student before a member of the management team [36]". According to Kutsyuruba and Walker [37], trust is critical; to the survival of leaders. Where trust; is lacking, it will affect the leaders. The wrong perception of followers can break the speed of trust. The destruction of trust can also make followers take malevolent action. It constitutes an impediment to the productivity of undergraduate leaders in the discharge of their duties.

8. Lack of leadership skills

Respondents argue that lack of leadership is a critical challenge. The 100 L FGD respondents agree that majority of their leaders lack basic leadership skills. Seven out of the ten respondents concurred leadership skills are lacking among their leaders. A Hall Representative in the male hostel admitted that "we need to be trained, in basic leadership skills; especially now that it has to do with leading our peers [38]". Another Hall Representative in the female hostel remarked that "sometimes, the manner they communicate with their peers shows that they need training in fundamental leadership skills [39]". One of the Lecturers mentioned that "you still find that modicum, of impatience among some leaders. Well, since they are youth, it is expected. But patience is a virtue needed for leadership. They need training in

Leadership Challenges among Undergraduate Students: Case Study of Dominion University...
DOI: http://dx.doi.org/10.5772/intechopen.102056

that respect [40]". It corroborates the thesis of Gonfa [41] that the possession of leadership skills is essential to motivation, persuasion, and mobilizing followers to achieve set goals. Gonfa [41] believes that leadership is an all-inclusive word. He contends that it encompasses communication, management, developing visions, and establishing goals. Leadership skills are critical to the seamless of an organization. Leadership skills resonated in all the FGDs. In the 100 L FGD, emphasis was on communication skills. It validates Gonfa [41] that communication; is an essential tool for leadership to thrive. The 200 L FGD Respondents; are more particular about the listening skills, mobilization skills, and manner of approach. One of the respondents in the 300 L FGD stated that "some of them are acting as bosses since they are course representatives. They forget that we are peers and classmates [42]". The majority of the respondents contend that leadership skills; can be learned. Accordingly, to enjoy cooperation, peers that are leaders; should seek to develop the needed skills to be effective in the tasks assigned to them. Gonfa [41] submits that the absence of leadership skills will make leading difficult. The dearth of leadership skills reduces the effectiveness of leaders and leads to the fall of productivity. Therefore, the lack of leadership skills can be, removed by the training of undergraduates at all levels. Gonfa [41] affirms that leadership skills development for students can produce a lasting impact.

9. Student exhibiting deviant actions

The three FGDs affirmed that the university is a common ground for all kinds of people. Some are morally defiant and non-morally defiant. The Dean of Students Affairs pointed out that "those who are bankrupt of morals try to exhibit their defiance. They are the ones who make the work and actions of the leaders more cumbersome [43]". Through their defiant attitude, they attempt to lure other students. According to another female Hall Warden, "the morally defiant ones; that cause chaos for the leadership. They make the work of the leaders more cumbersome [44]". This submission signifies the need for the student leader to develop the capacity to deal with such groups of students. Sherman [45] attributes to the promulgation of certain; rules and regulations by the leadership of an organization. The deviant tendencies of Dominion University students towards their leaders are traceable to their not accepting some of the extant rules and regulations. Manifestation of deviance is also linked; with the lack of knowledge. Sherman [45] believes that not knowing the rules and regulations can lead to deviance from the followers against the leaders. Also, defiance and violation of the rules can be caused by malice from the students against their leaders.

10. Power struggle between two different classes

All the respondents noted an unholy power struggle between three different classes. The researcher observed that the 300 L students believe they deserve more respect from the 200 L and 100 L students. The 300 L students think that attention is; given to the 200 L and 100 L students. So, they longer command respect from lower-level classes. The students still believed that the school authority must be involved in such matters. Equally, some respondents attested that a clash of leadership goals ultimately constitutes a challenge among students. It can also lead to a power struggle because each side wants to establish its authority. Managing such clashes for undergraduate leadership can be frustrating. Karl Marx discussed the concept of power or class struggle within an economic context. He contends that conflict is endemic because society is structured to favor certain; classes of people. However, power or class struggle, as a leadership challenge among undergraduate students is not in the thesis of Karl Marx. It is a distinctive finding in this study.

11. Conclusion

One of the basic instincts and features that man shared with other organized creatures of creation is not just the ability to live in a communal way or a community. Both man and animals have seen the need to live together communally to preserve their species; for continuous existence. In this light, the bees lived in such an organized community to the extent that a queen bee can lead and direct all other bees for protection and the necessity of sustenance. Still, in the same vein, Gorillas also live a communal life organized around an alpha male for protection and procreation. Human beings are the apex of created beings by God. They have the quality uniquely projected. As a sentient being, everyone has the ability and capability to use intelligence as they desire. However, to care for and cater to the human species, human beings need more organization than the primitive organization found in nature. To achieve this common goal, all must work together without coercion. While some are to guide and lead, others are to follow. It brings up the quest for leadership. Against this background, this paper interrogated the leadership challenges among undergraduate students of Dominion University. Leadership challenges are not limited to the corporate world. It is also evident among university graduates. However, there is a need for consistent capacity building in terms of leadership skills for undergraduate students. It is expected leadership skills acquisition can transform the plethora of challenges facing undergraduate leaders in Dominion University.

Author details

Afatakpa Fortune* and Okedare David Olubunkunmi
Department of General Studies, Dominion University, Ibadan, Nigeria

*Address all correspondence to: fortuneafatakpa@gmail.com

IntechOpen

© 2022 The Author(s). Licensee IntechOpen. This chapter is distributed under the terms of the Creative Commons Attribution License (http://creativecommons.org/licenses/by/3.0), which permits unrestricted use, distribution, and reproduction in any medium, provided the original work is properly cited.

References

[1] Kunz GI, Garner MB. Going Global: The Textile and Apparel Industry. New York, NY: Fairchild Publications; 2007

[2] Aymoldanovnaa AA, Zhetpisbaevab BA, Kozybaevnac KU, Kadirovna SM. Leadership development university students in the activities of student government. Procedia—Social and Behavioral Sciences. 2015;**197**: 2131-2136

[3] Zuokemefa EP, Sese TE. Leadership and student unionism, challenges and solutions in the Nigerian tertiary education system (colleges of education, polytechnics and universities). European Scientific Journal. 2015;**11**(25):382-392

[4] Ezekwem EC. Student Unionism and University Administration in Nigeria. 2006. Available from: http://publisher. com/proposal 1568/index/html

[5] Rachel DU, Odey EO. Leadership conflicts among students on nigerian university campuses: The experience of the University of Calabar, Calabar Nigeria. British Journal of Education. 2017;**5**(3):1-8

[6] Usman SM. Electoral violence and rigging in Nigeria: A comparative analysis of 2003 and 2007 general elections. Paper presented at a one-day workshop of Youth Against Electoral Violence. Abuja: International Conference Centre; 2009

[7] Olaniyi OB. Leadership Challenges in Nigeria Universities: Redirection for World Class Leaders. 2021. Available from: https://www.academia. edu/41771976/Leadership_Challenges_ In_Nigeria_Universities_Redirection_ For_World_Class_Leaders [Accessed: November 20, 2021]

[8] Anunobi O. Leadership access to the 21st century university education in Nigeria: Issues and prospects.

International Journal of Institutional Leadership, Policy and Management. 2020;**2**(3):460-471

[9] Muftahu M. Why leadership training should be institutionalised. 2021. Available from: https://www. universityworldnews.com/post. php?story=20210126105819254 [Accessed: November 25, 2020]

[10] Leadership. Available from: https:// www.merriam-webster.com/thesaurus/ leadership [Accessed: September 25, 2021]

[11] Bowman M. Why is having a company vision so important for business? 2019. Available from: https:// thriveagency.com/news/business-vision/ [Accessed: December 9, 2021]

[12] Adelakun TV. Personal Communication. July 16, 2021

[13] Fishman R. 5 Reasons Why Having a Vision is Important. 2020. Available from: https://mymeadowreport.com/ reneefishman/2020/5-reasons-why-having-a-vision-is-important/ [Accessed: December 2, 2021]

[14] Patil YY. Role of Value-Based Education in Society. 2013. Available from: https://www.researchgate.net/ publication/286933664_Role_of_Value-Based_Education_In_Society

[15] Ademola I. Personal Communication. April 7, 2021

[16] David O. Personal Communication. April 9, 2021

[17] Ighodaro L. Personal Communication. April 15, 2021

[18] Ibironke A. Personal Communication. May 3, 2021

[19] Ibeneme P. Personal Communication. May 14, 2021

[20] Rudolph CW, Katz IM, Ruppel R, Zacher H. A systematic and critical review of research on respect in leadership. Leadership Quarterly. 2020;**32**(1):101492. DOI: 10.1016/j.leaqua.2020.101492. Retrieved on October 10, 2021 from https://www.researchgate.net/publication/346107750_A_Systematic_and_Critical_Review_of_Research_on_Respect_in_Leadership

[21] Olaonipekun A. Personal Communication. May 18, 2021

[22] Rogers K, Ashforth B. Respect in Organizations: Feeling Valued as "We" and "Me". Journal of Management. 2017;**43**(5):1578-1608. DOI: 10.1177/0149206314557159

[23] Ayo A. Personal Communication. July 7, 2021

[24] Pont B, Nusche D, Moorman H. Improving School Leadership Volume 1: Policy and Practice. 2008. Available from: https://www.oecd.org/education/school/44374889.pdf [Accessed: December 6, 2021]

[25] Dumebi I. Personal Communication. July 22, 2021

[26] Aderogba B. Personal Communication. April 25, 2021

[27] Sashkin M. Leadership. In: Rosebach WE, editor. Contemporary Issues in Leadership. New York: Taylor & Francis; 2018. pp. 7-20

[28] Siddaway AP, Wood AM, Hedges LV. How to do a systematic review: A best practice guide for conducting and reporting narrative reviews, meta-analyses, and metasyntheses. Annual Review of Psychology. 2019;**70**: 747-770. DOI: 10.1146/annurev-psych010418-102,803

[29] The Neuroscience of Respectful Leadership. The American Genius.

2020. Available from: https://theamericangenius.com/business-marketing/the-neuroscience-of-respectful-leadership-preventing-professional-disrespect/

[30] Van Quaquebeke N, Felps W. Respectful inquiry: A motivational account of leading through asking questions and listening. Academy of Management Review. 2018;**43**(1):1-27. DOI: 10.5465/amr.2014.0537

[31] Helms PM. Effective Leadership: Perceptions of Principals and the Teachers They Lead. 2012. Education Theses, Dissertations and Projects. Paper 56

[32] Evaristus L. Personal Communication. June 8, 2021

[33] Igbekele G. Personal Communication. June 15, 2021

[34] Thompson G, Buch R, Glasø L. Follower jealousy at work: A test of vecchio's model of antecedents and consequences of jealousy. The Journal of Psychology. 2018;**152**(1):60-74. DOI: 10.1080/00223980.2017.1407740

[35] Ibidun W. Personal Communication. July 25, 2021

[36] Haastrup H. Personal Communication. June 18, 2021

[37] Kutsyuruba B, Walker KD. The destructive effects of distrust: Leaders as brokers of trust in organizations. In: Normore AH, Brooks JS, editors. The Dark Side of Leadership: Identifying and Overcoming Unethical Practice in Organizations. Bingley, UK: Emerald Group Publishing Limited; 2016. pp. 133-154

[38] Okoronkwo P. Personal Communication. May 20, 2021

[39] Kosheunti K. Personal Communication. May 29, 2021

[40] Desalu W. Personal Communication. May 5, 2021

[41] Gonfa BD. Review of effects of poor leadership skill in organization: Evidences. Arabian Journal of Business and Management Review. 2019;**9**:381-386

[42] Sakpra M. Personal Communication. July 11, 2021

[43] Osahon A. Personal Communication. May 12, 2021

[44] Saseyi I. Personal Communication. July 29, 2021

[45] Sherman RO. Normalization of Deviance: A Nursing Leadership Challenge. 2014. Available from: https://www.emergingrnleader.com/normalization-deviance-nursing-leadership-challenge/ [Accessed: December 9, 2021]

Chapter 9

Positive Leadership Experiences of Software Professionals in Information Technology Organisations

Harold Andrew Patrick, Sunil Kumar Ramdas and Jacqueline Kareem

Abstract

Today's corporate culture frequently treats distrust like a virtue; however positive teams are more effective. A workplace that instils confidence, and supports collaboration and creativity attracts committed and talented employees. Positive psychology plays a pivotal role in influencing numerous conceptual leadership models of which, positive leadership is one such concept. The purpose of this chapter is to highlight and recognise the value of positive leadership at workplace, this chapter aims to provide evidences of how positive leadership and its sub-dimension's act as a link between employees and organisations positive outcomes. Judgement and stratified sampling technique was adopted to draw software professionals and to select information technology organisations (ITOs). Nine hundred and eighty three software professionals participated from around 25 IT organisations. The positive leadership measure (PLM) was administered. Results indicate that software professionals did experience positive leadership and the immediate supervisor's positive behaviour lays down the foundation for a successful organisation. The sub-dimensions significantly impacted positive outcomes. The chapter details the results, discussion, implications and suggestions.

Keywords: positive psychology, positive leadership, recognition, positive perspective, strength based approach, software professionals, information technology organisations

1. Introduction

Leadership is one among the most sought after topics spoken among corporates and academic researchers. It can be traced back to the Indian, Egyptians and Greek civilisation where philosophers such as Pluto, Socrates, and Aristotle spoke about it length. The author of epic literature Ramayana, Maharishi Valmiki defines leadership and its characteristics precisely during his conversation with Sage Narada at the beginning of Ramayana. This resonates with the theory of multiple intelligence (1983) by Howard Gardner (Harvard psychologist) to the current society or environment about leader's versatility, characteristic while they are in their pinnacle. Leadership lessons can be traced to the bhakti movement prominent during the eighth-century

IntechOpen

in southern India, and spread towards other parts of the world. The spiritual leaders, social reformer and philosophers like Sri Ramanujacharya, a great exponent of the Sri Vaishnavism who presented the epistemic and soteriological importance of bhakti, was also known for his charismatic and virtuous behaviour, administrative acumen and managerial ability to balance inspiring followers as well as getting the task accomplished. His ability to conceive and execute the construction of the Thondanur Lake (Melukote-Karnataka-India) 1000 years back is a major irrigation source even today for both agriculture and drinking for that region. Through his virtuous behaviour and altruistic love for his devotees, he intrinsically motivated, empowered them to practice spiritual values, which lead to the ultimate goal of devotional service. Yet the understanding and significance of leadership studies begun only during the twentieth century however the social-scientific approach towards leadership studies only started during the 1930s. As the research progressed, leadership has been continuously redefined and several theories on leadership have been proposed, developed and still developing. The last quarter century has seen a positive orientation driven by cultural values towards a shared vision. As positive psychology plays an important role in the human behaviour and it is not about a feel-good concept. Leaders today have a disproportionate impact on workplace positivity and have undermined its power to improve organisational effectiveness. The fundamental characteristic that stands out among leaders are positivity, authenticity, to serve, share power and feel others wholeness. Similarly another spiritual leader Srila Prabhupada was known for his acumen for management principles and entrepreneurial skills in temple administration, revenue generation through publication besides people management influenced thousands of youth from across the world towards Krishna consciousness by applying positive psychology and affirmative behaviour via love, trust, empowerment and affection. These spiritual leaders demonstrated the components of having a vision (big picture thinking), positive attitude, and altruistic love for their followers to experience intrinsic self-value and satisfaction of life purpose. Which corporates leaders are incorporating based on spirituality and positivity to develop their virtuous behaviour, perceptions of trust, organisational support, and commitment among employees, which could have positive effects on organisational performance [1, 2]. Positive psychology has major influence on leader's behaviour at workplace and research indicates that positive approaches to empower people and building trust are a must-have leadership trait. Organisations are group of people who pursue common goals: leadership has been central to organisations because leadership has been a process by which groups create or achieve goals. Most of us right from childhood looked around those people who are achievers and automatically equated those achievers with leaders and assumed whatever the individual did to achieve the outcomes that they did constitute leadership. Part of the challenge of leadership education and leadership development in organisation is to overcome the implicit understanding that people come into the organisation based on the individuals inspired by in their past. Since last 30 years of leadership research, organisations and scholars have been looking at the subject of leadership. There are three things about leadership which we need to be understood.

- Leadership is about generating voluntary commitment on the part of the people towards group goals which means "leadership is not about achieving goals through any means i.e. one's authority or individual position but it's about "inducing individuals to voluntarily commit themselves to certain long term goals which are beneficial for the group.

- Leadership is not so much about the individual (the leaders) it's more about the relationship. What we mean here is there are three things associated to this aspect "Leader-follower-context": leadership relationship is very important

Positive Leadership Experiences of Software Professionals in Information Technology Organisations
DOI: http://dx.doi.org/10.5772/intechopen.100805

(e.g. many organisations hire star performers from competitors. They try to replicate the success of the star performer in prior organisation but that does not work (always). Often the result of the star performer is due to his unique team composition, their strengths, organisational culture (context).

• Today leadership is associated with positive psychology, positive change and positive deviance. The concept called positive leadership.

Great leaders build significant economic value, excel under pressure and align meticulously with organisational business strategy to drive better performance. They try to bring employees together around the organisational objectives, motivate them to deliver by creating value for both. Various studies indicate that organisations which are value based enhance their performance and most likely sustain their long term objectives commercially. Leaders who practice positivity follow these basics to achieve their goals.

It is about practicing positivity continuously with virtuous behaviour; demonstrate organisational values, beliefs and integrity. They have a clear vision, shared values and set goals aligned to the organisational objectives. They recognise the importance of a team and develop them to excel in their tasks.

The chapter details positive leadership, significance and importance, the execution and benefits of positive leadership, the sub dimensions of positive leadership—recognition, strength based and perspective based approach, methodology adopted, sample, tools of measurement, results, discussion, theoretical and practical implications of positive leadership and conclusion.

2. Positive leadership

Leadership is optimistic or positive, when it is virtuous leading to heliotropic effect. It's about demonstrating high degree of excellence, such as optimism, compassion, integrity, and audacity. However, virtuousness takes place when an individual exhibits fineness in his actions that are pertinent in every situation at workplace. For example, in India, the National Disaster Rescue Force (NDRF) team members take up various rescue operations in challenging circumstances (both natural and man-made disasters) by exhibiting valour to venture, acumen to handle the situations of threat, empathy to aid the individual who are trapped, and the self-effacement to acknowledge what is beyond their capability. In contrast, let us look at a corporate performance appraisal scenario, where the supervisor needs to provide adverse feedback to his team member. At the same time expected to be candid in sharing the information about the performance is not unto to the expected standards. The supervisor is expected to be sensitive to the team member's feelings/emotions and also understand why his performance is suffering and what measures needs to be taken to improve it. Every state of affair or circumstance needs a divergent set of virtues to be practiced based on the situation and also upholding the interest of the team members who too upkeep the circumstances exhibiting excellence. To maintain the higher standards of performance, it needs both the supervisor and team member to demonstrate the pertinent intrinsic worth in their actions within a given circumstances. Therefore, leader's optimism or positivity may be a comparatively unusual episode. However, literature indicates leader's positivity exists alongside the continuum. At any given circumstance during the engagement between the supervisor and team member, the supervisors may demonstrate positivity. These positive actions and reactions of both may be due to virtuousness.

Positive leadership is a proprietary leadership strategy which helps organisations and leaders (at all levels within the organisation) excel under pressure. Positive leadership is heliotropic. It involves experiencing, modelling, and purposefully enhancing positive emotions. It is built around the application of positive psychology [3], positive organisational scholarship [4] and positive change [5]. These facilitate and nurture positive deviance in order to accomplish both individual and organisational objectives with effectiveness. Positive deviance herein, refers to the 'X' factor that distinguishes positive leaders from the rest. Positivity is about leaders having disproportionate stimulus in the workplace positivity by practising affirmative behaviour. It is based on the scientific evidence and theoretically-grounded principles to endorse consequences such as virtuous behaviours, interpersonal flourishing, and revitalising association [6]. Those who embrace positive leadership are authentic and passionate individuals, who enable positively deviant performance, foster an affirmative orientation in organisation by focusing on virtuousness. That is exhibiting positive emotions which influence, inspire, and empower them by building trust and showing keen interest in their follower's progression along with organisational bottom line. They continuously engage in positivity and have clarity about what they want, why and how in achieving their objectives through building positive work environment, relationship, communication and meaning.

3. How positive leadership is different from other leadership styles

A leader's positive outlook, self-awareness, servant hood, authenticity, social exchange, virtuous behaviours and charisma to influence, form the basis of positive leadership theories that include authentic, transformation, servant, empowering, and ethical. The basic difference amid these styles is that a servant leaders focus on the followers' needs in terms of reinforcing positive climate and meaning, whereas transformational leader emphasises on positive relationships and communication towards organisational goals. Authentic leaders emphasise on positive behaviour in terms of transparent communication and ethical organisational climate whereas Ethical leaders, focus on ethical standards, beliefs and values, while empowering leaders focus on enhancing employees through sharing power. However, the common thread among these is positivity which enhances employees experiencing more trust, engagement and empowerment [7]. Traditionally, these "leadership theories have been inclined towards positivity, yet none have defined positive leadership" [8]. Further, asserting that positive leaders need to remain methodical and cohesive over time and across situations. While focusing on heliotropic effect and positive deviance [6], this chapter explores leader's affirmative behaviour focusing employee's strengths, positive perspective and recognition.

4. What positive leaders do differently?

Positive leaders play an important role in influencing the organisational performance via virtuous and affirmative behaviour due to their direct influence they have on their employees. They align the performance of their employees with all-embracing objectives of the organisation and shaping a positive workplace culture. During the transformation (2006) period of Ford Ltd., Mr. Alan Mulally, CEO talks about his leadership lessons learnt during his career and how effectively he applied positive leadership style. He advocates that "positive leadership conveys the notion that there is always a way forward". Further reinstating that positive leadership is about strengthening the opinion that every employee is counted in. When the workforces are involved in driving the organisational objective, it is more rewarding. The leader's personality and actions have an influence on his employees and does affects the organisation. Hence it is significant to adopt a positive attitude and positive practices. When leaders communicate their vision and expectation with clarity it stimulates workplace trust and self-reliance among employees to look beyond call of duty. Positive leader's emphasis on strength based approach that builds the necessary competency for long-term goals by creating a performance work culture over a period of time. Leader's positive perspective clears the path of obstacles and challenges as opportunities to achieve their objectives. However, appreciation, recognition and positive feedback creates more engagement leading to higher productivity.

5. Create a vision that stimulates employees and stake holders

The organisational vision statement has to inspire and stimulate the employees to focus on their goals aligning to the organisational goals for development and accomplishment. Similarly leadership and vision are considered to be indistinguishable. They focus on what matters utmost and try to accomplish it along with the team by addressing the future and its realities in a transparent manner with optimism. Leaders take the opportunity to communicate the vision to its employees, so it is embraced and implemented to enhance the outcomes to achieve the bottom line. It is very important from the leadership perspective to constantly engage the employees via communicating the company vision and value statement. Example: when the leaders reinforce the organisation vision by correlating or binding it to the individual employee or teams goals. When leaders effectively share the vision statements, it narrates a story that is beneficial for both the organisation and employees and has an impact over the products and services by creating a higher value. However, if employees are uncertain about the story narrated or the story does not bring desired change, then they are not likely to embrace the vision. So leaders need to create visibility so the employees link their objectives and also share their success stories towards comprehending the organisation vision. Organisation's positive practice is always credited to the leader's vision of defining the higher purpose. Many organisations understood that focusing on customers' needs makes a difference, which in turn develops individual and organisational prosperity. Organisation with higher purpose or drive out-performed the ordinary organisations (8:1) ratio. Example: the Nike leadership talks about innovation to inspire sports champions or athlete focusing on to do everything imaginable towards enhancing human potential to perform.

6. Cultivate positive practices at workplace

Positivity breeds self-reliant, zealous and affirmative employees. Positive practices are a powerful process that can influence individuals in many ways professionally and personally. They stimulate individuals to perform better. When employee's experience positive emotions at work place, the affirmative sense is formed by associating their effort with its impact on their performance. Prof. Grant (Wharton Business School) advocates that leaders can achieve more by outsourcing inspiration through various means and practices. Example: it is vital for leaders to recruit employees based on their strengths which will enhance the organisations productivity and work culture. Organisations need employees who can work in teams and willing to challenge the problem arising at workplace with positive perspective with confidence. These factors encourage them to perform and improve their productivity and also focus on developing their competencies than tearing them down. Periodic feedback, recognition, positive perspective helps enhances employees to achieve better output even if it's systematic assignments. Positive leaders understand the challenges at workplace and approach them with positive perspective. They look at these challenges as opportunities to perform based on the competencies and abilities of the team and self. They feel self-assured that they can overcome the challenges they encounter at workplace by reducing workplace stress levels: enhances productivity, problem solving, decision making abilities, resiliency, better interaction with teams avoiding conflicts etc. [9]. Positive workplace has various benefits in terms of motivating employees to have better engagement at workplace and being happier. Employees who are satisfied and happier surpass expectations and have a longer life cycle with the organisation. Example: Kjerulf, Alexander founding member of Woohoo Inc., stated that, "Happiness is the ultimate productivity booster" and employees who are cheerful at workplace exhibit more optimism, better leadership skills and manage their time well. They also practice positive leadership via improving competency, recognition and having optimistic perspective.

7. Being proactive and also encouraging team members to take initiative

Leaders need to explore the opportunities for employees learning and growth. Leaders have to realise and explore the potential strengths of employees together for their success. Innovation and critical feedback is necessary for the progression of the organisation. Leaders need to look at solutions rather than problems and ask the right questions to employees to help them look at different perspective. Example: the Apple way of looking at things "Is it possible for a phone to do more than make calls?" When leaders empower and provide opportunities to co-create and enable employees to feel wound up to initiate proactive behaviours and continue to face experiment with assignments without burning out. These factors build the self-confidence of the team members as they see their leader's positive perspective. Employees exhibit more engagement at workplace when there are passionate about they work and have a good work life balance. Employees who are proactive are looking at futuristic roles, assignments and projects by anticipating the requirements, challenges and likely consequences. They demonstrate their affirmative behaviour in terms of volunteering them to support their team member when their have issues in their projects. These behaviours exhibit their leadership skills.

8. Positive psychology plays a significant role in the human behaviour and it is not about a feel-good concept

Today's leaders have a lopsided influence on place of work's positivity and undermined its influence to improve organisational efficiency. The essential physiognomies that standout amid effective leaders are their positivity in testing times by being authentic to work, share power and empower followers to experience growth and advancement to strive towards assimilation of objectives. Research indicates that positive approaches to empower people and building trust are a must-have leadership trait. Their aptitude to introspect around their feelings and actions in what way it influences employees is extremely go forward and seek for feedback for improvisation. Positive leaders stimulate confidence, grow employee's strengths, positive perspective and recognise one's contribution to transform big picture thinking into certainty [10]. Based on the positive leadership theories (authentic, transformation, ethical, participative, empowering servant leadership), researchers started looking at positive psychology which has a major influence on

Positive Leadership Experiences of Software Professionals in Information Technology Organisations
DOI: http://dx.doi.org/10.5772/intechopen.100805

leader behaviour. The progress of positive leadership theories in the last two decades has lacked "the considerate, developing procedure, putting into practices states that positive leadership still remains an under investigated". The authors defined positive leadership as an individual who aligns closely with business strategy to drive higher level of performance by promoting optimism and focusing on employee's strengths, positive perspective and recognition.

- Positive leaders support their employees to by providing opportunities to perform based on strengths and constructive feedback.

- Appreciate and provide meaningful recognition for employees, that their contributions are valued towards achieving organizational objectives and also motivate them to maintain or enhance their good work.

- Connect between team members and organisational goal through positive relationship and meaningfulness and its outcomes.

- Strengthen and promote contribution goals rather than self-interest goals by building a positive work climate.

9. Positive leadership sub-dimensions

9.1 Recognition

Recognition, reward and appreciation practices by the immediate supervisors at workplace bind employees towards having an affirmative approach in their assignments helping them develop self-efficacy to endure better performance and creating positive reminiscences. Appreciation and recognition influence employees in driving better output efficiency and higher level of engagement. Research indicates that simple recognition increases (31%) productivity in information technology organisation [11], also the performance enhances by (3.1) than negative interactions [12]. When there is encouragement, there is upsurge in employee performance [13] and development leading to employees experiencing a feeling of fulfilment towards the organisation [14]. These factors do create a positive environment for employee's commitment, enthusiasm, rendezvous, achievement, retention. Reward and recognitions means a lot to the employees, it not only creates positive emotions but also enhances one's commitment by creating a psychological feeling of being an integral part of the organisation which is worth more than the reward one receives. It also provides an opportunity to be an ambassador of the organisation and to cultivate an appreciative mind-set and a more collaborative attitude.

9.2 Strength based approach

It is a way of looking at people as resourceful and is based on social work practice theory, highlighting or giving importance to developing individual's self-determination and competency. A holistic and multidisciplinary approach towards promoting individuals wellbeing. Positive leadership is about fostering employee's strengths to effectively build employees competencies or skills towards utilising them for better performance. Research indicates that there is a relationship amid strengths and engagement, which is central towards employee's affirmative experiences at workplace towards better perform. Gallup study indicates that strength-based approach and development leads to increase in sales by (10–19%): profits (14–29%), customer engagement (3–7%) and engaged employees (9–15%). Positive leader's strengths-based approach is more effective focussing on individual's strengths to higher performance. This promotes employees to thrive by enhancing individual's strengths. Strengths-based practice by leaders empowers employees to nurture vigorous and optimistic workplace environment towards excellence.

9.3 Positive perspective

Provides a positive platform towards handling uncertainties, it's about how leaders look at challenges as opportunities and provide governance to achieve organisational objectives. They look at challenges as chance for growth and development. It includes de-catastrophizing setbacks, where leaders control perception and provide support or solution towards solving the problems encountered by the team or individuals in their tasks. From leadership point of view, understanding their one perspective and being rational about employee's view point increase their aptitude to lead and serve better. Leaders adopting positive perspective enhance positive outcomes through solution-oriented perspective [8, 15, 16]. The key constituent of resilience is about having a solution approach to problems encountered. When leaders have an optimistic perspective they look at solution than problems and have higher resilience. Due to this factors team members are not possible to flounder in frustration and dissuasion. They confront obstacles head-on, regain lost impetus, and move forward along with team in achieving their objectives. Sometime every individual comes across an uphill situation or tasks. How they handle these situations with positivity matters as set-backs are temporary, having positive perspective is key towards well-being.

10. Methodology

The study adopted judgmental and stratified sampling to identify the organisations and the employees need for administrating the questionnaire in information technology organisations (ITOs). The inclusion criteria for the employee to qualify for participating in the study was that they must have been employed in the current organisation for 18 months and have minimum experience of 36 months in ITO. About 1800 questionnaires were distributed and 983 fully completed questionnaires were compiled for analysis (54.6% response rate).

Positive leadership measure (PLM), designed by Arakawa and Greenberg [11] was adopted. It measures positive leadership and its sub-dimensions—(i) strengths-based approach (five items), (ii) positive perspective (five items) and (iii) recognition (seven items). The scale consists of twenty (20) items (17 items and (3) three open-ended qualitative questions) with Cronbach's α = 0.885 for the entire scale. Each sub dimension had one open-ended question. Two (2) items were reverse coded. This chapter only focuses on the qualitative analysis of the three sub-dimensions of positive leadership.

The data collected, aided in reporting the perception of the software professionals about their immediate supervisor's positive leadership practices they experienced. The interview was scheduled for a period of 15 min with three open-ended questions addressed to the participant. The design incorporated in framing the questions to map how they perceived their immediate supervisor's strength based approach, positive perspective approach and recognition practices at workplace. The three open-ended questions provided an opportunity for the employees to share their perception or experiences on the three sub-dimensions of positive leadership as experienced from their immediate supervisor. The researcher believes that the employee's perception of experiencing positive

Positive Leadership Experiences of Software Professionals in Information Technology Organisations
DOI: http://dx.doi.org/10.5772/intechopen.100805

leadership practices at workplace would be influenced by their immediate supervisor's positive leadership behaviour or practices exhibited at workplace. The responses provided by the sample were classified under the three sub-dimension of positive leadership relating to approaches of strength based, positive perspective and appreciation and recognition. The responses were stratified into positive and negative responses. Further the statements were content analysed to calculate and examine certain words, their meaning etc. to examine the leadership behaviours experienced by employees at workplace based on the sub-dimension of positive leadership. **Strength based responses** were further segregated into immediate supervisors develop strengths to perform better via (a) encouragement, support, guidance and similar tasks, (b) provide feedback for improvement, (c) opportunity to learn and develop via technology support, training programs and mentoring, (d) do not develop their strengths. **Positive perspective responses** were based on immediate supervisor's emotional support, towards his team members via (a) providing positive interpretation to past experiences to solve problems, (b) assign another technical resource for support and guidance, (c) participate in problem solving exercise, provide alternate views and solves problems, (d) do not support or participate when problems arise. **Appreciation and recognition responses** were grouped in to how often the immediate supervisor uses appreciation, acknowledges and encourages i.e. (a) once in a way, (b) sometimes, (c) frequently or regularly, (d) quarterly or during appraisals. These responses were calculated in percentage to understand the importance of these sub-themes and their influence on the team members towards enhancing their positive outcomes at workplace.

11. Respondent sample

Positive leadership and its sub-dimensions are explored to understand how they influence employees towards positive outcomes based on the study in ITO with a sample of 1800 software professionals.

Nine hundred and eighty three software professionals participated in this study and shared their feedback on positive leadership behaviour of their immediate supervisor. Male (60%) male and women (40%) participated in the study. They are working in the current ITOs for more than 18 months and been a software professional for more than three years.

12. Results

The results indicate that the employee's experienced positive leadership practices due to of their immediate supervisors at workplace. They exhibited affirmative behaviour at workplace which created an optimistic environment influencing employees to perform. They also supported and provided solution orientation suggestions to the challenges faced at workplace to achieve the objectives. They emphasised on developing team member's strengths towards better execution of tasks and also appreciated and rewarded their contributions towards the projects or tasks.

The employees indicated that they experiencing strength-based approach @ 76% i.e. appreciate team member's strengths, focus on their development and match competence as per tasks. The supervisors exhibited support and encouragement at workplace by developing individual strengths. That is "appreciating employees' strengths, matching talents to tasks, and focusing on strengths more than weaknesses". Around 37% expressed that their immediate supervisors provided positive feedback and support to learn and develop for improving the competency. Around 29% expressed there was opportunity towards learning in terms of training programs, workshops and webinars. Apart from technical support and mentoring by supervisors.10% felt, they were given similar task based on their strengths to excel in their assignment. However, 30% felt there was no effort from their supervisors to develop their strengths.

The open end question asked respondent if the supervisor supported by appreciating individual competence, provided assignments as per their strengths and paid less attention towards their weakness. Encouragement of supervisors through (a) mentoring and coaching, (b) training programs, (c) provide similar task as per strength were experienced under strength based approach.

Sample positive responses were:

R6: supervisor provides work based on my skills, which creates confidence in me to perform.
R667: uses my strength in situations I would not have thought of. Makes me realise my potential.
R858: she identifies the gap in my performance and encourages me to fix the gap and improve the strength.

Sample negative or neutral responses were:

R26. does not develop our strength, just interested in getting the work done.
R510: not really. By providing opportunities and forcing you to build your strength on your own.
R579: we have good training support system and career development programs. Supervisors shares information and does not support much in our development.

Employees experienced appreciation and recognition @ 86.5% i.e. frequent encouragement, appreciation and rewards for team-member's accomplishments. Among the employees who share their perspectives, 64.2% say that there is some kind of appreciation and recognition at workplace. At least once in a way or sometimes they are acknowledged for their contribution. Around 13.6% say they experience frequent, regular or monthly recognition and 8.2% say once in a quarter or during their appraisal (half-yearly or annual) they are recognised. In contrast, 23.5% did not experience the support of immediate supervisors in their development, among them 13% felt there was no support or guidance and 14% felt there was lack of recognition and encouragement. The open ended question elicited experiences if employees experienced recognition and acknowledgement for their contribution by their immediate supervisors.

Sample positive responses were:

R180: he sends out a mail to the team recognising and appreciating the accomplishment or shares it in the team meeting. It is almost instantaneous...
R302: regularly, through mails appreciating the good work, rewards with smileys, recommend for reward and recognition.
R525: quite often, recognises our performance. Both formally and informally.
R976: every quarterly, appreciates during team meetings and nominates for rewards.

Sample negative or neutral responses were:

R91: at our level, we do not expect these, as we need to be self-motivated and accountable.

Positive Leadership Experiences of Software Professionals in Information Technology Organisations
DOI: http://dx.doi.org/10.5772/intechopen.100805

R633: really every senior has to encourage and recognise for juniors and has to motivate the people to achieve the committed targets.
R866: no recognition or encouragement for any amount of hard work and accomplishment done.

Employees experienced immediate supervisor's positive perspective @ 87% i.e. de-catastrophizing stumbling block, emotive coping, solution orientation, and positive elucidation of issues. Around 61% of the employees expressed they receive good support and guidance whenever they need assistance. They support them by sharing their experience to solve the issue or they themselves do it. Around 19% says that their supervisors dive deep to understand the root cause, make them understand the issue and provide solutions. Around 7% say that their supervisors assign another resource for technical support when required. Around 13% expressed that their immediate supervisor's never demonstrated positive perspective, which indicates there was no support or guidance in their assignments even if they required completing the tasks. The open ended question asked if the immediate supervisor was very supportive, addressed their project issues and were empathetic towards them.
Sample positive responses were:

R2: take up the issue from where it could not be resolved at my end.
R266: gives a patient hearing to the issues faced, understand the issues and suggest measure to overcome the problem.
R302: corrective action by analysing the problem and helping us to understand the issue. Make us re-do the work based on his inputs. Suggests alternatives and also solves the problem.
R565: guide me on what i can do better and what is important for delivery.

Sample negative or neutral responses were:

R653: no support, it's a daily routine, so need to manage on own.
R866: fault finding/identify a scape goat in the project.

These responses of all the three dimensions of positive leadership describe the software professional's emotions or perceptions about their positive leadership experiences at the workplace. This provided an understanding about the importance of how virtuous behaviour is vital at workplace and these behaviours are the basic qualities that enhance the well-being and happiness of employees. When leaders understand and recognise the importance of practicing virtuous behaviour at workplace it will lead to positive organisational outcomes.

13. Discussion

The fundamental characteristics that stand out among positive leaders are their heliotropic effect across situations, and authenticity to serve both in the group and out-group members, share power as well empower members to experience growth and development by striving towards wholeness and integration of goals. The study significantly indicates that employees do experience affirmative and virtuous behaviour at the workplace, demonstrated by their immediate supervisor which influences them towards positive performance or outcomes. The leader's positive practices enhanced the team members rendezvous and well-being due to the positive leadership approaches. The supervisors exhibited positive deviance at workplace via (i) respect individuals and acknowledge them as the first customer at the workplace, (ii) shape optimism, formulate positive strategy and introduce positive organisational design, (iii) engage employees and deliver better results through trust and empowerment, (iv) not only focus on hard behaviours, but unleash the softer behaviour to experience independence and autonomy in a true sense of employees. The leaders need to cultivate and manage a combination of technical, business and people management skills to manage projects and teams effectively in ITO. When they exhibit affirmative behaviour, it creates an environment trust and empowerment at work place. These factors support them to manage challenges better, and ensure holistic employee engagement, resulting thereby in enhanced stakeholder management. Importantly, they play the role of a facilitator, a coach and a mentor, an observer and supervisor. By and large, they look to develop competences that are essential for developing via providing positive perspective and recognising the accomplishments.

Positive leaders have a clear sense of resolution towards achieving the organisational objectives and to develop employee's competencies aligned with the organisational objectives. They allow employees to participate and work on the strengths or competencies to perform well. Due to which they set clear expectation and direction for team members to achieve. Among the positive leadership sub-dimensions, immediate supervisor's positive perspective had the highest traction. This could be due to leaders playing an (i) significant role in managing uncertainty of change and (ii) controlling the perceptions and implementation of strategies that reduce the stumbling blocks, and looks at the pitfalls as an opportunity for growth and development. The leaders with positive perspective demonstrate resilience in terms of developing employee's character and gravity of their capabilities by sharing their experiences and perspective in handling the challenging situation or assignments at workplace. The ability to be authentic, trust their team and analysis the issue either by providing solutions or recommending alternative measures are appreciated. They not only inspire and influence the teams but build organisational capability via team building and manage change to perform and deliver under pressure. At the same time through strength based approach enhance the performance of the team towards organisational objectives. They encourage and recognise team members which motivate them to work more cohesively, share statistical data or information and also engage with one another towards achieve the set objectives and have positive solutions towards problems encountered. Positive leaders are resilient and therefore do better in challenging situations and also reinforce preferred performance from employees. They exhibit that via recognising the employees for their contribution influences others to perform better and build a positive image of the organisational practices. These factors recognise the leader's affirmative behaviour, winning attitude and momentum and sustainability to deliver against all odds.

14. Theoretical implications and future research

The study supports the theoretical models of broaden-and-build theory, contingency theory and put forward that characteristics demonstrated by positive leadership based on the application of positive behavioural principles emerging from disciplines such as positive psychology [3] and positive organisational psychology [4] and positive change [5], where leader's positive approach and virtuous behaviour enhances empowerment, trust, engagement and flourishing. Further studies can look at the impact of trust, psychological capital directly and indirectly on employee's happiness and productivity via positive leadership. Another area to

Positive Leadership Experiences of Software Professionals in Information Technology Organisations
DOI: http://dx.doi.org/10.5772/intechopen.100805

explore is efficacy of constructive feedback through leaders and supervisor-team member relationship [17] can be investigated empirically to state whether positive leadership adds to the literature with reference to the relationship at workplace. The motivational theories that explore delegation of responsibilities call for more trust in workplace can be furthered investigated to understand how they lead to positive outcomes and enhance the team member's competencies to perform more effectively [18]. The study also aids forthcoming researchers to investigate other possible positive leadership variables among employees in the IT organisations. Longitudinal empirical studies to support a robust association among positive leadership variable using new empirical models, such as authentic leadership, servant leadership, ethical and transformational leadership can be explored. Study positive leadership behaviour only among women employees to understand 'gender-balanced and inclusive leadership' to attract, retain and develop talented women workforce for leadership roles in the IT Organisations.

15. Practical implication

Organisational leaders directly impact both organisation and its people. So it's important for leaders to practice positive deviant performance, so employees can accept change and work towards the set objectives. The research indicates that application of positive leadership does create a difference in terms of out-put efficiency, employee-satisfaction, and well-being at workplace [6]. When organisations practice and encourage virtuous behaviour, positive emotions and self-determination at workplace, it leads to flourishing environment.

The following practiced must be encouraged at workplace for better outcomes

- Creating positive climate through 'positive' communication, relationship and meaning towards optimistic social exchanges for better performances

- Develop authentic relationships, virtues, and acknowledging contribution of every individuals

- Promote empowerment, teamwork and collaboration having positive perspectives

- Strengthen employees' competencies to perform, and achieve mastery in their domain through mentoring and coaching

- Practice frequent recognition and appreciation to engage better towards well-being

16. Limitations

The present investigation contributes to positive leadership and its behavioural consequences of software professionals the study included only software professionals restricting its generalizability. The self-report technique brings about the respondents' emotional state, attitudes, and views and opinions at one point in time and hence it suffers from common method bias. Though the researcher used a globally proven scale, to measure the relationship and employee experience on the constructs. It was not treated to find out if it was culture free and culture fair.

17. Conclusion

Positive leaders do not merely create positive emotions at workplace but enhance organisational performance. This study increases the understanding of positive leadership and its sub-dimensions, vis a vis how it influences employees and positive outcomes in organisations. What differentiates positive leaders from the rest is the positive deviance and the approach adopted strategies for "extraordinary performance by creating positive climate, building relationship, communication and meaning" [6]. They explore for opportunities to capitalise in employees who work with them towards increasing the positive emotions of both. "Positive Psychology" is not about feel-good activity or false synchronisation. Leaders have a disproportionate influence on workplace positivity. So it's important to be positive and to spread optimism in their workplace. As negative temperaments need to be bottled-up, due to their "infectious" nature as leader's positive approach creates an aura towards positive outcomes. Employees acquire through positivity by placing their stumbling block and botches in circumstance as chances to build "resilience" and practice modus operandi for cultivating one's positivity. Positive leadership brings "positivity" a business concept than can get-up-and-go after engagement and output-efficiency. They build a positive workforce, align employees 'character, role and accountability as per their strength and strengthen positivity by frequent recognition for their hard contributions. As organisational leaders, engage employees for their optimism, cultural fit and reasoning for better performance. Skills, experience and knowledge are secondary. Positive leader's increases positive emotions within their organisation and team spirit. They choose this style for improving morale and performance by enhancing job satisfaction and higher level of engagement. Further, it provides inputs to design employee growth, development and retention strategies in Indian ITOs. Positive organisational leaders influence and mentorship would reduce internal competition for mutual benefit (i.e. both for the employee & the employer), while enhancing the spirit of support, collaboration and teamwork, which would go a long way in creating a holistic and positive work environment.

Author details

Harold Andrew Patrick[1], Sunil Kumar Ramdas[1*] and Jacqueline Kareem[2]

1 CMS Business School, Jain University, India

2 Christ University, India

*Address all correspondence to: rsunilkr@rediffmail.com

IntechOpen

© 2022 The Author(s). Licensee IntechOpen. This chapter is distributed under the terms of the Creative Commons Attribution License (http://creativecommons.org/licenses/by/3.0), which permits unrestricted use, distribution, and reproduction in any medium, provided the original work is properly cited.

References

[1] Fry LW, Cohen MP. Spiritual leadership as a paradigm for organizational transformation and recovery from extended work hours cultures. Journal of Business Ethics. 2009;**84**:265-278. DOI: 10.1007/s10551-008-9695-2

[2] Fairholm GW. Spiritual leadership: Fulfilling whole-self needs at work. Leadership & Organization Development Journal. 1996;**17**(5):11-17. DOI: 10.1108/01437739610127469

[3] Seligman MEP. Positive social science. The APA Monitor Online. Vol. 29. No. 4. 1998. Available from: http://www.apa.org/monitor/apr98/pres.html

[4] Cameron KS, Dutton JE, Quinn RE. Positive Organizational Scholarship—Foundations of a New Discipline. San Francisco, CA: Berrett-Koehler Publishers; 2003

[5] Cooperrider DL, Srivastva S. Appreciative inquiry in organizational life. Research in Organizational Change and Development. 1987;**1**:129-169

[6] Cameron KS. Positive Leadership: Strategies for Extraordinary Performance. San Francisco, CA: Berrett-Koehler; 2012

[7] Ramdas SK, Patrick HA. Psychological empowerment experiences of software professionals in post lockdown information technology organisations. Transnational Marketing Journal. 2021;**9**(2):301-318. DOI: 10.33182/tmj.v9i2.1577

[8] Youssef-Morgan CM, Luthans F. Positive leadership: Meaning and application across cultures. Organizational Dynamics. 2013;**42**:198-208. DOI: 10.1016/j.orgdyn.2013.06.005

[9] Ramdas SK, Patrick HA. Driving performance through positive leadership. Journal of Positive Management. 2018;**9**(3):17-33. DOI: 10.12775/JPM.2018.146

[10] Bennis W. The leadership advantage. Leader to Leader. 1999;**12**:18-23. DOI: 10.1002/ltl.40619991205

[11] Arakawa D, Greenberg M. Optimistic managers and their influence on productivity and employee engagement in a technology organisation: Implications for coaching psychologists. International Coaching Psychology Review. 2007;**2**(1):78-89

[12] Fredrickson BL, Losada MF. Positive affect and complex dynamics of human flourishing. American Psychologist. 2005;**60**:678-686

[13] Kouzer MJ, Posner ZB. Encouraging the Heart: A leader's guide to rewarding and recognizing others. Jossey –Bass, San Francisco, Calif, Jossey-Bass. http://www.books24x7.com/marc.asp?bookid=4838

[14] Henryhand CJ. The effect of employee recognition and employee engagement on job satisfaction and intent to leave in the public sector [thesis]. 2009. https://www.proquest.com/openview/9f1df00711437559b64536f4b482a7af/1.pdf?pq-origsite=gscholar&cbl=18750

[15] Zbierowski P, Góra K. Positive leadership: Its nature, antecedents and consequences. Journal of Positive Management. 2014;**5**(1):85-99. DOI: 10.12775/JPM.2014.008

[16] Ramdas SK, Patrick HA. Positive leadership behaviour and flourishing: The mediating role of trust in information technology organizations. South Asian Journal of Human Resources Management. 2019;**6**(2):258-277. DOI: 10.1177/2322093719870024

[17] Gerstner CR, Day D. Meta-analytic review of leader-member exchange theory: Correlates and construct issues. Journal of Applied Psychology. 1997;**82**:827-844. DOI: 10.1037// 0021-9010.82.6.827

[18] Wegner J. The manifestations of positive leader roles in classical theories of leadership. Journal of Corporate Responsibility and Leadership. 2016;**3**(3):91-104. DOI: 10.12775/ JCRL.2016.018

Chapter 10

Process Management: A Requirement for Organizational Excellence in the Twenty-First Century Business Environment?

Ken Kalala Ndalamba and Euzália do Rosário Botelho Tomé

Abstract

The purpose of this study is to define process management as a requirement of organizational excellence in the twenty-first century business environment. The business environment in the twenty-first century has reached a new height as far as challenges are concerned. The Covid-19 pandemic and its consequences have shaped a new business environment that requires organizations and businesses to raise the bar for themselves in honoring their obligation to achieve excellence. This means that competitive advantage, quality service, and product are achieved through organizational excellence. How can process management help organizations and businesses achieve organizational excellence in such a hostile and turbulent business environment? Applying a conceptual approach, the study attempts to answer the question through a comprehensive literature review. Testable propositions have been formulated, action steps defined, and implications of the study established. By identifying workflow design (WFD), control and correction of workflow processes (CCWFP), monitoring of workflow processes (MWFP), and workflow promotion of process-related learning in organizations (WPPRLO) against the background of conceptualization, operationalization, and context, the study findings suggest that process management is indeed a requirement for organizational excellence in the twenty-first century business environment. Scholars and practitioners have the opportunity to confirm or disconfirm the validity of the assumptions and ideas presented in the study.

Keywords: twenty-first century, business environment, Covid-19, organizational excellence process management, product quality, service quality, workflow

1. Introduction

The emergence of the Covid-19 pandemic in late 2019 and its gradual spreading across the globe in 2020 urged countries to shut down businesses as the global efforts to fight the pandemic [1]. Such measures signaled the new height that the business environment in the twenty-first century has reached as far as challenges are concerned.

The Covid-19 pandemic and its consequences have shaped a new business environment that has raised strain on the relationship between businesses, customers, and suppliers requiring organizations and businesses to be at their very best if they are to survive in such an environment. In other words, the new business environment compels organizations and businesses to sustain their competitive advantage through excellence.

Twenty-first century organizational development (OD) scholars Harrington [2], Rad [3], Dahlgaard-Park [4], Brown [5], and Samawi et al. [6] identified process management (PM) as a critical success factor for organizational excellence (OE). Although much has been written about business process management (BPM), the concept of process management in organizations (PMO) is not widely understood, is far more complex than is commonly perceived.

The purpose of this study is to examine the importance of process management as a requirement for organizational excellence. Six testable propositions about process management have presented that address the nature of process management and organizational excellence.

Based on a comprehensive literature review [7], the study begins with an examination of the complex nature of excellence and organizational excellence. After defining process management, the study identifies key elements considered integration facilitating factors and six propositions that practitioners and scholars can test to assess the nature of that process management. The study concludes by identifying five contributions and suggests opportunities for additional research.

2. Organizational excellence: a conceptual framework

Excellence is conceived as "superiority, greatness, distinction" [8]. To excel implies "to do or be better than; surpass; to show superiority, surpass others". In other words, excellence can describe, in the words of Paul, "whatever is true, whatever is honorable, whatever is just, whatever is pure, whatever is lovely, whatever is gracious, if there is any excellence, if there is anything worthy of praise" [4].

Scholars and practitioners have scrutinized the word "excellence" in an attempt to establish its essence. From a practical perspective, countries and regions across the globe attempted to establish particular frameworks of excellence. The European foundation for quality management (EFQM), for instance, considers adding value for customers, creating a sustainable future, developing organizational capability, harnessing creativity and innovation, leading with vision, inspiration, and integrity, managing with agility, succeeding through the talent of people and sustaining outstanding results, as attributes of excellence [9]. In Australia, leadership, strategy and planning, data, information and knowledge, people, customer and market focus, innovation, quality and improvement, success, and sustainability are all regarded defining factors of the business excellence framework [10].

The Malcolm Baldrige National Quality Award (MBNQA) in the USA, considers leadership, strategic planning, customer and market focus, information and analysis, human resources focus, and process management as quality associated with excellence [11]. The same applies to the Canada Awards for Excellence program, which promotes leadership, governance, strategy, planning, customer experience, employee engagement, innovation, and wellness as qualities for excellence [12]. The Union of Japanese Scientists and Engineers (JUSE) is consistent with the above-mentioned frameworks of excellence by considering organization and its management, education, quality information, planning, analysis, standardization, control, quality assurance, and results as contributing factors to excellence [13]. It is evident that practitioners, by pursuing quality as an end, established excellence as means. Therefore, by establishing a framework of excellence it is more likely to have quality as an outcome.

Process Management: A Requirement for Organizational Excellence in the Twenty-First Century...
DOI: http://dx.doi.org/10.5772/intechopen.101769

While practitioners converged their views on the concept of excellence, OD scholars have over decades invested in research with a view of developing a framework for OE [5, 14–19].

For many scholars, such a framework encompasses the likes of performance of management, knowledge as a source of value creation, culture, and values of the organization, sustainable change, measures relating to leadership, processes, people, communication, and strategy to mention but a few.

Literature suggests that organizational effectiveness (OEf) was previously the focus of scholarly debates. In this respect, Yuchtman and Seashore consider the concept effectiveness deficient for making reference to goal attainment. For the authors when the term effectiveness is associated to the organization this should emphasize both the distinctiveness of the organization as an identifiable social structure and the interdependence of the organization with its environment [20]. The conceptual conflict amongst scholars led Connolly et al. to propose a "multiple-constituency" approach to the concept [21].

The proposed approach assumes that an organization's different constituencies will form different assessments of its effectiveness. Quinn and Rohrbaugh went further arguing in favor of what they refer to as "a competing values approach to organizational effectiveness" [22]. This approach encompasses three value dimensions including focus (task—people), structure (control—flexibility), and time (short-term—long-term).

Dragging the conceptual debates, Cameron's view is consistent with Quinn et al. by arguing that organizational effectiveness is a construct that is grounded in the values and preferences of evaluators [23]. Consequently, no single and correct concept exists. For Cameron, the approaches that emerged over time attempted to address specific purposes which prompted scholars to conceptualize effectiveness in the organization in various ways including matching the ideal characteristics of a bureaucratic organization, accomplishing goals, obtaining needed resources, satisfying important stakeholders, high quality internal processes, the presence of simultaneous opposites, producing flourishing and virtuousness. These are all useful approaches to assessing and producing valuable outcomes.

Significantly is the "4P" model (people' partnership, processes, and products). The model, by assuming that "excellent products and services are a result of building excellence into people, partnership and processes, and this requires a strong foundation—leadership", shifted the paradigm from organizational effectiveness (OEf) to organizational excellence—OE [4]. Interestingly, the "4P" model integrates both the mechanistic and organic approaches to organizational management pointing at leadership as the integration facilitating factor. The significance of the approach lies in the fact that OE can be achieved and sustained when variables from both the mechanistic and organic approaches complement one another.

Moreover, many research favors the organic approach for promoting the human resource dimension and its critical role in organization management. Such is the view of Alan Brown who affirms that "Organizations that fail to adopt an organic approach are unlikely to embed quality and excellence and engage both managers and employees. Without these key ingredients, sustainability is unlikely, and their quality efforts are likely to remain at the tool pusher and drifter stages" [5]. Importantly, the success of the organic approach is measured through the effectiveness of the mechanistic approach. Therefore, the need to establish well-functioning workflow processes that should guarantee the intended and expected quality as an outcome.

3. Process management: A concept and its scope

It is widely acknowledged that efficient and effective process management improves organizational dynamism, readiness, and reactiveness capability to challenges [24–27]. Scholars including Wagner and Patzak argue that leading companies without PM are no longer imaginable [28].

While its main objective is to increase efficiency and effectiveness, the understanding of the concept in both theory and practice revealed a mutual contradiction in some aspects along the years [29]. If not addressed adequately such inconsistencies may harm the very notion of PM by leaving gaps in the understanding and practice of PM. Therefore, the need to engage scholars and practitioners to address the inconsistencies in the understanding and practice of PM within the context of the twenty-first century.

Paim and Flexa conceptualize PM as "a coordinated set of permanent tasks required to design processes and assure they function properly and to foster process-related learning" [30]. Evidently, PM is all about aligning processes with the strategic goals of an organization. In this respect, business process management (BPM) has been the focus of many studies over several decades restricting the very concept of PM to business only. Moreover, the scope of PM in this study goes beyond business. It is broader involving both for-profit and not-for-profit organizations.

Research reveals that the call for the shift or integration between the traditional functional management model with the famous "business process management" approach has proved challenging [31]. However, the lack of a universally accepted definition of BPM does not stop scholars and practitioners from attaching connotations to it. Significantly, people involvement through the leadership of the line managers is the most important component that BPM offers to process management favoring the organic approach to management [32].

To this effect, Kohlbacher stresses that BPM goes beyond designing, developing, and executing business processes. It promotes interaction between these processes, managing and analyzing, and optimizing them [33]. On this basis, literature considers

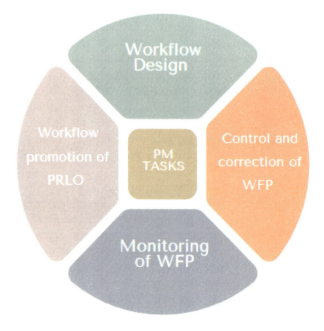

Figure 1.
PM tasks.

Process Management: A Requirement for Organizational Excellence in the Twenty-First Century...
DOI: http://dx.doi.org/10.5772/intechopen.101769

the following as tasks associated with process management: the design, monitoring, control, and correction of processes, and the promotion of process-related learning in organizations [24, 30, 34, 35]. These tasks are summed up in **Figure 1**.

3.1 Workflow design (WFD)

Scholars and practitioners identify workflow design as an engineering activity that schemes and shapes what they refer to as the sequential tasks involved to take an item from "initiated" to "processed" one step at a time. Significantly the activity requires an intention to contrive for a purpose [36–38].

Research suggests that workflow design is based on the structure and characteristics of the product [39, 40]. These premises prompted Reijers et al. to offer a method referred to as product-based workflow design (PBWD) [41]. The authors argue that PBWD takes the product specification and three design criteria as a starting point, after which formal models and techniques are used to derive a favorable new design of the workflow process. Consistent with Reijers et al., Lee and Suh established and recommended a workflow matrix (WfM) with a view to analyze and reengineer strategies to improve the design process [42]. For the author, Workflow design establishes well-defined procedures and an operational-level sophisticated workflow.

Held and Blochinger enriched the workflow design discussion by introducing a concept of the collaborative workflow design. The concept combines cooperation and workflow model analysis [43]. Held and Blochinger argue that workflow design is often an effort of distributed and heterogeneous teams, therefore making tool support for collaboration a necessity.

The above scholars' discussion has brought to the shore the utmost importance of workflow design. On the basis of the arguments presented by scholars, workflow design enables organizations and businesses to see their entire activity processes and how data moves seamlessly from step to step. Therefore, workflow design is an indispensable strategy towards OE.

3.2 Control and correction of workflow processes (CCWFP)

The success of a workflow design rests upon the resilience of its structures. This implies how robust, effective and efficient the process structures are when facing pressure. Thus the need for control and correction of workflow processes on a regular and permanent basis. Control means "to check the accuracy of, verify; to regulate," [44]. On this basis, control and correction of workflow processes are mostly methodical and technical support activities that aim at identifying the strengths and weaknesses of the process structures.

Ideally, the strategy, with regard to weaknesses, in particular, would be to reduce and or transform them into strengths to reinforce the resilience capability of the process structures. In this way, the desired outcomes are most likely to be achieved because of the continuous improvement of the process structures.

3.3 Monitoring of workflow processes (MWFP)

Monitoring is understood as a general sense of "observe, keep under review, to guide" [45]. Characterized by a broader scope, monitoring of workflow processes entails keeping track of and gathering data about the performance of workflow processes.

Previous studies indicate that monitoring is "a continuing function that aims primarily to provide... an ongoing intervention with early indications of progress, or lack thereof, in the achievement of results" [46]. Importantly, monitoring offers a "metric for tracking progress towards project goals through a logical framework documenting intermediate and long-term measurable objectives" [47].

Consistent with the above, the monitoring process starts with the definition of a logical framework that establishes a pragmatic approach to monitoring. Such an approach should ensure that actions are taken in order to "frequently facilitate the need to modify processes that can be used in instances where there are limited resources, limited financial capital, and limited human capital to determine whether programs and projects have had an impact" [48]. Unless monitoring of workflow processes is done effectively, control and correction of workflow processes will be undermined and thus jeopardize the outcome.

3.4 Workflow promotion of process-related learning in organizations (WPPRLO)

PM tasks are activities that promote learning experiences in organizations by linking research to practice with respect to workflow processes. From business and management perspectives, learning is key to both survival and success [49]. The significance of learning organizations has been discussed over the years. Scholars' arguments are consistent in suggesting that a learning organization is one that builds and strengthens resilience capabilities to secure the intended outcome [50, 51].

Design, control, and monitoring of workflow processes constitute an integrated approach to the workflow management cycle (WFMC). As such, a benchmark of learning organizations.

It transpires, from the above, that the successful implementation of process management relies on the efficiency and effectiveness with which its four tasks are executed. Thus the need to shift to or integrate BPM because of the promotion of people involvement in the process. This suggests that unless workflow processes are managed adequately through perfect execution of the above-identified tasks, it will prove difficult to affect the efficiency of an organization's actions and development—improving organizational dynamism, readiness, and reactiveness capability to face challenges of the global business environment [52, 53].

4. Process management and organizational excellence: the integration facilitating factor (IFF)

Research reveals that OE can be achieved and sustained when variables from both mechanistic and organic approaches complement one another. Furthermore, the success of the organic approach is measured through the effectiveness of the mechanistic approach. Hence, the need to establish well-functioning workflow processes that would guarantee the intended and expected quality of the outcome.

PM is recognized as one of the pillars for OE [2, 5, 6]. On the evidence of the discussed WFMC, it has become transparent that organizations cannot achieve excellence if WFMC is not established and does not function effectively and efficiently to produce quality bound outcomes. WFMC is an execution of PM tasks—design, control, monitoring of workflow processes, and workflow promotion of process-related learning in organizations. Therefore, OE is perceived as a means to a quality outcome. It depends on the successful implementation of PM from a mechanistic perspective. **Figure 2** below captures the process.

Figure 2 above, presents the relationship between PM and OE which leads to quality of service or product. However, the effectiveness of PM depends on three conditions namely conceptualization and operationalization of PM, and the context

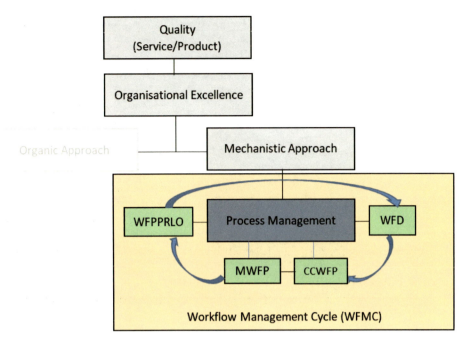

Figure 2.
An integration of PM and OE.

in which PM is implemented [54]. These conditions determine when and how PM may have a stronger or weaker impact on OE.

4.1 Conceptualization and operationalization

Conceptualization and operationalization of PM encompass how formal, participatory and comprehensive PM has been defined and established. PM is a formal process because it incorporates and promotes a systematic way (e.g. thinking, doing, and applying) to reaching a possible outcome. This is bureaucracy by excellence [55–59]. It is participatory because it encompasses the involvement of all stakeholders (e.g. the superior and subordinate) in the process, therefore consistent with the theory of management by objectives [60–62]. The comprehensiveness refers to how aligned both employees and the management are. It emerges as a result of PM formality and the participation of the stakeholders in the process. Our first three propositions reflect the impact of these the integration facilitating factors between PM and OE:

P1: Formalized processes in organizations are most likely to be managed with efficiency and effectiveness for establishing a systematic way of completing tasks (doing things).

P2: Organizations that involve all the stakeholders (i.e. employees and the management) in the design and operationalization of processes are most likely to achieve success in formalizing processes.

P3: Unless all the stakeholders (i.e. employees and the management) are involved in the conceptualization and operationalization of processes, it would prove challenging to share a common understanding and comprehend the workflow management cycle.

Therefore, it becomes evident that the conceptualization and operationalization of PM help align the understanding of the workflow management cycle following the involvement of all the stakeholders. Consequently, processes will be engineered and run with efficiency and effectiveness because they have been formalized. When they have been designed to show conformance to standards such as ISO 9001, ISO 14001, and OSHAS 18001 in particular, formalized processes establish consistency in performance and results saving time and money to organizations [63–66].

4.2 Context

The context encompasses the management and administration of public and private organizations in both developed and developing countries. A school of thoughts advances that distinctions between public, private, and non-profit become confusing and misleading because of diverse sets of management settings involved in them [67].

However, practitioners and a growing number of scholars joined Harvard Business School Joseph L. Bower in distinguishing that public management and administration entails dealing with the needs and interests of a nation as a whole [68, 69]. Private management and administration, on the other side, focus on the needs and interests of individuals or a narrower group of people. **Table 1** below illustrates the difference.

Significantly, the difference lies in values. While public management and administration value amongst others sustainability by trying to balance public interest, public needs, and political interests [70]. Private management and administration values promote business profit by focusing on "risk-taking", "customer focus", and "bottom-line orientation" [71, 72].

It is argued that both public and private management and administration in developed countries yield better results than in developing countries. In fact, one of the common characteristics of developing nations is the struggle portrayed in matching the level of results produced by developed nations as far as public management and administration is concerned. Most countries in sub-Saharan Africa are an example of such characteristics. They lag very much behind developed nations in ensuring that everyone benefits equally from provided goods and services such as mail service, public health services, schooling, and highway systems to mention but a few. In the light of the above, the last three propositions read.

P4: Effective management of organizational processes helps generate outputs equal to or beyond the expectations of stakeholders.

P5: Values promoted in either public or private sectors influence the conceptualization and operationalization of organizational processes towards effective management.

P6: Developed and developing country contexts are separated by the ways in which both contexts approach and associate values to organizational process management.

A well-established and functioning PM promotes an organizational culture of excellence. The opposite destroys trust with employees and reduces their commitment and creativity—resulting in lost profits and lowered productivity [73].

Public management	Private management
Entails dealing with and controlling the needs and interests of the whole as a nation	Focuses on narrower needs and interests of an individual or particular groups

Table 1.
The difference between public and private management and administration.

Process Management: A Requirement for Organizational Excellence in the Twenty-First Century...
DOI: http://dx.doi.org/10.5772/intechopen.101769

5. Actions steps

1. Establish firm's strategic plan involving all the stakeholders aiming to earn the trust and commitment of all [74, 75];

2. Conceptualize and operationalize a business workflow with the involvement of all the stakeholders aiming to improve firm productivity and profitability [76];

3. Adopt and adapt to context without losing own identity and culture [77].

6. Implications of the study

In addressing the importance of PM as a requirement for OE in the twenty-first century business environment, this study makes five meaningful contributions:

1. It defines OE within the context of the twenty-first century business environment and its challenges: OE acknowledges both the organic and mechanistic approaches. Focus, however, was on the mechanistic approach (PM). This must be verified at every type of business and organization;

2. It identifies and discusses the tasks of PM within the context of the twenty-first century business environment and its challenges;

3. It clarifies the integration facilitating factor between PM and OE: Each factor plays a significant role to the degree that it seeks to facilitate the integration between PM and OE;

4. It suggests six propositions associated with PM and OE: in framing these propositions, the study identifies the importance of individuals and organizations carefully re-evaluating their missions, choices, and responsibilities;

5. It establishes three actions steps for PM that promote OE: Although many organizations are outstanding examples of OE, each organization and individual has the responsibility to assess their own choices with regard to PM to identify how they can raise the bar for themselves in honoring their obligation to achieve excellence.

Each of these practical implications has value as organizations and businesses seek to achieve excellence, which will result in the trust, followership, commitment, and extra-role behavior of their employees [78].

7. Conclusion

One of the challenges of the twenty-first century business environment is the Covid-19 pandemic. Its consequences have shaped a new business environment requiring excellence in the way in which businesses are conducted. Process management (PM) is identified as a requirement for organizational excellence (OE).

The purpose of the study was to examine the importance of process management as a requirement for organizational excellence. Six testable propositions about process management that addressed the nature of process management and organizational excellence were formulated. Opportunities for future research abound in testing the elements and propositions of this study. Each of the propositions suggests measurable elements of PM and OE that have practical implications for modern organizations.

As organizations and businesses struggle to find their feet in order to earn and retain the trust of those whom they seek to lead and to serve, they require wisdom, experience, and a broad range of skills that are important to understand and establish PM that promotes OE [79]. As scholars and practitioners work together to examine the propositions of this study, they have the opportunity to confirm or disconfirm the validity of the assumptions and ideas contained herein.

Author details

Ken Kalala Ndalamba[1*] and Euzália do Rosário Botelho Tomé[2]

1 Gregório Semedo University (UGS), Luanda, Angola

2 African Field Epidemiology Network (AFENET Angola), Luanda, Angola

*Address all correspondence to: ndalambaken@gmail.com

IntechOpen

© 2021 The Author(s). Licensee IntechOpen. This chapter is distributed under the terms of the Creative Commons Attribution License (http://creativecommons.org/licenses/by/3.0), which permits unrestricted use, distribution, and reproduction in any medium, provided the original work is properly cited.

References

[1] WHO. Timeline: WHO's COVID-19 Response [Internet]. 2021. Available from: https://www.who.int/emergencies/diseases/novel-coronavirus-2019/interactive-timeline [Accessed: August 6, 2021]

[2] Harrington HJ. The five pillars of organizational excellence. Handbook of Business Strategy. 2005;6:107-114

[3] Rad AM, Yarmohammadian MH. A study of relationship between managers' leadership style and employees' job satisfaction. International Journal of Health Care Quality Assurance Incorporating Leadership in Health Services. 2006;19:11-28. DOI: 10.1108/13660750610665008

[4] Dahlgaard-Park SM. Decoding the code of excellence—For achieving sustainable excellence. International Journal of Quality and Service Sciences. 2009;1:5-28

[5] Brown A. Organisational paradigms and sustainability in excellence: From mechanistic approaches to learning and innovation. International Journal of Quality and Service Sciences. 2014;6:181-190

[6] Samawi GA, Abutayeh B, Yosef FA, Mdanat MF, Al-Qatawneh M. Relation between total quality management practices and business excellence: Evidence from private service firms in Jordan. International Review of Management and Marketing. 2018;8:28-35

[7] Gibson CB. Elaboration, generalization, triangulation, and interpretation: On enhancing the value of mixed method research. Organizational Research Methods. 2017;29:193-223

[8] "Excellence", Online Etymology Dictionary, n.d. Available from: https://www.etymonline.com/search?q=excellence [Accessed: August 6, 2021]

[9] EFQM. EFQM Model 2013 [Internet]. 2013. Available from: https://www.efqm.org/ [Accessed: August 23, 2021]

[10] SAI. The Australian Business Excellence Framework [Internet]. 2004. Available from: https://www.saiglobal.com/ [Accessed: August 23, 2021]

[11] NIST. National Institute of Standard and technology: US Department of Commerce [Internet]. 2017. Available from: https://www.nist.gov/ [Accessed: August 23, 2021]

[12] EC. Excellence Canada [Internet]. 2019. Available from: https://excellence.ca/ [Accessed: August 23, 2021]

[13] JUSE. The Union of Japanese Scientists and Engineers [Internet]. 2015. Available from: http://www.juse.or.jp/english/ [Accessed: August 23, 2021]

[14] Zenger J. Training for organisational excellence. Journal of European Industrial Training. 1985;9:3-8

[15] King AS. Criteria for excellence in organization development: Perceptions and actualities. American Journal of Business. 1989;4:29-34

[16] Bornemann M, Sammer M. Assessment methodology to prioritize knowledge management related activities to support organizational excellence. Measuring Business Excellence. 2003;7:21-28

[17] Ringrose D. Development of an organizational excellence framework. The TQM Journal. 2013;25:441-452

[18] Vora MK. Business excellence through sustainable change management. The TQM Journal. 2013;25:625-640

[19] Rao MS. Embrace change effectively to achieve organizational excellence

and effectiveness. Industrial and Commercial Training. 2015;**47**:145-150

[20] Yuchtman E, Seashore SE. A system resource approach to organizational effectiveness. American Sociological Review. 1967;**32**:891-903

[21] Connolly T, Conlon EJ, Deutsch SJ. Organizational effectiveness: A multiple-constituency approach. Academy of Management Review. 1980;**5**:211-217. DOI: 10.5465/amr.1980.4288727

[22] Quinn RE, Rohrbaugh JA. Competing values approach to organizational effectiveness. Public Productivity Review. 1981;**5**:122-144

[23] Cameron K, Organizational Effectiveness. Organizational Behavior. 2015;**11**. DOI: 10.1002/9781118785317.weom110202

[24] Da Silva LA, Damian IP, De Pádua SID. Process management tasks and barriers: Functional to processes approach. Business Process Management Journal. 2012;**18**:762-776

[25] Rialti R, Marzi G, Silic M, Ciappei C. Ambidextrous organization and agility in big data era: The role of business process management systems. Business Process Management Journal. 2018;**24**:1091-1109

[26] Rowell J. Do organisations have a mission for mapping processes? Business Process Management Journal. 2018;**24**:2-22

[27] Zelt S, Recker J, Schmiedel T, Vom Brocke J. A theory of contingent business process management. Business Process Management Journal. 2019;**25**:1291-1316. DOI: 10.1108/BPMJ-05-2018-0129

[28] Wagner KW, Patzak G. Performance Excellence—Der Praxisleitfaden zum effektiven Prozessmanagement. 2nd ed. München: Carl Hanser Verla; 2015

[29] Meerkamm S. The concept of process management in theory and practice—A qualitative analysis. In: Rinderle-Ma S, Sadiq S, Leymann F, editors. Business Process Management Workshops. BPM 2009. Lecture Notes in Business Information Processing. Vol. 43. Berlin, Heidelberg: Springer; 2010. DOI: 10.1007/978-3-642-12186-9_41

[30] Paim R, Flexa R. Process Governance: Definitions and Framework, Part 1 [Internet]. 2011. BPTrends. Available from: https://www.bptrends.com/ [Accessed: August 23, 2021]

[31] Hammer M, Champy J. Business Reengineering—Die Radikalkur für das Unternehmen. 7th ed. Frankfurt, New York: Campus Verlag; 2003

[32] Jeston J, Nelis J. Business Process Management: Practical Guidelines to Successful Implementations. Oxford: Butterworth-Heinemann; 2006

[33] Kohlbacher M. The effects of process orientation: A literature review. Business Process Management Journal. 2010;**16**:135-152

[34] Matuszak-Flejszman A. Product & Process Management: Process Management in Companies. Poznań: Poznań University of Economics and Business; 2018

[35] Ahrens V. Complementarity of project and process management [Internet]. 2018. Available from: https://www.nordakademie.de/ [Accessed: August 23, 2021]

[36] Reijers HA. Design and Control of Workflow Processes: Business Process Management for the Service Industry. Berlin: Springer-Verlag Berlin Heidelberg; 2003

[37] IBM. Workflow design process [Internet]. 2014. Available from: https://www.ibm.com/docs/en/mam/7.6.0?topic=wo-workflow-design-process [Accessed: July 12, 2021]

[38] KF. Workflow Design That Works in the Real World [Internet]. 2019. Available from: https://kissflow.com/workflow/workflow-design-that-works-in-the-real-world/ [Accessed: July 12, 2021]

[39] Vajna S. Workflow for design. In: Clarkson J, Eckert C, editors. Design Process Improvement. London: Springer; 2005. DOI: 10.1007/978-1-84628-061-0_16

[40] Naboni E, Natanian J, Brizzi G, Florio P, Chokhachian A, Galanos T, et al. A digital workflow to quantify regenerative urban design in the context of a changing climate. Renewable and Sustainable Energy Reviews. 2019;**113**. DOI: 10.1016/j.rser.2019.109255

[41] Reijers HA, Limam S, Van der Aalst WMP. Product-Based workflow design. Journal of Management Information Systems. 2003;**20**:229-262. DOI: 10.1080/07421222.2003.11045753

[42] Lee H, Suh HW. Workflow structuring and reengineering method for design process. Computers & Industrial Engineering. 2006;**51**:698-714

[43] Held M, Blochinger W. Structured collaborative workflow design. Future Generation Computer Systems. 2009;**25**:638-653

[44] "Control", Online Etymology Dictionary, n.d. Available from: https://www.etymonline.com/search?q=Control [Accessed: August 6, 2021]

[45] "Monitoring", Online Etymology Dictionary, n.d. Available from: https://www.etymonline.com/search?q=Monitoring [Accessed: August 6, 2021]

[46] World Bank. Monitoring and Evaluation: Tips for Strengthening Organizational Capacity [Internet]. 2007. Available from https://journals.sagepub.com/doi/10.1177/1098214018775845 [Accessed: September 22, 2021]

[47] Aceituno A, Stanhope K, Rebolledo P. Using a monitoring and evaluation framework to improve study efficiency and quality during a prospective cohort study in infants receiving rotavirus vaccination in El Alto, Bolivia: The Infant Nutrition, Inflammation, and Diarrheal Illness (NIDI) study. BMC Public Health. 2017;**17**:911. DOI: 10.1186/s12889-017-4904-5

[48] Myrick D. A logical framework for monitoring and evaluation: A pragmatic approach to M&E. Mediterranean Journal of Social Sciences. 2013;**4**:14. DOI: 10.5901/mjss.2013.v4n14p423

[49] Serrat O. Knowledge Solutions: Tools, Methods, and Approaches to Drive Organizational Performance. Singapore: Springer; 2017

[50] Mills DQ, Friesen B. The learning organization. European Management Journal. 1992;**10**:146-156

[51] Tortorella GL, Vergara AMC, Garza-Reyes JA, Sawhney R. Organizational learning paths based upon industry 4.0 adoption: An empirical study with Brazilian manufacturers. International Journal of Production Economics. 2020;**219**:284-294

[52] Flynn BB, Schroeder RG, Sakakibara S. A framework for quality management research and an associated measurement instrument. Journal of Operations Management. 1994;**11**:339-366

[53] Ahrens V. Complementarity of Project and Process Management, Arbeitspapiere der Nordakademie. Nordakademie. Elmshorn: Hochschule der Wirtschaft; 2018

[54] George B, Walker RM, Monster J. Does strategic planning improve organizational performance? A Meta-Analysis. Public Administration Review. 2019;**79**:810-819

[55] Weber M. Economy and Society: An Outline of Interpretive Sociology. California: University of California Press; 1978

[56] Wilson JQ. Bureaucracy: What Government Agencies do and Why They Do it. New York: Basic Books; 2019

[57] Cornell A, Knutsen CH, Teorell J. Bureaucracy and Growth. Comparative Political Studies. 2020;**53**:2246-2282

[58] Adler PS. The sociological ambivalence of bureaucracy: From Weber to Gouldner to Marx. Organization Science. 2012;**23**:244-266

[59] Adler PS, Borys B. Two types of bureaucracy: Enabling and coercive. Administrative Science Quarterly. 1996;**41**:61-89

[60] Drucker P. The Practice of Management. New York: Harper; 1954

[61] Khan WA. Management by Objectives (Mbo) in Enterprises. Independently Published; 2018

[62] Solansky ST. Team identification: A determining factor of performance. Journal of Managerial Psychology. 2011;**26**:247-258

[63] Gibson CB, Dunlop PD, Cordery JL. Managing formalization to increase global team effectiveness and meaningfulness of work in multinational organizations. Journal of International Business Studies. 2019;**50**:1021-1052. DOI: 10.1057/s41267-019-00226-8

[64] Pertusa-Ortega EM, Zaragoza-Saez P, Claver-Cortes E. Can formalization, complexity, and centralization influence knowledge performance? Journal of Business Research. 2010;**63**:310-320

[65] Adler PS, Chen CX. Combining creativity and control: Understanding individual motivation in large-scale collaborative creativity. Accounting, Organization and Society. 2011;**26**:63-85

[66] Hutchins E. Organizing work by adaptation. Organization Science. 1991;**2**:14-39

[67] Rainey HG, Chun YH. Public and private management compared. In: Ferlie E, Lynn LE Jr, Pollitt C, editors. The Oxford Handbook of Public Management. Oxford: Oxford University Press; 2007

[68] Bower JL. Effective Public Management [Internet]. 1977. Strategic Planning. Available from: https://hbr.org/1977/03/effective-public-management [Accessed: July 22, 2021]

[69] GM. The Difference between Public and Private Sector Management [Internet]. 2017. Available from: https://www.getsmarter.com/blog/career-advice/public-and-private-management/ [Accessed: July 22, 2021]

[70] Marques I, Leitão J, Carvalho A, Pereira D. Public administration and values oriented to sustainability: A systematic approach to the literature. Sustainability. 2021;**13**:1-27. DOI: 10.3390/su13052566

[71] Larson P. Public and private values at odds: Can private sector values be transplanted into public sector institutions? Public Administration and Development. 1998;**17**:131-139

[72] Murray J. Public Sector vs. Private Sector: What's the Difference? How Public and Private Sectors of the U.S. Economy Work [Internet]. 2021. Available from: https://www.thebalancesmb.com/public-sector-vs-private-sector-5097547 [Accessed: July 25, 2021]

[73] Pfeffer J. The Human Equation; Building Profits by Putting People First. Boston, MA: Harvard Business School Press; 1998

Process Management: A Requirement for Organizational Excellence in the Twenty-First Century...
DOI: http://dx.doi.org/10.5772/intechopen.101769

[74] Caldwell C, Ndalamba KK. Trust and being "worthy"—The key to creating wealth. Journal of Management Development. 2017;**36**:1076-1086

[75] Esfahani P, Rad MAM, Akbari AB. The success of strategic planning in health care organizations of Iran. International Journal of Health Care Quality Assurance. 2018;**31**:563-574 10.1108/IJHCQA-08-2017-0145

[76] Seitanidi MM, Crane A. Social Partnerships and Responsible Business: A Research Handbook. New York, NY: Routledge; 2014

[77] Quinn RE. Deep change: Discovering the Leader Within. San Francisco, CA: Jossey-Bass Publishers; 1996

[78] Beer M. High commitment high performance: How to build a resilient organization for sustained advantage. San Francisco, CA: Jossey-Bass; 2009

[79] Kouzes JM, Posner BZ. The Leadership Challenge, San Francisco. CA: Jossey-Bass; 2012

Chapter 11

Improving Higher Education Instructional Delivery in the Developing World: The Role of University Teachers as Digital Leaders

Inusah Salifu and Eugene Owusu-Acheampong

Abstract

The last couple of years have seen an increasing demand on university teachers, especially in the developing world, to apply innovations to their instructional delivery to meet students' needs and cater to national aspirations. To succeed in this, a digital leadership initiative that ensures effective use of technology-mediated instruction is indispensable. This study used the context of Ghana to examine the kinds of digital technology tools university teachers in the developing world often used in their teaching as digital leaders and whether the tools were effective in promoting academic work. The study used the embedded mixed method design based on which 252 teachers of the country's universities were accidentally selected to complete questionnaires. Data were analysed using descriptive and inferential statistics. The study mainly found laptops, mobile phones, and projectors as the commonest digital technology tools used in teaching by the participants, and they thought that the tools effectively promoted academic work. The findings have global implications because knowing the effectiveness of digital technology use in higher education teaching in Ghana could serve as a source of information on measures to mitigate the impact of the Covid-19 pandemic on the academic work of HEIs in developing countries.

Keywords: digital leadership, developing world, Ghana, higher education, technology-mediated instruction, university teachers

1. Introduction

In today's world, rapid technology advancement and globalization seem to significantly influence the creation of a new knowledge-based economy. In other words, technology appears to be the critical factor in this knowledge-based economy for many nations across the globe [1, 2]. Most governments in the world, especially those in developing countries, have recognized that advancement in technology has an immense influence on the socio-economic development of their citizenry. Based on this development, some governments have invested heavily in technology developments to build the human resource base to address and conveniently cope with the demands and pressure of the current information and digital age [3, 4].

The concept "digital technology tools" was used since the post-World War II period in the United States of America to allow the integration of equipment such as audiotapes, television, and slide projectors in teaching [5, 6]. In our contemporary society, digital technology tools include computer-related hardware and software integrated into teaching and learning [7]. In this research, the use of digital technology tools refers to all electronic devices used in instructional delivery.

Digital technology has long been identified as a means to bridging the gap between access to higher education and improvements in learning outcomes, and university teachers have been recognized to play a leading role in the use of digital technology tools [8]. Many arguments posited for digital technology integration indicate that technology makes teaching and learning effective [9]. Trinidad et al. [10] explained teaching and learning effectiveness as "the degree to which a teaching tool contributes to students' retention of learning or skills...Effectiveness is measured through students' grades, acquired skills, transfer of knowledge, or retention of ideas" (p. 162).

In Ghana, the initiative to use digital technology devices to improve access, equity, and quality in education delivery was taken only a couple of years ago. In 2003, the country formulated a policy called Ghana ICT in Education Policy. The main aim of the policy was to integrate technology into education to promote teaching and learning, especially in the higher education sector. At the time, the policy framework recognized the essential role of technology in creating an opportunity for teachers to enhance their instructional delivery [11]. Although the policy document was timely because it served as a platform for the promotion of a systematic technology-driven education [12], our engagement with the literature revealed that there was a paucity of information as to whether teachers in the country, especially those teaching at the university level, saw themselves as digital leaders whose critical role was to promote the use of digital technology in teaching. Consequently, there appeared to be a knowledge gap as to the nature of digital technology tools used in instructional delivery at the university level in Ghana, and whether the tools effectively promoted teaching and learning.

The aim of the research was to use the context of Ghana to examine the extent to which university teachers in the developing world effectively used their digital leadership role to promote the use of digital technology in instructional delivery. Specifically, the research was to examine the kinds of digital technology tools university teachers in Ghana often used in their teaching. It was also to find out whether the tools were effective in promoting teaching and learning. Based on the objectives, we posed questions as follows:

1. What kinds of digital technology tools do university teachers in Ghana often apply in their instructional delivery as digital leaders?

2. How effective are digital technology tools in promoting academic work in Ghanaian universities?

The research was compelling because earlier studies by Boakye and Banini [13] and Mercader [14] claimed that despite the increasing number of research on digital technology integration in teaching, the concentration had been on the Western world, and little was known about the extent of the use of digital technology in the education system of the developing world.

Thus far, the Section 1 of this chapter has given the background, problem, objectives, and questions guiding the research. Next will be a review of the literature on the theoretical framework and the global use of digital technology tools in higher education. To be followed is the Section 4 detailing the processes involved in conducting the research. The findings and discussion will also be presented

Improving Higher Education Instructional Delivery in the Developing World: The Role...
DOI: http://dx.doi.org/10.5772/intechopen.100546

subsequently. The chapter will conclude by highlighting the implications of the research for global higher education, especially in the developing world.

2. Higher education teaching in the Ghanaian context

Ghana has 180 higher education institutions (HEIs) out of which there are 99 public and 81 private universities [15]. Most of the public universities operate the collegiate system. According to NCTE, about 70% of students in the universities enroll to acquire a bachelor's degree, while about 22% pursue diploma programs mostly by the distance education mode. The enrolment in graduate programs (masters' and doctoral degrees) is, however, minimal, according to the NCTE.

Recruitment of teachers in Ghana's HEIs is mainly based on the acquisition of a terminal degree (usually a Ph.D.) and a satisfactory publication record. Recruited teachers serve on a contract basis, usually 6 years with the opportunity for renewal. The promotion criteria for teachers vary from university to university. However, for promotion purposes, the universities commonly emphasize teaching, research, scholarly work (publications), and community service. After recruitment, university teachers in Ghana normally begin as Lecturers and may rise to Senior Lecturer, Associate Professor up to Professor. With regard to reporting lines, teachers and students are directly managed by Heads of Departments (HODs). The HOD's are also supervised by Deans who manage Schools or Faculties. The Deans also report Provosts of Colleges in the collegiate system or directly to Pro Vice-Chancellors who also reports to Vice-Chancellors. The Vice-Chancellors are ultimately answerable to University Councils.

3. Review of the literature

3.1 Theoretical framework: Roger's diffusion of innovation (DoN) theory

Roger's [16] innovation-decision activities vividly define a framework on how people choose to accept or reject a particular technology. The four key ingredients in the framework depicted in **Figure 1** concern innovation, communication, the context of the social system, and time. The four key components interrelate to describe how a person's adoption represents diffusion. Beyond these components, Casmar [17] identified five critical characteristics of adoption decisions. These include the relative merits associated with the adoption of the technology (relative advantage), the complex nature of the technology (complexity), ability to access and try the technology (triability), the availability and visibility of the technology (observability), and compatibility [18].

3.2 Digital technology tools used in higher education teaching context around the globe

Chevers and Whyte [19], Shelton [20], and Tondeur et al. [21] argued that the most frequently applied technology in teaching and learning are projectors and laptops/computers for presentation. According to Farmery [22], most instructors integrate blogs, wikis, and podcasts in teaching and learning. Amory [23], Bagheri et al. [24], Bates and Sangra [25], and Cheung and Slavin [26] also reported that instructional technologies would modify how learners and instructors collect and gather information and collaborate.

Makewa et al.'s [27] study on instructor's competence in integrating digital technologies into teaching and learning found that majority of the study participants

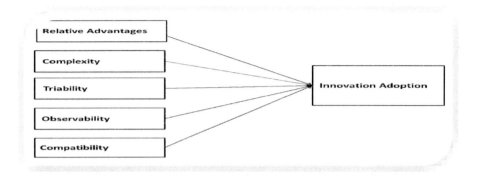

Figure 1.
Adoption decisions. Source: [16].

disagreed with being knowledgeable in applying online technology tools such as the podcast, wikis, and blogs. Besides, Montrieux et al.'s [28] qualitative study revealed that mobile tools such as mobile quizzes, blogs, and podcasts were famous for their integration in classroom teaching and learning. However, lecturers tended to be more confident and knowledgeable in using projectors. Other researchers such as Makewa et al. [27], Shelton [20], and Farmery [22] also found projectors and computers as the most frequently used technology tools in teaching. For their part, Alkash and Al-Dersi [29], Rumble and Harry [30], and Rashid and Elahi [31] found that technology-related resources such as the Internet, e-mobile, and computers facilitate distance learning.

In another related research, Alqurashi [32] found that there was a statistically significant relationship between familiarity and proficiency in using digital technologies and integrating them in teaching. Kumar and Daniel's [33] comparative study on the technology integration into instructional delivery at Fijian further established that 36.67% of the studied population indicated they were knowledgeable and skillful in incorporating digital technologies in teaching. In Fleischer's [34] view, integrating digital technology tools in teaching enhances students' creativity and inspires them to explore and learn new things independently. Fleischer's study found that teachers and students used laptops for academic work for long hours.

3.3 Institutional challenges in the use of digital technology in teaching

According to Bozkurt [35], the breakdown of technology devices and inadequate wireless services, limited time for integration in lessons, unreliable Internet speed, the lack of computers, and inadequate accessibility to technology tools for effective integration are some institutional factors affecting digital technology integration in teaching and learning.

Chertovskikh's [36] research also identified the following as barriers to technology integration: insufficient digital learning resources, insufficient pedagogical support, the lack of institutional policies for technology integration, insufficient technology equipment, poor connectivity, and insufficient technical support. In similar research, Adedokun-Shittu and Shittu [37] also found technical problems and constraints such as power failure, Internet interruption, and inadequate training for instructors as some of the critical challenges confronting technology integration in teaching and learning. Furthermore, Bagheri et al.'s [24] research rather found the challenges to include inadequate human resource capacity, low bandwidth for Internet connectivity, and poor penetration of technology in higher institutions.

3.4 Summarizing the literature and locating the gaps

Thus far, the literature reviewed highlighted the fact that there was scholarly information on various digital technology tools integrated into teaching in higher education institutions. It also revealed the fact that there were challenges confronting digital leaders in using the technologies in teaching. Conspicuously missing, however, was information on which of the digital technology tools were commonly used in the developing world, and whether or not they effectively promoted academic work. This was the gap this research intended to fill.

4. Methods

4.1 Research design and sample

The study used the embedded/nested mixed-method design to concurrently collect both quantitative and qualitative data. However, the latter played a complementary role in supporting the former [38]. The choice of the design enabled us to give a holistic picture and broader perspective of the extent to which university teachers in the developing world effectively used their digital leadership role to promote the use of digital technology in instructional delivery. The study used the accidental sampling technique to select 252 university teachers across Ghana. The sample size was considered appropriate based on Krejcie and Morgan's [39] standard criteria for determining sample size. **Table 1** presents details of the demographic characteristics of the sample.

4.2 Research instrument

A self-developed questionnaire was used for the research. The instrument had three sections. The first section ("A") was on the demographic background of respondents. The second section ("B") dealt with kinds of digital technology tools university teachers often applied in their instructional delivery. The third and final section ("C") also elicited responses on the effectiveness of the tools in promoting academic work. Although the instrument was mainly structured, the second and third sections gave respondents an opportunity to express their own qualitative opinions not captured in the structured items. The design of the items in the two sections was informed by the authoritative views expressed in the extant literature gleaned for this research. The items were put on a five-point Likert scale in both sections as follows: Section "B": (1) never used; (2) rarely used; (3) occasionally used; (4) frequently used; and (5) more frequently used. Section "C": (1) strongly disagree; (2) Disagree; (3) Unsure; (4) Agree; and (5) Strongly agree. Prior to using the instrument, a face validity test was conducted on it to ascertain the extent to which the items in the second and third sections met the objective of the research and the findings proved positive. Again, the instrument was piloted among accidentally selected 63 (i.e., a quarter of the sample size) university teachers in Ghana who were not part of the sample. A Cronbach's alpha test yielded a reliability coefficient of 0.81 making the instrument undoubtedly reliable for use in the research.

4.3 Data collection and analysis

The data collection exercise was done using the self-constructed questionnaire and took a period of 102 days to complete. As explained already, the accidental technique was used, and it allowed the distribution of the instrument among university

Variable	No.	%
Gender		
Male	97	38.49
Female	155	61.50
Total	252	100.0
Age		
30–39	74	5.95
40–49	113	28.17
50–59	65	25.79
Total	252	100.0
University teaching experience		
1–5 years	121	48.02
6–10 years	88	34.92
11 years+	43	17.06
Total	252	100.0

Source: Fieldwork (2021).

Table 1.
Demographic characteristics of participants.

teachers on the basis of availability and willingness to participate. Using the SPSS version 21, preliminary analyses were done by organizing the data according to the five-point Likert scale and subjecting them to frequency and percentage analyses. The same data were subsequently converted into means and standard deviations. The qualitative data were grouped into common themes to be analyzed using descriptive statistics. However, because the themes generated did not yield new issues remarkably different from the main items already captured in the questionnaire, the intention was shelved.

4.4 Ethics

A written consent was obtained from the participants before their involvement in the study. To ensure confidentiality and to check that the rights of the participants are not disregarded and abused, ethical clearance with reference number ECH 101/19-20 was obtained from one of the universities' ethics committees for the humanities. Besides, participation in the research process was voluntary, and participants could withdraw at any point in the research process. Participants' identities were also concealed.

5. Findings

This section presents analyses of the field data obtained from our investigation on the extent to which university teachers in a developing country like Ghana effectively used their digital leadership role to promote the use of digital technology in instructional delivery. The presentation in this section is based on only the quantitative aspect of the embedded/nested mixed-method design because, as indicated in Section 4 (see Subsection 4.3), the qualitative data did not yield new issues remarkably different from the main quantitative data.

Improving Higher Education Instructional Delivery in the Developing World: The Role...
DOI: http://dx.doi.org/10.5772/intechopen.100546

The first research question asks: What kinds of digital technology tools do university teachers in Ghana often apply in their instructional delivery as digital leaders?

Table 2 presents the means (M) and standard deviations (SD) of the various digital technology tools used for teaching in Ghanaian universities. It further shows the frequency (in mean rank) of their usage for instructional delivery. Looking at the measure of central tendencies on the table, an examination of only the extreme measures of the means (i.e., variable with the highest mean and the variable with the lowest mean) shows that the participants' responses for the variable "laptops" has the highest mean score ($m = 4.28$) indicating a skew toward the agreement scale, responses for the variable "digital speakers" has the lowest mean score ($m = 1.52$) indicating a skew toward the disapproval scale. By implication, whereas laptops were the most frequently used digital technology tool by the participants, digital speakers were the least used by them.

Having examined the measure of central tendencies on the table, it is equally important to also consider the measure of dispersion. From the table, two extreme measures of standard deviations (i.e., the most dispersed variable from its mean and the least dispersed variable from its mean) show that whereas responses for the variable "Television sets" are the farthest apart and most dispersed (SD = 1.63). On the opposite, responses for the variable "Digital cameras" are the closest and least dispersed (SD = 1.08).

The second research question also asks: How effective are digital technology tools in promoting academic work in Ghanaian universities?

Table 3 shows respondents' opinions regarding the effectiveness of digital technology tools in promoting teaching and learning in Ghanaian universities. For the measure of central tendencies, an examination of only the extreme measures of the means gives the impression that while the responses for the variable contending that digital technology tools allowed students to easily retain and recollect learning concepts have the highest mean score ($m = 4.51$) indicating a skew toward the strong agreement scale, responses for the variable claiming that digital technology tools made it easy to attract students' attention has the lowest mean score ($m = 2.20$) manifesting a skew toward the disagreement scale.

In the case of the measure of dispersion, a perusal of the table also reveals two extreme measures of standard deviations showing that responses for the variable on the assertion that digital technology tools enhanced the learning experience of

Digital technology tools	N	M	SD	Mean rank
Laptops	252	4.28	1.32	1
Mobile phones	252	3.94	1.42	2
Projectors	252	3.75	1.27	3
Desktop computers	252	3.03	1.48	4
Television sets	252	2.99	1.63	5
IPads	252	2.10	1.57	6
Smartboard	252	1.81	1.19	8
Digital cameras	252	1.61	1.08	7
Digital speakers	252	1.52	1.11	9
Source: Fieldwork (2021).				

Table 2.
Kinds digital technology tools frequently used by Ghanaian universities.

Digital technology tools...	M	SD
Allows students to easily retain and recollect learning concepts	4.51	0.88
Allows students to access information at any time and place	4.27	0.89
Motivates and sustains students' interest in teaching	3.68	1.22
Allows easy transfer of knowledge by students	3.67	0.97
Helps students to explore opportunities for further learning	3.51	1.06
Enhance the learning experience of students	3.42	1.51
Leads to better acquisition of skills by students	3.23	1.40
Enable students to obtain desirable findings	3.12	1.39
Helps students to learn independently	2.36	1.07
Makes it easy to attract students' attention	2.20	1.30

Source: Fieldwork (2021).

Table 3.
Effectiveness of digital technology tools in promoting instructional delivery.

students are the farthest apart and most dispersed (SD = 1.51). On the contrary, responses for the variable on the view that digital technology tools enabled students to easily retain and recollect learning concepts are the closest and least dispersed (SD = 0.88).

6. Discussion

The study found high average usage for laptops, mobile, and phones as the usually used educational technology for teaching by the participants in playing their roles as digital leaders. The study, however, revealed the speaker as the least used educational technology device by the teachers. The findings further show that although most of the participants used digital technology tools, only a few effectively applied the tools in their instructional delivery. This result is interesting, given that a burgeoning body of the literature such as Amory [23], Bagheri et al. [24], Bates and Sangra [25], and Cheung and Slavin [26] found their integration into instructional delivery of most higher education institutions in the world. These digital technology tools are common, easy to operate, accessible, and have numerous advantages [40]. These merits perhaps account for the reason most teachers would want to use them to teach. Alkash and Al-Dersi [29] and Chevers and Whyte [19] believed that these tools make teaching lively, less stressful, and flexible.

Another possible explanation could be that most of the university teachers owned laptops and mobile phones and used them for various social activities. Research has shown that most university teachers believe that the use of these technology tools enhances teaching and fosters collaboration between students and faculty members. For instance, Tondeur et al. [21] pointed out that educational technology integration in the instructional process has become common because technology has assumed a pivotal role in enhancing teaching and learning. It is therefore not surprising that the participants deployed the digital devices to teach. It is also believed that most students have laptops and mobile phones; therefore, the participants would naturally find it ideal to share information and educational resources with the students [5].

Again, the use of the digital tools in teaching by the participants as digital leaders appears to give credence to the finding that digital technology tools increase teachers' ability to speedily search for information [2, 7] and library databases [1]. By implication, the findings mean that if university teachers in the developing world are assisted with technology devices, it would boost their morale and encourage them to integrate educational technology into teaching [41]. It would also enhance the quality of their instructional delivery and impact positively on students' learning outcomes.

Comparing the findings of this research with previous studies reveals some consistencies. For example, the findings appear to confirm a key finding of Bozalek et al. [1] who revealed that educational technology devices are used in teaching in higher institutions in South Africa. Furthermore, Sife et al. [6] found that in Tanzania, higher institutions faculty members use educational technology for many educational purposes. The findings also corroborate Jackson and Chapman's [4] research who reported that most lecturers were proficient in using PowerPoint and Word applications for teaching.

Arguing from the perspective of Roger's [42] diffusion of innovation theory, which anchors this research, one would reason that if digital technology tools are not easy to use, not accessible, and do not offer relative advantages to university teachers in the developing world, they might decline their usage in teaching. It appears obvious that university teachers in Ghana, like all other teachers in the higher education sector in the developing world, may have positive attitudes toward the usage of digital technology tools in teaching but they need support to procure them.

7. Conclusion and recommendations

This study aimed to use the context of Ghana to examine the kinds of digital technology tools university teachers in the developing world often used in their teaching as digital leaders, and whether the tools were effective in promoting academic work. The study mainly found laptops, mobile phones, and projectors as the commonest digital technology tools used in teaching by the participants, and they thought that the tools effectively promoted academic work.

The study has two major limitations. First, the accidental technique used to recruit participants from Ghanaian universities does not allow the findings to generalize beyond the present sample. Second, because the study used the cross-sectional survey design, it cannot offer causal interpretations. Based on the limitations, we recommend that future research should compare the experiences of university teachers playing digital leadership roles in different geographical contexts across several developing countries. Because the research found that digital technology tools were effective in promoting academic work, we wish to also suggest that universities in Ghana should provide allowances to teachers to assist them to procure digital technology tools needed for teaching.

Despite the limitations, substantially, the findings are original because, to the best of our knowledge, there has not been previous research that has focused on the same issue on HEIs in the developing world. The study is also novel because of its use of the Diffusion of Innovation (DoN) theory to discuss pertinent issues about digital technology use in higher education. Most importantly, because developing countries arguably have similar characteristics, the findings may apply favorably with other developing countries.

Again, the findings may have global implications because knowing the effectiveness of the use of digital technology in higher education teaching in Ghana as a developing country could serve as a source of information on measures HEIs in developing countries have put in place to deal with the negative impact of the Covid-19 pandemic on academic work. Finally, research also contributes to existing knowledge about how HEIs in the developing are using digital leadership to address the issue of large class size teaching bedeviling most universities.

Acknowledgements

The authors acknowledge the immense contributions of colleagues who read through the manuscript and provided the needed feedback to improve the quality of the paper.

Funding

The authors received no financial support for the research, authorship, and/or publication of this article.

Conflicts of interest

There are no potential conflicts of interest/competing interests with respect to the research, authorship, and/or publication of this article.

Consent to publish

The authors consent to the publication of the manuscript titled above in the journal "Australian Education Researcher."

Availability of data and material

All data generated or analyzed during this research are included in this manuscript (and its supplementary file).

Improving Higher Education Instructional Delivery in the Developing World: The Role...
DOI: http://dx.doi.org/10.5772/intechopen.100546

Author details

Inusah Salifu[1]* and Eugene Owusu-Acheampong[2]

1 Department of Adult Education and Human Resource Studies, School of Continuing and Distance Education, College of Education, University of Ghana, Legon, Ghana

2 Department of Secretaryship and Management Studies, Cape Coast Technical University, Cape Coast, Ghana

*Address all correspondence to: isalifu@ug.edu.gh; insalifu1@yahoo.co.uk

IntechOpen

© 2021 The Author(s). Licensee IntechOpen. This chapter is distributed under the terms of the Creative Commons Attribution License (http://creativecommons.org/licenses/by/3.0), which permits unrestricted use, distribution, and reproduction in any medium, provided the original work is properly cited. (cc) BY

References

[1] Bozalek V, Ng'ambi D, Gachago D. Transforming teaching with emerging technologies: Implications for higher education institutions. South African Journal of Higher Education. 2013; **27**(2):419-436

[2] Latchem C. Using ICTs and Blended Learning in Transforming Technical and Vocational Education and Training. Paris, UNESCO Publishing; 2017

[3] Boden R, Nedeva M. Employing discourse: Universities and graduate 'employability'. Journal of Education Policy. 2010;**25**(1):37-54

[4] Jackson D, Chapman E. Non-technical skill gaps in Australian business graduates. Education and Training. 2012;**54**(2/3):95-113

[5] Delgado, A. J., Wardlow, L., McKnight, K., and O'Malley, K. (2015). Digital technology: A review of the integration, resources, and effectiveness of technology in K-12 classrooms. Journal of Information Technology Education, 14:397-416.

[6] Sife A, Lwoga E, Sanga C. New technologies for teaching and learning: Challenges for higher learning institutions in developing countries. International Journal of Education and Development using ICT. 2007;**3**(2): 57-67

[7] Kachalov N, Velsh A, Antonova Z, Konysheva A, Proschaeva N. Application of modern digital technologies at the research university. Procedia-Social and Behavioral Sciences. 2015;**206**:225-231

[8] Dzobelova VB, Yablochnikov SL, Cherkasova OV, Gerasimov SV. Digital educational technology in a higher education institution. In: "New Silk Road: Business Cooperation and Prospective of Economic Development"

(NSRBCPED 2019). Amsterdam, Atlantis Press; 2020. pp. 153-156

[9] Quaye, F., Ametepe, W., and Annan, N. K. (2015). The impact of ICT on teaching and learning in tertiary institutions: A case study of Wisconsin International University College, Ghana. Journal of Information Engineering and Applications, 5(5), 8-14.

[10] Trinidad JS, Ngo GR, Nevada AM, Morales JA. Engaging and/or effective? Students' evaluation of pedagogical practices in higher education. College Teaching. 2020;**68**(4):161-171. DOI: 10.1080/87567555.2020.1769017

[11] Addy NA, Ofori-Boateng P. ICT and education: An analysis into Ghana's universities. International Journal of ICT and Management. 2015;**3**(2):23-28

[12] Natia J, Al-hassan S. Promoting teaching and learning in Ghanaian basic schools through ICT. International Journal of Education and Development using ICT. 2015;**11**(2):113-125

[13] Boakye KB, Banini DA. 11. Teacher ICT Readiness in Ghana. In: ICT and Changing Mindsets in Education/ Repenser l'éducation à l'aide des TIC. 2008. p. 147

[14] Mercader C. Explanatory model of barriers to integration of digital technologies in higher education institutions. Education and Information Technologies. 2020;**25**:5133-5147

[15] National Council for Tertiary Education. Statistical report on tertiary education for 2016/2017 academic year. Accra, Ghana. 2018

[16] Rogers EM. Diffusion of innovations: Modifications of a model for telecommunications. In: Die diffusion von innovationen in der

telekommunikation. Berlin, Heidelberg: Springer; 1995. pp. 25-38

[17] Casmar SP. The adoption of computer technology by faculty in a college of education: An analysis of administrative planning issues [doctoral dissertation]. Washington State University; 2001 [ProQuest Digital Dissertations (UMI No. AAT 3025011)]

[18] Surendra S. Acceptance of Web Technology-Based Education by Professors and Administrators of a College of Applied Arts and Technology in Ontario. Toronto, Canada: University of Toronto; 2001. pp. 1-164

[19] Chevers DA, Whyte CC. Gender difference in the knowledge and adoption of digital technology by faculty: The case of a Business School in Jamaica. In: CONF-IRM 2015 Proceedings. 2015. p. 23

[20] Shelton C. Giving up technology and social media: Why university lecturers stop using technology in teaching. Technology, Pedagogy and Education. 2017;**26**(3):303-321

[21] Tondeur, J., van Braak, J., Siddiq, F., and Scherer, R. (2016). Time for a new approach to prepare future teachers for educational technology use: Its meaning and measurement. Computers and Education, 94 134-150

[22] Farmery R. The integration and use of ICT across the secondary school [doctoral dissertation]. Cardiff University; 2014

[23] Amory A. Tool-mediated authentic learning in a digital technology course: A designed-based innovation. Interactive Learning Environments. 2014;**22**(4):497-513

[24] Bagheri M, Ali WZW, Abdullah MCB, Daud SM. Effects of project-based learning strategy on self-directed learning skills of digital technology students. Contemporary Educational Technology. 2013;**4**(1):15-29

[25] Bates AT, Sangra A. Managing Technology in Higher Education: Strategies for Transforming Teaching and Learning. New Jersey, John Wiley and Sons; 2011

[26] Cheung AC, Slavin RE. How features of digital technology applications affect student reading outcomes: A meta-analysis. Educational Research Review. 2012;7(3):198-215.

[27] Makewa LN, Kuboja JM, Yango M, Ngussa BM. ICT-integration in higher education and student behavioral change: Observations at University of Arusha, Tanzania. American Journal of Educational Research. 2014;**11**: 30-38

[28] Montrieux H, Vanderlinde R, Schellens T, De Marez L. Teaching and learning with mobile technology: A qualitative explorative study about the introduction of tablet devices in secondary education. PLoS One. 2015;**10**(12):e0144008

[29] Alkash KAM, Al-Dersi ZEM. Advantages of using PowerPoint presentation in EFL classroom & the status of its use in Sebha University. International Journal of English Language and Translation Studies. 2017;**1**:3-16

[30] Rumble G, Harry K. The Distance Teaching Universities. Oxford, Routledge; 2018

[31] Rashid M, Elahi U. Use of digital technology in promoting distance education. Turkish Online Journal of Distance Education. 2012;**13**(1):79-86

[32] Alqurashi E. Technology tools for teaching and learning in real time. In: Educational Technology and Resources for Synchronous Learning in Higher

Education. Pennsylvania, IGI Global; 2019. pp. 255-278

[33] Kumar S, Daniel BK. Integration of learning technologies into teaching within Fijian Polytechnic Institutions. International Journal of Educational Technology in Higher Education. 2016;**13**(1):36

[34] Fleischer H. What is our current understanding of one-to-one computer projects: A systematic narrative research review? Educational Research Review. 2012;**7**(2):107-122

[35] Bozkurt A. Educational technology research patterns in the realm of the digital knowledge age. Journal of Interactive Media in Education. 2020;**1**(18):1-17. DOI: https://doi.org/10.5334/jime.570

[36] Chertovskikh O. Prospects for integrating artificial intelligence and new digital technologies into tertiary education. 2020. Available from: SSRN 3746561

[37] Adedokun-Shittu NA, Shittu AJK. Evaluating the impact of technology integration in teaching and learning. Malaysian Online Journal of Educational Technology. 2014;**2**(1):23-29

[38] Creswell JW. Research Design: Qualitative, Quantitative, and Evaluating Quantitative and Qualitative Research. 3rd ed. Newcastle, Sage; 2009

[39] Krejcie RV, Morgan DW. Determining sample size for research activities. Educational and Psychological Measurement. 1970;**30**:607-610. DOI: 10.1177/001 316447003000308

[40] Jordan LA, Papp R. Powerpoint: It's not "yes" or "no"—it's "when" and "how". Research in Higher Education Journal. 2014;**22**:1-11

[41] Allahawiah S, Tarawneh S. Factors affecting information and communication technology (ICT) use by southern college's teachers in Balqa Applied University. In: Proceedings of the West East Institute International Academic Conference on Education, Humanities and Social Sciences. 2015. pp. 138-145

[42] Rogers, E. M. (2003). The Diffusion of Innovation. 5th ed. New York: Free Press.